ORALITY, LITERACY, AND COLONIALISM IN ANTIQUITY

Edited by
Jonathan A. Draper

Society of Biblical Literature
Atlanta

ORALITY, LITERACY, AND COLONIALISM IN ANTIQUITY

Library of Congress Cataloging-in-Publication Data

Orality, literacy, and colonialism in antiquity / edited by Jonathan A. Draper.
    p. cm. — (Semeia studies ; no. 47)
    Includes bibliographical references.
    ISBN 1-58983-131-4 (paper bdg. : alk. paper)
    1. Mediterranean Region—Religion—Congresses. 2. Oral communication—Religious aspects—History—To 1500—Congresses. 3. Written communication—Religious aspects—History—To 1500—Congresses. 4. Colonies—Religious aspects—History—To 1500—Congresses. 5. Oral communication—Mediterranean Region—History—To 1500—Congresses. 6. Written communication—Mediterranean Region—History—To 1500—Congresses. 7. Mediterranean Region—History—To 476—Congresses. I. Draper, Jonathan A. II. Semeia studies ; no. 47.
    BL687.O73 2004b
    302.2'24'093—dc22
                                               2004004749

CONTENTS

RESPONSES

ABBREVIATIONS

AB	Anchor Bible
ABRL	Anchor Bible Reference Library
AGSU	Arbeiten zur Geschichte des Spätjudentums und Urchristentums
BA	*Biblical Archaeologist*
CBQ	*Catholic Biblical Quarterly*
CRINT	Compendia rerum iudaicarum ad Novum Testamentum
HDR	Harvard Dissertations in Religion
HTR	*Harvard Theological Review*
HUCA	*Hebrew Union College Annual*
HvTSt	*Hervormde teologiese studies*
Int	*Interpretation*
JA	*Journal asiatique*
JBL	*Journal of Biblical Literature*
JJS	*Journal of Jewish Studies*
JSNT	*Journal for the Study of the New Testament*
JSNTSup	Journal for the Study of the New Testament Supplement Series
JSOTSup	Journal for the Study of the Old Testament Supplement Series
LCL	Loeb Classical Library
Neot	*Neotestamentica*
NGTT	*Nederduitse gereformeerde teologiese tydskrif*
NovTSup	Supplements to Novum Testamentum
NTS	*New Testament Studies*
RevQ	*Revue de Qumran*
SBLDS	Society of Biblical Literature Dissertation Series
SBLSymS	Society of Biblical Literature Symposium Series
SemeiaSt	Semeia Studies
SJLA	Studies in Judaism in Late Antiquity
SNTSMS	Society for New Testament Studies Monograph Series
Spec	*Speculum*
StPB	Studia post-biblica
TSAJ	Texte und Studien zum antiken Judentum

ABBREVIATIONS

VT	*Vetus Testamentum*
WUNT	Wissenschaftliche Untersuchungen zum Alten und Neuen Testament

ORALITY, LITERACY, AND COLONIALISM IN ANTIQUITY

Jonathan A. Draper
University of Natal

1. INTRODUCTION

In a narrative cameo reflecting on a botched visit to an itinerant and illiterate Nambikwara group in the Amazon, Claude Lévi-Strauss notes that the primary function of writing in the evolution of humankind has not been intellectual in nature. Rather, it has functioned for social control:

> The only phenomenon with which writing has always been concomitant is the creation of cities and empires, that is the integration of large numbers of individuals into a political system, and their grading into castes or classes.... It seems to have favoured the exploitation of human beings rather than their enlightenment.... My hypothesis, if correct, would oblige us to recognize the fact that the primary function of written communication is to facilitate slavery. The use of writing for disinterested pleasure, is a secondary result, and more often than not it may even be turned into a means of strengthening, justifying or concealing the other. (1976:392–93)

Lévi-Strauss notes that the dissemination of literacy in modern Europe has also been related to the need to militarize and control the new proletariat and to increase the authority of government over citizens.

In the ancient world, where there was no separation between politics, economics, and religion, narrative and legal texts revealed by the gods served to cement and legitimate the power of the ruling elite (W. V. Harris: 39). The building of empires requires carefully compiled records, laws, genealogies, means of communication, and propaganda. Closely associated with this hegemony, writing was also central to various forms of control related to property and commerce. This can easily be overlooked when "religious" and "literary" texts are read in a modern context, as if they are somehow separate from, and superior to, the mundane exercise of material domination. The connection between the emergence of the great empires and the emergence of written texts in the ancient world is not accidental but integral.

While literacy and the use of texts in one form or another is pervasive throughout the ancient world, only a tiny minority were able to read and write. According to W. V. Harris (22, 329), less than 10 percent of the population were able to read even in the most favorable circumstances. The majority had access to texts only through scribes, who could be hired for particular purposes to read and interpret texts and who consequently had considerable power in the community. The access of the majority to text was the access of "outsiders" who interacted with it through intermediaries and appropriated it in oral forms (Lévi-Strauss: 391). Even the imperial elite relied, for the most part, on professional scribes for their access to texts.

The studies in this book take up various questions relating to the relationship between orality and literacy in the context of colonized people in antiquity and explore the role of orality in relation to this hegemony. The essays emerge out of a colloquium in which scholars of the ancient world engaged in dialogue with scholars in oral culture in the colonial and post-colonial period in Southern Africa.[1] The reasons for the interdisciplinary exchange were as follows. The study of ancient cultures in the light of cognate contemporary cultures provides a useful yardstick against which to judge claims about what might have happened in antiquity (cf. the 1982 study of slavery by Patterson and the usefulness of his interdisciplinary approach for the interpretation of New Testament texts in the articles in Callahan, Horsley, and Smith). The intention of the volume, then, is partly to bring together two discourses in New Testament scholarship, which have to this point been conducted largely in isolation from each other: the study of orality and literacy, and the study of colonialism. In addition, these essays bring together in an interdisciplinary dialogue scholars of classical and biblical antiquity on the one hand and scholars of African oral culture on the other. Contemporary Africa provides an example in its life and recent history of the kinds of dynamics around orality and literacy that characterized the ancient world and that are so alien to the experience of Western scholars. The project was designed as a unity so that, while the papers have been published in two volumes for convenience, they should be read together.

---

1 The Colloquium on Orality, Literacy and Colonialism was held in Pietermaritzburg, South Africa, 28–30 August 2001 as part of a project funded by the Indigenous Knowledge Systems Focus Group of the National Research Foundation of South Africa and the University of Natal Research Fund. The essays on Southern Africa were published in *Orality, Literacy, and Colonialism in Southern Africa* (Draper 2003a). The funding of the NRF and UNRF is gratefully acknowledged, while the views expressed here are not necessarily the views of the NRF.

2. The Nature of Oral Communication in Relation to Text

Three of the essays in this volume provide theoretical explorations of the nature of orality and its relation to text. John Miles Foley examines diversity and complexity of the interface, especially in view of the fact that oral tradition survives largely in textual form. Hence he problematizes the separation of oral and textual forms. He provides a strategy for tracking the elusive features of oral poetry and argues for a variety of interpretive tools to read "oral texts." Pieter Botha, on the other hand, reopens the question of the "great divide" between orality and literacy by challenging the well-known findings of Scribner and Cole. He argues that to ignore the differences between oral cultures and text-based cultures is to fall into ethnocentrism. Bobby Loubser seeks to find a way out of the impasse of the debate around the difference between oral and literary communication by means of a theory of media as an aspect of culture. From this aspect orality and literacy are different media that are related specifically to particular cultural matrices and that each has its own particular range of possibilities and limitations. Some things can be done only by means of one medium but not by another.

3. Orality, Literacy, and Hegemony

In colonial and postcolonial Southern Africa, the relationship between text and hegemony is particularly clear, since the subjugated peoples had an entirely oral culture. Like the Native American chief described by Lévi-Strauss, they recognized instinctively the role that texts played in the conquest (Opland 1999). Moreover, colonial intrusion was accompanied by an officially sanctioned attempt to convert the indigenous people to a largely Protestant form of Christianity, a religion of a book. So mission was accompanied from the beginning with an attempt at widespread literacy training. However, the missionaries attempted to maintain ideological control of both text and interpretation in support of the imperial enterprise. The first volume of essays (Draper 2003b) arising from the colloquium has charted the complex and intricate process by which text was both appropriated and subverted in multiple oral forms and traditions in Southern Africa. It also revealed the interaction of text and orality in the emerging resistance to colonialism. This second volume takes up these insights in a focus on the dynamics of orality, literacy, and colonialism in antiquity.

In antiquity, oral forms were the usual and preferred cultural norms for both the ruling elite and the underclasses, in spite of the pervasiveness of literacy in the culture. Jean-Luc Solère has shown that the Platonists, for instance, did not consider it proper to write down their philosophy, yet they did so, choosing esoteric forms not readily accessible to the masses in order to protect their doctrines. The cult of Mithras, on the other hand, as Baudouin Decharneux demonstrates, eschewed written forms of transmission of the teaching of the cult altogether, even though its members were largely literate.

However, since the ruling elite and their retainers controlled the knowledge of and use of writing to a large extent, what survives in writing from antiquity is largely the official transcript of the elite:

> The theatrical imperatives that normally prevail in situations of domination produce a public transcript in close conformity with how the dominant group would wish things to appear. The dominant never control the stage absolutely, but their wishes normally prevail. In the short run it is in the interest of the subordinate to produce a more or less credible performance, speaking the lines and making the gestures he knows are expected of him. The result is that the public transcript is—barring a crisis—systematically skewed in the direction of the libretto, the discourse, represented by the dominant. In ideological terms the public transcript will typically by its accommodationist tone, provide convincing evidence for the hegemony of dominant values, for the hegemony of dominant discourse. It is in precisely this public domain where the effects of power relations are most manifest, and any analysis based exclusively on the public transcript is likely to conclude that subordinate groups endorse the terms of their subordination and are willing, even enthusiastic, partners in that subordination. (Scott 1990:4)

There may be dissident literature from an alienated or dispossessed section of the elite, as at Qumran or in the apocalyptic literature in the intertestamental period, but the voice of the illiterate subordinated classes is largely silenced by writing.

Nevertheless, James Scott argues that the poor have a "hidden transcript" of resistance to domination, which they seek to insert as much as they can within the limits of safety. Periodically this hidden transcript may also explode onto the public stage, in times of catastrophe or unbearable oppression. This will be swiftly and brutally silenced by the ruling elite but remembered and celebrated by the poor in oral forms long after the event in song and story. One need only think of the continuing modern singing of oral peasant carols of the Drummer and Jesus, which are based on a medieval resistance movement of the poor that was violently suppressed. Such oral expressions of continuing resistance after such a quelled breach of the public transcript may find their way into writing, often when the ruling elite or the retainer class no longer know their origin. In addition, the occasions of the "breach of the public transcript" and their suppression usually make literary waves, so that texts can be read between the lines or "against the grain" (Eagleton; Mosala;

West) to hear the suppressed voices of the "hidden transcript" expressed otherwise only in lost oral forms.

4. ORALITY AND LITERACY IN THE NEW TESTAMENT

In the case of Jesus, for instance, a peasant who publicly breached the public transcript by his demonstration in the temple in Jerusalem (and perhaps rode kinglike into the city in a deliberate mockery of the elite and a simultaneous assertion of the popular nature of kingship in Israel), the memory would have been celebrated in orally mediated story and sayings among his own people in Galilee long after his death. Resurrection would not have been a prerequisite for such a phenomenon, as he would have become a hero to the poor regardless of the outcome.

> The first public declaration of the hidden transcript, then, has a prehistory that explains its capacity to produce political breakthroughs. If, of course, the first act of defiance meets with a decisive defeat it is unlikely to be emulated by others. The courage of those who fail, however, is likely to be noted, admired, and even mythologized in stories of bravery, social banditry, and noble sacrifice. They become themselves part of the hidden transcript. When the first declaration of the hidden transcript succeeds, its mobilizing capacity as a symbolic act is potentially awesome. At the level of tactics and strategy, it is a powerful straw in the wind. It portends a possible turning of the tables (Scott 1990:227)

The sayings of Jesus prior to his death, as they were repeatedly performed orally in the "little tradition" of the underclasses are likely to show the dynamics of the hidden transcript. This will include an insinuation of the protests of the poor into public discourse with the retainer class without initially producing a direct breach. They will have been remembered within a particular context and recited on particular occasions.

Richard Horsley undertakes a broad overview of the emergence of the Hebrew Scriptures in the context of various imperial administrations after the destruction of the independent kingdoms of Judah and Samaria. He views the emergence of text in late Second Temple times as the product of a series of arrangements between imperial regimes and restored factions in Judea to control the peoples and revenues in Judea. However, the covenantal traditions of Israel continued to be performed and transmitted orally among the peasants of Galilee. Jesus was the champion of this popular tradition over against the scribes and Pharisees, who were the proponents of the official textual transcript of the temple state of Judah.

Werner Kelber views scribality as central to Roman control over the empire. He argues that the Christians were in a particularly weak position because it was known that their founder had been executed as a criminal. Consequently, the Gospel writers were forced to defend the position of Christians and enhance their status by means of the dangerously exposed medium of text. He explores the range of Christian scribal strategies in response to and in competition with Roman imperialism.

In my own essay I examine the way in which John's Gospel opposes orally mediated Word internalized by meditation on Scripture to scribal halakah designed to settle disputes and control the people by reference to text. John undertakes this task after the collapse of the temple state and the emergence of the scribes as the preferred ethnarchs of the Roman imperial administration.

5. OPEN QUESTIONS

Two responses to the papers probe the findings of the contributors to the colloquium in considerable detail. Martin Jaffee, who has done pioneering work on rabbinic oral culture (2001), responds from the perspective of rabbinic oral-traditional culture. He argues for a nuanced approach to the interaction of orality and textuality in the rabbinic tradition, in which scribes receive the textually transmitted oral tradition by memorization, which rerenders it as "voices from the past." Their dialogue with these voices results in new textually encoded oral productions. In this case, the insistence on oral methods of instruction, the sages achieve direct control over the text. The rabbinic claim to stand in an unbroken line of oral transmission from Sinai is seen as a defensive response to Christian hegemony in the Byzantine period.

Claudia Camp focuses on the theoretical issues raised by orality, literacy, and colonialism. She calls for methodological rigor and sophistication in approaching what is a complex and many-faceted issue. Her insightful critique of the volume points the way to work remaining to be undertaken. How can studies on oral-dominated cultures acknowledge and respond to differences from text-dominated cultures without falling into ethnocentrism? How do texts come to determine identity when few can read? Can issues of imperial hegemony be explored historically and "theoretically" without stepping over into "theological" or ideological valorization? Are there "different understandings of "writtenness" (and thus orality) in early Christianity? The debate continues.

ESSAYS

Indigenous Poems, Colonialist Texts

John Miles Foley
University of Missouri-Columbia

Introduction: Two Laments for "Oral Poetry"

I begin with two laments, both of which you have heard before in one or another performance-version. The first is intoned by the folklorist or ethnographer and proceeds as follows:

> Oral poems inhere in a culture as indigenous property, but they are ever subject to colonialist "take-over" by texts. Textualization begins with fieldwork collection, continues through the denaturing process we call editing and translating, and reaches its zenith with publication and reading. Benevolent though the intention may be at every stage, compromise is inescapable: wrenched out of its most immediate performative context, an oral poem becomes something else as soon as it is inscribed—whether on tablets, vellum, papyrus, acid-free paper, audio tape, video tape, or digital media. Editing means resorting its cognitive categories, constraining it to mean in our terms, and translating means shuffling its semiotics.

The upshot is only too predictable. By the time enthusiastic scholars get ready to plug their cocreated poems into the network of print and Internet publication, with the benign hope of winning their attendant audiences, textual colonialism has won the day. The price of gaining such audiences is, effectively, losing the oral poem.

The second dirge, typically that of the literary scholar, reverses some of these priorities. For many page-trained investigators, textual colonialism amounts to a necessary polishing of the rough-cut jewel of indigenous oral poetry. Here is a variant:

> Verbal art truly matures only in texts. Only by inscription can we manage complex literary maneuvering. Oral poetry is all well and good, but it fulfills its promise only when the new vehicle of literacy (our own vehicle) comes to prominence. Writing restructures consciousness, makes reasoning more analytical, and clears the way for major Western monuments such as the ancient Greek *Iliad* and *Odyssey*, which are simply unimaginable without a textual underpinning.

Never mind, of course, that the Homeric epics are rather short and unelaborate on the international scale of oral epic. Never mind that in placing Homer's poems on an unapproachable pinnacle we are merely reifying Western cultural egocentrism. Never mind that in speaking of Homer's inherited medium as something he superseded in a stroke of original genius we are forsaking much of the poems' idiomatic meaning. The literary bias runs deep, conveniently camouflaged as a set of sacrosanct, unexamined assumptions about verbal art. As part of the very "operating system" of everyday scholarly investigation, this bias sets strict limits on what we can imagine. Here is the colonialist mentality in full control.

These twin laments may seem to reflect opposite conceptions about verbal art, and in many ways they certainly do. The former favors on-site experience and cultural embedding; its more fervent advocates argue against consideration of any "oral poem" not encountered firsthand as a living performance. Pressed to such an extreme, this viewpoint rules out not only African or Native American forms taken down in dictation before the advent of more modern inscriptional media (which are, after all, still inscriptional media) but also all premodern forms that survive only as texts. So much for the *Iliad*, the *Odyssey, Beowulf,* and not least the New Testament. If the pristine orality of verbal art has been sabotaged by the incursive forces of writing and texts, so goes the argument, then it is a text, and if it is a text, it is not oral tradition. Such an attitude has the advantage of whittling down an enormously complicated field to manageable size and complexity, but of course it does so only by defining most of the field's contents out of existence.

The latter lament, on the other hand, valorizes the textual avatar, privileging the artifact as cultural epitome. While often content to credit a given form's roots in oral tradition, this approach customarily downplays the relationship between those submerged, invisible roots and the only-too-visible flowering that textual imperialists can immediately see and appreciate. As we wend our way through a culture's garden of verbal art, we are encouraged to focus on such flowers as freestanding phenomena that interbreed only through intertextuality, as expressions of original and individual genius. We are discouraged from botanical pursuits that in probing beneath the surface would help us appreciate the systemic reality of those blooms more fully and responsibly. What matters to us— by definition—is what our (cognitively predisposed) interpretive procedures can capture.

Different as they are, however, the two complaints or perspectives share a number of preconceptions, deep-seated ideas that have long remained immune to reexamination and that have conditioned the way we think about oral traditions. First and foremost is the dichotomous

model that Ruth Finnegan (1977) has called the Great Divide, the convic-
tion that orality and literacy—or oral traditions and texts—are mutually
exclusive phenomena. Although evidence from fieldwork continues to
pile up, putting the lie to the "airtight container" model, the Great Divide
dies hard. We seem to want to theorize in terms of cataclysmic shifts
(which harbor unsustainable corollaries of evolutionism), as if orality,
manuscripts, printed documents, and electronic communication were
separable layers of human history. Full in the face of reports from all over
the world that this just is not so, many of us cling to the false dichotomy
as at least a first approximation, a guiding principle that we can shape to
the particular situation at hand. Admittedly, the binary model did have
an important role to play in the development of studies in oral tradition:
it helped us to prescribe an "other," to get some distance from our subject. However, the "either-or" strategy has run its course; in the present
state of knowledge it only distorts what we can learn about oral poetry.
We need a model that corresponds to the messy and delightfully complex
reality of verbal art in multiple media.

Second is the inordinate fascination with composition over reception,
with virtually all attention devoted to the performer's work over that of
the audience. It is easy enough to see how scholars who spend nearly
every waking moment with book or pen or mouse in hand are fascinated
by how one might possibly manage without these cognitive prostheses.
How do we seek to understand and explain oral poetries? By reading and
writing about them, of course. Even our fieldwork is teleologically aimed
at sharing insights via the inscriptional network. But in focusing so hard
on how the job gets done without what we assume to be the customary
tools, we have very often ignored the living reality of what gets built.
What if the "product" we glimpse cannot be satisfactorily appreciated
without some sense of the process that framed it? How do we know that
the performer's idiom squares with our own? What, in short, can we
know or discover about the reception of oral poetry, about the audience's
participatory role in the overall communication?

Connected to these two premises is a third: the dimension of social
embedding. We often strip oral poetry of all or most such context in order
to enshrine it in the network of print or electronic publication, to create a
suitable exhibit for the Museum of Verbal Art,[1] thereby ritualistically and
colonially making it our own. That is one aspect of the problem. But a
second, more insidious aspect also rears its ugly head: because we train
ourselves to recognize the forms that literature has privileged, we tend to

---

1 On the metaphor of the Museum of Verbal Art, see my essay on "The Impossibility of
Canon" (Foley 1998a).

"discover" and privilege those forms in fieldwork investigation. The South Slavic tradition provides an example of this dynamic. In the beginning was epic, fieldworkers supposed, as nineteenth-century scholars sought to disinter nationalistic roots by collecting what the folk preserved. The Brothers Grimm had their counterpart in Vuk Stefanović Karadžić, who along with a dictionary and ethnographic studies published four volumes of Serbian songs that were to become a people's heritage.[2] Little or no attention was paid to the other oral poetic forms that proliferate through village culture even today: the funeral laments, genealogies, and magical charms were almost entirely ignored, the fairy tales and folktales received somewhat better treatment, but only the epic won a large scholarly following. In fact, we would not go far wrong by stating this dynamic proverbially: the more socially functional and the less literary a South Slavic poetic genre proved, the more consistently scholars have ignored it.

Instead of subscribing to the Great Divide, valuing composition over reception or downplaying social function—all three impulses being versions of a literary bias—I will propose a less centralized, more open-ended model for oral poetry. Let me openly stipulate my own bias in these matters, which will privilege difference and heterogeneity over universalism by arguing for diversity not only of content and form but also (and necessarily) of perspective. That is, we need urgently to become more aware of the broad, remarkably many-sided spectrum of what we call oral poetry. But even that ever-developing awareness, that push for pluralism is not by itself enough to do real justice to oral poetry. We also need to affirm a corresponding variety of approaches—*a diversity in frame of reference*—that can help us to wrap our text-bound minds around a highly elusive collection of phenomena. Make no mistake about it: internationally speaking, oral traditions dwarf textual traditions in both size and complexity, and that is the foremost reason why "defaulting" to cognitive categories invented for, suited to, and daily reinforced by texts will not serve our agenda. Cultural pride and familiarity of usage aside, those tools are not up to the task.

In what follows below, I will offer a more inclusive and diverse model for oral poetry, expandable to oral traditions as a whole.[3] My hope is that laying bare some of our unexamined assumptions about what oral

---

2 See Karadžić; available translations of selected poems from these volumes include Holton and Mihailovich; Matthias and Vučković; and Pennington and Levi.
3 This model is discussed at length in Foley 2002, as is the vexed question of what constitutes "poetry," a much more culturally and ideologically charged term than is commonly recognized.

poetry is and how it means will be useful to colleagues who have contributed so variously to this initial meeting in the three-year series of colloquia. Ideally, since all exchanges worth the name are two-way streets, I also hope that this call for pluralism in content and approach will prompt reactions that will help me to deepen and productively complicate the model. In short, I want to leave room for the natural morphology of indigenous oral poems without imposing a colonialist, textual blueprint.

A Spectrum of Oral Poetry

Instead of a narrow conception or a dichotomous model, I advocate a four-part spectrum of oral poetry that reaches from live performance to authored, silent texts and involves reading and writing in three of its four very flexible categories. Let me be explicit about what using the term spectrum entails. Speaking metaphorically, it means that infinite different colors are possible, that one hue blends into the next, and that each wavelength has both its own individual identity as well as a natural relationship with myriad other colors. Where even this metaphor falls short, however, is in its linearity. Oral poetry shows no straight-line "progression" from one stage to another either historically or developmentally. All hues that make up the spectrum are possible in any given culture. I emphasize this point because the last thing we need in oral-tradition studies is another lockstep system that "simplifies" or organizes by exclusion or by forcing boilerplate structures onto the natural heterogeneity of oral poetic forms. What is required is a system that accommodates what we have discovered and makes room for the many forms we have yet to learn about.

With this goal in mind, I sketch below four generalized but fact-based situations for the composition, performance, and reception of oral poetry.[4] Settling on these four patterns naturally requires some simplification, some sacrifice of individual details to principles of explanation. For our purposes, however, this is as it must be. As indicated above, we seek a reasonable middle ground: a set of categories that together offer a rough outline of various media possibilities, a flexible taxonomy that can boost our understanding by organizing myriad individual cases under a few meaningful headings. If configured with due attention to features that truly matter, such a model can serve as a sort of filing system for the diverse collection of oral poetries from around the world and from ancient times to the present.

---

4 See further Foley 2002.

Here, then, is a proposed system of media categories, each illustrated by a single example:

	Composition	Performance	Reception	Example
1. Oral per-formance	Oral	Oral	Aural	Tibetan paper-singer
2. Voiced texts	Written	Oral	Aural	Slam poetry
3. Voices from the past	O/W	O/W	A/W	Homer's *Odyssey*
4. Written oral poems	Written	Written	Written	Bishop Njegoš

Our categories begin, expectably perhaps, with *oral performance*, which entails oral composition, oral performance, and aural reception; they end, perhaps not so expectably, with *written oral poems*, that is, with texts composed in writing and meant for silent, individual reading. Oral poetry can be detected across this entire spectrum of media, even when camouflaged in textual form, and we need to be aware of its many guises.

Let me prefix two cautionary statements to our discussion. First, as explained above, I intend no hierarchy among the four categories. *Oral performance* describes one situation in which we discover oral poetry; it is not necessarily either the "finest" or the purest or the most valuable. Correspondingly, as written technology enters the picture in various ways, it does not degrade or pollute or diminish something pristine any more than it moves poetry forward in quality or complexity; it simply makes for other brands or types of oral poetry. Media combine and interact in interesting ways.

Second, and this goes to the heart of our unexamined assumptions, I offer this four-part system as a true spectrum and not as a series of discrete categories. In other words, I have plotted these four points to map the breadth of the spectrum and to suggest some organizational benchmarks, but the most faithful representation of oral poetry will also be the least categorical. Systems of analysis are necessarily imposed from outside, not generated from the inside; for that reason, they can make no claim to universal, archetypal solutions. We need to grant every culture, tradition, genre, poem, and individual poet and audience the license to complicate the system, to add their own footnotes to whatever assertion we make in the spirit of overall explanation. With these flexible and non-hierarchical categories in mind, then, let's see how each of them works.

1. *Oral Performance*

For many people, the designation *oral poetry* means only one thing: verse composed and performed orally in front of a listening audience. In this first category the processes of composition and performance are usually simultaneous, as in South Slavic epic. When these paired processes are separated, we are sometimes dealing with a memorized text for later performance (not seldom by a different person), a situation that falls into our second category of *voiced texts*. In oral performance, however, reception is customarily live and immediate. Poet and audience participate together, and everything takes place in present time and experience. This is the easiest kind of oral poetry for us text-consumers to grasp, chiefly because it is so opposite to literature in every respect. Indeed, for some of us oral performance is the only scenario that qualifies. Change any part of the equation—composition, performance, or reception—and it no longer adds up; we no longer have oral poetry. But this kind of fundamentalism will prove indefensible because it disenfranchises a great many oral poems that have also involved writing and texts as part of their development.

Of course, there can be no question that oral performance is far the most widespread and copious of our four patterns, with scores of examples from six of the seven continents. Alongside Jack tales and folk sermons from North America and the *romances* of Spain and its diaspora stand, for example, the traditional songs of the Maori from Australia, Basotho migrant songs from Africa, the *Pabuji Epic* from southern India, and Sibundoy oral sayings from Colombia, South America.[5] Even a selective catalogue would soon reach heroic proportions. And this is to say nothing of the myriad instances of oral performance that have been lost simply because they were never documented, indeed could not be *document*-ed because they flowered and expired before the invention of writing or the onset of field collection. Even in our own time, however, a relatively small percentage of such oral/aural performances are ever collected, and fewer still ever reach publication, broad dissemination, and either the academic or the general reader. On theoretical grounds alone, the case for limiting oral poetry to category one is critically weak; what do we do with poems that weave in and out of performance, that are composed in writing but performed orally and received aurally, that audiences can experience only via books, and so forth? Categories two

---

5 See, e.g., Coplan (Basotho); McCarthy 1994 (Jack tales); McDowell (Sibundoy sayings); McLean and Orbell (Maori); Rosenberg 1988 and Titon 1988:253–358 (folk sermons); J. Smith (Pabuji epic); and C. Smith (Spanish ballads).

through four will cover these and other possibilities. Practically, the case is just as weak; in many parts of the world there simply are not many opportunities for many of us to experience oral performance firsthand or secondhand.

Indeed, it is impossible to overemphasize the fact that most of us get to know oral performance only in a textual format, whether in manuscripts or books or perhaps via audio or video facsimiles (which are still texts). We are not part of the Tibetan paper-singer's audience, the Xhosa praise-poet's usual constituency, or the rapt participant-audience of Mexican folk-drama.[6] Rather we are restricted to reading frozen, carefully configured editions of these real-life events; even when full of contextualizing information and analysis, these objects are by no stretch of the imagination equivalent to actual experience of the events themselves. That is a natural sort of situation, of course: relatively few of us do original fieldwork, and even those who do will limit their activities to one or a couple of cultures and languages. But let us be absolutely clear on this most basic point: our treasured editions, though piled high with versions, notes, and context, are not themselves oral performance. Why not? Simply because another medium has intervened. Nonetheless, as flawed and partial as such editions endemically are, I would staunchly maintain that what they (re)present is oral poetry.

Take a related if not identical case. Suppose someone shoots a multimedia video of an oral performance, encoding not just the words we enshrine in texts, with whatever accompanying textual information can be tacked on, but also the visual images, sounds, audience involvement, and so forth. This still is not oral performance. Although the video preserves more of the original performance dynamics than the printed page, it is still a text, fixed and unchanging no matter who views it, no matter when or where one "reads" it. In place of the poet's creation in the here-and-now we experience a distanced, cinematographic refraction of the performance, shot from a certain point of view under certain assumptions and qualified by whatever film-editing occurs from the moment of recording onward. Even if we think of playing the video as something approaching oral performance and watching it as something akin to aural reception, the basis of the experience is still a text. Book, acoustic tape, and film may represent oral performance, but strictly speaking they are not equivalent to it.

Then, too, research has unearthed examples of what is called "oralizing" or "reoralizing." Such discoveries productively call into question the

---

6 On Tibetan oral traditions, see Yang Enhong; on Xhosa praise-poetry, Opland 1983, 1998, and Kaschula 1995, 2000; on Mexican folk-drama, Bauman and Ritch.

evolutionary paradigm of oral-to-written, turning the imagined one-way street leading from oral poetry to literary texts into a broader thoroughfare that permits and even fosters two-way traffic as well as streets leading in many other directions. The Anglo-American folk ballad is a striking example of this natural volatility, circulating back and forth among tradition-bearers, collectors, printed broadsides, and the like. Pushkin's *Eugene Onegin*, originally a highly literary document, has entered Russian oral tradition as dramatic poetry in its own right and earned a place in category one. Balinese poetry in oral tradition interacts in substantive ways with the textual culture and record, not only putting the lie to the Great Divide model but giving clear evidence of two-way migration across the imagined gap.[7] These and other such cases illustrate why a doctrinaire, purist conception of oral poetry as restricted to oral performance cannot work. What we need is a more complete and sensitive system of media dynamics that makes room for the innate diversity of human expressive arts.

2. Voiced Texts

Real-life observations, as distinct from mere theorizing, can help us toward this kind of pluralism. There is another type of oral poetry that begins life as a written composition only to modulate to oral performance before a live audience. For poems that cluster around this node in the spectrum I suggest the designation of *voiced texts*. What separates this kind of verbal art from contemporary written poetry enshrined in literary reviews, chapbooks, and anthologies is precisely its intended medium of publication, the means by which it reaches its audience. Voiced texts aim solely at oral performance and are by definition incomplete without that performance. Compare this trajectory with the more usual and familiar kind of written poetry, which aims primarily at transmission through print to an audience of silent, individual readers. Of course, poets of any sort may read their poetry aloud and often choose to do so, but only in the case of voiced texts is the spoken word the necessary and defining outcome of the composition-performance-reception process.

---

7 See, e.g., de Vet (Balinese epic); McCarthy 1990, M. E. Brown, and Niles 1998 (ballads); and Warner (Russian folk-plays). We should also note the initiative associated with the Universität Freiburg working group on orality and literacy, which has applied orality-literacy studies across a wide disciplinary scope in the humanities and social sciences, including literature (as opposed to oral poetry). For a sense of that school's interpretative program as applied to literature, see Erzgräber and Volk (on medieval English texts), Goetsch (on modern literature, mostly novels, in English, German, and other languages), and Habermalz (on James Joyce's *Ulysses*).

Slam poetry offers us a ready example of voiced texts that can be experienced in urban centers across the United States and increasingly in Western Europe and elsewhere. While it customarily begins life as a penned or word-processed composition, slam does not really live until it is orally performed before a live audience. It may reach publication later on, but that stage is secondary and completely unnecessary. This species of oral poetry is not as widespread internationally as oral performance, of course, but its easy and increasing accessibility makes it an attractive opportunity for directly experiencing oral poetry. Unfortunately, however, slam poetry and other voiced texts suffer from some of the same media prejudice as does oral performance. Because it does not usually intersect with the print network that supports documentation and literature, oral poetry in this second category has usually met with one of two equally discouraging outcomes. Either it has been judged unworthy of comparison with elite, mainstream poetry or simply gone unnoticed because it operates below the literary radar. Colonialist attitudes have impeded its recognition as a living, indigenous oral poetry.

Audience is hardly a problem for most contemporary popular music, some of which also belongs in the voiced texts category of oral poetry. Although a fixed, written text lies at the basis of most rock songs, for example, musicians such as Sting and Dave Matthews regularly speak of how a song evolves as a band works with it over the succession of live performances that make up a tour. The instrumentation may change, a harmony may be deleted or added, various members of the band may experiment with rhythms or insert instrumental solos (leading to extended versions), the lead singer can modify phrasing or even lyrics. A particular song may begin life as the fixed text copyrighted with a record company and burned onto a mass-market CD—essentially providing an identical "book" for everyone to "read." But by the time the tour is finished, that same tune may have evolved quite a distance from the original text, taking on a new shape each time it is performed and reperformed for live audiences. Indeed, "live" albums of well-known songs make their mark by taking advantage of the distance between "canned" versions and fresh reinterpretations of what is recognizably the same song, but with a difference.

Blues, an African American genre in origin, is perhaps most profitably understood as straddling the oral performance and voiced texts categories.[8] At one end of the spectrum, many blues songs are traditional; we can no more say who "wrote" them than we can attribute this or that

---

[8] For an excellent contextual study of traditional country blues, see Titon 1994. Other modern genres straddling categories include, for example, rap and hip hop.

South Slavic epic or Hispanic ballad to a single creator. What is more, blues is more often than not learned and transmitted wholly without texts—written or acoustic—via face-to-face transmission from one player to another. That is not to say that texts do not enter the mix in some situations: a musician may learn from a recording or, more rarely, from sheet music or written-down verses. And we must make room for the blues songs whose lyrics are in fact penned by one individual, though characteristically within the melodic, verbal, and instrumental context of the blues tradition. Regular melodies and guitar licks, always varying within limits, are part of the cueing mechanism that identifies a blues song as what it is.

Voiced texts can also be performed orally by someone other than the person who composed them in writing. Our team's fieldwork in the former Yugoslavia turned up the interesting case of a *guslar* who did just that: Živomir Milojević, a singer of epic songs from the Christian tradition of Serbia who preferred to be known as "Čika Žika," or "Uncle Žika." But he did not voice (or wholly remake) a text-story that was read aloud to him, as in the famous instance involving the preliterate Parry-Lord *guslar* Avdo Medjedović and his *Odyssey*-length performance of *The Wedding of Smailagić Meho*, a feat we would have to call oral performance.[9] No, Čika Žika proudly informed us that he had learned his best song by reading it himself from a songbook or *pjesmarica*. Intrigued over his boast of having personally consulted a written medium as his source, we asked to see the songbook and were presented with a brief pamphlet that did indeed house the song in question, attributed to a *guslar* from the nearby market-town of Arandjelovac.

It was true, then: Čika Žika had apparently learned his favorite song from this small text by reading it himself. Using literacy skills gained during his four years of formal schooling, he had crossed out a line here or there and scrawled a few words on some of the pages. But when he began to play "live"—and this was confirmed more precisely via later analysis of his text and the tape of his performance—the source quickly faded into the background. Notwithstanding his claims and our initial expectations, there was little to compare in the text and his performance. Lines corresponded here and there, while parallel sequences of ideas rolled along without much overlap in actual expression. The text had started the process, there was no denying that. But in voicing it Čika Žika's own traditional competence had taken over, molding the song to his personal idiomatic shape.[10]

---

9 See further Medjedović.

10 Milman Parry reports a parallel case involving his field assistant Nikola Vujnović (who was both literate and a *guslar*) in his unpublished field notes, entitled "Ćor Huso,"

In a sense, voiced texts are the opposite of what happens when oral performance gets recorded and distributed as a print, audio, or video edition. In both cases we are still dealing with oral poetry, only now mediated through a text that becomes the newly created source for everything that follows. However, there is also a difference. In oral performance that text comes into play as the medium for those not present at the performance, while with voiced texts the fixed form exerts its influence— whatever that influence may be—at the beginning of the whole process. In the one case the oral poem is frozen and distributed to audiences as a fossil; in the other the text initiates a sequence of living events that lead to aural reception. Voiced texts live only in, and solely for, oral performance (with the exception of documentary videos of slam poetry and the like[11]), and their audience knows them only as oral poems.

3. Voices from the Past

Suppose that we are no longer able to hear the voice of oral poetry, at least not firsthand, no matter how hard we try? Consider this quandary. The poetic tradition we wish to understand has died many decades or centuries or millennia before, leaving us with textual shards of a once-living work of verbal art. Direct experience of that oral poetry lies forever beyond our reach. Under such conditions attending a performance, watching a video, even listening to an acoustic tape are of course all out of the question. Do we then collapse all distinctions between oral and written poetry? Do we stop trying to listen? Do we settle for the usual routines of textual gymnastics? Do we default to *littera*-ture?

As a first principle, I would argue that we cannot afford to ignore oral poetry simply because its original form flourished too early for it to be studied and recorded as such. Especially when various kinds of witnesses offer evidence that poems such as the Old English *Beowulf* or the ancient Greek *Odyssey* or the Indian *Mahabharata* or the Persian *Shâhnâma* existed first in oral tradition and were only later written down, how can

---

which I discovered in the Parry Collection archive in 2000, many years after our encounter with Čika Žika. Selections from "Ćor Huso" that bear directly on Homeric epic were published by Parry (437–64). For some examples of voiced texts from Africa, in which the original texts are memorized rather than written down and read, see the description of Urhobo and Somali oral poetry in Okpewho (esp. 68). Another example is the North Carolina storyteller Leonard Roberts's oral performance of "Raglif Jaglif Tetartlif Pole," which he recorded from his Aunt Columbia and published in two different collections; see further McCarthy 1994. On some similar but not identical phenomena covering both oral performance and other modes of oral poetry, see Duncan Brown's aptly entitled *Voicing the Text*.

11 See esp. Hemstreet et al. 2000.

we ignore a formative chapter in their biography? As a practical matter, we cannot allow mere chronology and the historical accident of available technologies to diminish or delimit our awareness of oral poetry. As an artistic matter, we cannot hope to read ancient, medieval, and other manuscript-based but oral-connected poetry without considering its true dynamics. Much is at stake here.

For these reasons I propose a third category of oral poetry: voices from the past. What does it include? Simply put, it offers a slot for those oral poetic traditions that time has eclipsed and that we can now consult only in textual form. Built into that capsule definition is a necessary flexibility. Any given poem's original composition may have been oral or written; in many cases we just cannot tell whether the document we hold in our hands is a direct transcription of an oral performance or an artifact some generations of editing and recopying removed from performance. The particular version that survives to us may even have been composed as a text, written down by a poet adhering to the rules of oral performance. All of these possibilities must be kept open or we run the risk of claiming more than we really know and as a result falsifying any conclusions we may try to draw.

Beowulf from medieval England and the *Iliad* and *Odyssey* from ancient Greece are two renowned examples of *voices from the past*. So too are the Mayan *Popol Vuh*, the Old French *Song of Roland* and medieval Spanish *Poem of the Cid*, the Persian *Shâhnâma*, the medieval Welsh *Mabinogion*, and numerous more poems that we can know only as texts. If we take a broad view of what we call poetry, we will certainly need to include parts of the Hebrew Bible and the New Testament.[12] Just how many scribes and editors stand between the last oral performances and these surviving documents—and what sorts of influence such intermediaries exerted—is for the most part beyond our ability to determine. Indeed, we cannot absolutely rule out a Homer who had enough literacy to write down his epics himself (though most would argue against that position) or a *Beowulf*-poet who memorized great chunks of his poem, partially fixing it in rote memory even before it was written down. Of course, flexibility and latitude are prime attributes of our model of media dynamics: all four categories of oral poetry readily accommodate the natural variety of individual circumstances and help forestall preemptive judgments. However, with voices from the past,

---

12 For further reading, see Kelber 1997, Horsley and Draper (New Testament); Niditch 1995, 1996 and Jaffee 1998, 1999, 2001 (Hebrew Bible); Tedlock 1996 (*Popol Vuh*); Duggan and Taylor (*Roland*); Webber and Zemke (*Cid*); S. Davies (*Mabinogion*), and Davidson (*Shâhnâma*). Voices from the past are the principal subject of books such as Zumthor 1990.

when so many of the facts surrounding the history of performances and traditions are lost to us, it is particularly important to keep an open mind. We must be willing to accept some blind spots in our knowledge of these works as we try to "hear" oral poetries exclusively through the texts they have left behind.

At first encounter, voices from the past may resemble the infamous "wastebasket" or "trapdoor" that some theories use to dispose of trouble-some, awkward phenomena that do not quite fit the hypothesis. But that is not the case here. This category renders a crucial service by helping us face up to the real-world challenge of fundamental diversity in human expressive forms. It also allows us to build a sensible agnosticism into the overall explanation, to admit forthrightly that we lack final answers to some questions. If we attempt to force too much order on such diversity, if we try to impose too much from the outside by making assertions we cannot substantiate, any system of media dynamics will be compromised. At that point it will be only too easy to collapse all verbal art back into our default category of text-bound literature. The baby will have gone the way of the bathwater.

What we can say—and here is the crucial point—is that all the poems in this category were composed according to the rules of the given oral poetry. They bear a telltale compositional stamp. Whatever the exact sce-nario of their commission to textual form and their history since that moment, they remain oral poetry. This has important implications for how we hear these voices from the past.

The evidence for calling them "oral poetry" is of two sorts: direct accounts of how they were composed and performed on the one hand, and structural symptoms of oral composition and performance on the other. The direct accounts are self-explanatory: the famous portraits of Hrothgar's singer (*scop*) in *Beowulf* or of the Ithacan bard (*aoidos*) Phemios or his Phaeacian counterpart Demodokos in the *Odyssey*. Of course, we must be very careful not to overestimate the ethnographic reliability of this kind of information, which is not at all the same thing as an anthropological analysis or a field report. Poetic depictions of oral performance, as idealizations with primary loyalty to their poetic tradi-tions, cannot be taken as on-site ethnography. Indeed, even fieldwork can produce stories of transparently legendary singers who serve as anthropomorphic images of the poetic tradition.[13] But in combination with references from other contemporary sources (Plato's *Republic* or

---

13 On the legendary singers described by the Parry-Lord *guslari* and their affinity to ancient descriptions of Homer as well as to modern Mongolian epic singers, see Foley 1999:49–62.

Ion, for example, for ancient Greek oral epic) or histories close to the period and place,[14] poetic accounts can give us confidence in what amounts to an oral-performance or voiced-text background for voices from the past.

The evidence of symptoms is less direct but no less dependable as long as we do not press it too hard. Research has isolated key features, different for each tradition and genre of course, that mark a poem's media heritage. These features are the residue of oral performance; they constitute "what's left" when an oral poem—however it was composed— is reduced to an unvoiced text. Recurrent phrases and scenes are a few of the more widely observed characteristics of voices from the past, but they are hardly the only such features. Thus the celebrated formulaic phrases in Homer, with "swift-footed Achilles" and "rosy-fingered dawn" recurring again and again; thus also the formulas in Coptic hymns from before the year 1000, in the Persian *Shânâhma* of the eleventh century, and in the Latvian *dainas* of the nineteenth, as also in the living tradition of African American rap music.[15] Homeric epic features a number of pliable recurrent scenes, such as the "Assembly" or "Feast," that vary within limits to suit the particular story and the singing style of a particular singer. Typical scenes such as these also populate the Old Norse sagas and once again the living traditions of central Asian epic and the Mongolian *Jangar* cycle as well.[16]

As noted, however, phrases and scenes hardly exhaust the inventory of expressive signs in oral poetry. Native American peoples of the Northwest Coast frame their oral stories in a complex, recognizable series of structures as small as the verse and as large as story-sections, using pattern-numbers as bedrock for their story-building. These keys to organization and meaning have been recovered from texts written out in the early and middle twentieth century, and they make a substantial difference in how we read the stories. Given the diversity of oral poetry in this third category, we cannot expect archetypal features across its wide expanse. But if the particular shape and texture of signals and structures is always idiosyncratic, the plain fact of patterning and of variation within limits is not. Voices from the past reveal their status as oral poetry through their recurrency and multiformity of language, however their

---

14 For a digest of available references to Old English oral poets in both the extant poems and the secondary sources, see Opland 1980.

15 On the Coptic hymns, see MacCoull. On the *Shâhnâma,* see Davidson, esp. 60–66. On the Latvian *dainas,* see Lord 1989; Vikis-Freibergs. On rap music as oral poetry, see Wehmeyer-Shaw; Pihel.

16 See Heissig; Chao.

special poetic language may happen to work. Oral poetry has left behind its footprints in these now-silent texts.

In the early going some specialists believed that the mere density of such patterning could serve as a litmus test, that it constituted "proof" of the actual orality or writtenness of a manuscript poem—whether the text in hand was originally an oral performance or not. We now claim much less but at the same time something much more fundamental: that these features signal a background in oral poetry, though they do not magically reveal the precise story behind any given text. In the case of voices from the past, we usually cannot honestly say whether this or that poem was actually an oral performance. But, on the basis of these two kinds of evidence—direct accounts and structural symptoms—we can confidently pronounce *Beowulf*, the *Odyssey*, the *Shâhnâma*, the *Mahabharata*, the *Roland*, the *Mabinogion*, the *Cid*, and many other manuscript works "oral poetry." And that identification carries with it a wealth of important implications for reading.

So much for composition. How were these voices from the past performed and received? Ascribing both oral and written performance and reception may seem like hedging, but it is a realistic representation of what we know and can figure out. In the ancient and medieval traditions cited above and many more poetries worldwide, there is every reason to conclude that both kinds of performance took place, sometimes side by side in the same era. Performers composed without texts in front of audiences, and they read aloud from texts for others; probably less frequently they read to themselves, whether aloud or silently.[17] Consider the real-life situations in the ancient and medieval periods. Few people controlled the arts of literacy, and what literacy there was enjoyed a limited range of applications. Few copies of oral poems existed in any user-friendly format, and mass readership had not yet been invented. Under such conditions the last thing we should expect is tidily organized modes of performance. *Beowulf* may well have been performed in Anglo-Saxon England both without a text and by voicing a text. Homer's oral poems seem to have been performed in numerous different venues, perhaps voiced from rote memory or from texts by rhapsodes (*rhapsoidoi*) as well as composed and recomposed by oral bards (*aoidoi*).[18] Artificially

---

[17] The idea of *vocality* developed by Zumthor (1987) and Schaefer (1992, 1993) and defined by Schaefer as "a cultural situation that very much depended and relied on the voice for mediation of verbal communication even though writing had already been well established" (1993:205) describes a phenomenon similar to voiced texts.

[18] On the performance of Old English poetry and comparative analogues, see also Niles 1999:89–119. Three recent hypotheses about the fixation of the Homeric poems are Janko; Jensen; and Nagy: 29–112.

compressing such natural variability for the sake of a well-ordered model can only cloud our perspective, not only on the oral poems in question but on voices from the past more generally.

As with composition and performance, so with reception. If anything, the spectrum of possible scenarios broadens even further at the far end of the chain of communication. We can imagine—and we have believable evidence for imagining—an oral poet performing before an audience. This is essentially oral performance as reflected in the versions of these poems that survive to us, though of course we can never personally verify that reflection. We also know that voiced texts were widely in play in the ancient and medieval periods, with a fixed version serving as the basis for the performance.[19] As we have learned, the voiced-text scenario demands that we allow for departures from that fixed version, in effect for recomposition during performance. It also requires that we allow for the composer and performer to be different people. Indeed, in a manuscript tradition such as the Anglo-Saxon, where even writing scribes recomposed formulaically as they copied, variable performance from manuscripts by a range of people seems a foregone conclusion.[20] Finally, the existence of a manuscript text, whether from ancient or medieval Europe, Asia, or the Americas, means that we cannot afford to deny the possibility of readers who read only to themselves. This is liable to be a very small group, given literacy rates, the uses to which writing is put, and contemporary textual technologies. But voices from the past must include all scenarios, forthrightly acknowledging what we do not know as well as recognizing the combination of media in play.

With what does this category of oral poetry finally present us? What is the underlying logic that sorts its various manifestations? We need to be clear and realistic in answering such questions: voices from the past are not—and can never be—as economically defined and delimited as oral performance or voiced texts. Too much remains either unknown or dependent on composite media to settle unambiguously on single options for composition, performance, and reception. Consider the intriguing case of the Finnish *Kalevala*, which derives from orally performed poems but reached epic form only through the active intervention of its collector Elias Lönnrot, a physician-folklorist whom some would call a ghost-writer and some would call a singer.[21] But

---

19 See Stock 1983, esp. 3–87 on interactions of oral and written and 88–92 on "textual communities," in which "the text itself ... was often re-performed orally" (91); also Stock 1990:1–29.

20 See O'Keeffe, esp. 23–46; Doane.

21 On the *Kalevala*, see esp. DuBois 1995; Honko: 8.

beyond an admittedly untidy spectrum of possibilities lies a saving grace: the rationalizing fact that, whatever guise they may take in their various histories and manuscript forms, voices from the past are still oral poetry. By allowing for the uncertainties generated by centuries of distance and by different mixes of performance and text in different cultures, we can focus on what really matters, namely, that the verbal art of Gilgamesh, the *Shâhnâma*, the *Mahabharata*, the Hebrew Bible, the New Testament, *Beowulf*, the *Odyssey*, the *Kalevala*, and other such works springs from oral tradition. Whether we know them as clay tablets, papyrus rolls, vellum codices, or printed books, these works are also—and vitally—oral poems.

4. Written Oral Poems

How can oral poetry exist as written verse read from texts meant for individual readers? What is oral about a process that begins and ends with writing technology and entirely lacks living voice and aural reception?[22] Is not a *written oral poem* a contradiction in terms?

Although this is far the smallest of our four categories, in some ways it is just as important as the others—not for what it contains but for what it reveals about what really constitutes oral poetry. Poets who write oral poetry are composing according to certain rules, just like readers who read oral poetry. Thus a learned figure from nineteenth-century Yugoslavia, Bishop Petar II Petrović Njegoš, accomplished what conventional wisdom once pronounced impossible: he composed oral poetry pen-in-hand for consumption by literate, reading audiences. Some investigators have termed his works "imitation oral," a designation that seems to question their quality or genuineness, but the fact is that Njegoš "sang" on the page. He wrote oral poetry.[23]

How he managed this apparent miracle is an important consideration for us as we try to learn how to read an oral poem. Born Rade Petrović in 1813 in a Montenegrin village, Njegoš was eventually to succeed his

---

22 I explicitly leave out of consideration novels that use oral strategies or refer to oral sources, on the grounds that they are neither poetry nor wholly oral (even in our fuller sense of "oral poetry"); see, e.g., Obiechina and Balogun (African); Rosenberg 1994 (African American), Brill de Ramírez (Native American). Another genre not treated is the complex hybrid known as the "frame tale" (see Irwin 1995, 1998), which occurs throughout South Asia, the Middle East, and Europe from the ancient world at least until the medieval period and "depicts ... storytelling events in all their variety and in the process carries many of the keys to oral performance onto the printed page" (Irwin 1998: 391).

23 For a brief biography of and commentary on Njegoš, see Lord 1986: 29–34; on another learned poet who wrote oral poetry, see Miletich 1978a, 1978b on Andrija Kačić-Miošić and "imitation oral" style.

uncle as bishop of Montenegro in 1833. His biography thus begins with early immersion in the South Slavic oral tradition of heroic stories, apparently both the Muslim and the Christian varieties. He even learned to sing the songs to the *gusle* himself, under the tutelage of his father and uncle. As for the "other world" of letters, as Albert Lord (1986) puts it, Njegoš received lessons in reading and writing in the monastery at Cetinje starting at age twelve. The trajectory of his own life mirrors the mixed context of orality and literacy that characterized nineteenth-century Montenegro.

Straddling these two worlds with a bilingual familiarity, Njegoš was able to use the traditional oral style at the same time that he could also stand outside it. We can see his multiple media-fluency in his early collection, *Pjevannija* (2nd ed., 1837), which runs the gamut of expressive forms. Some poems are reperformances of well-known traditional stories, some are "new" songs, and still others begin to introduce literary conventions into traditional song-making. These "new" poems were topical and locally situated but composed in the formulaic, decasyllabic idiom; their language and style came from one world and their subjects from another. Throughout this collection Njegoš displays a repertoire of registers or expressive strategies, the result of his dual competence in oral tradition and literary texts. In sum, his example shows us the importance of grasping the diversity of oral poetry across traditions, genres, and especially media. Njegoš probably composed entirely in writing (some say oral dictation may have figured into his work, but there is frankly no evidence for that); he "performed" the poems in a published text, and readers came to know them exclusively from that textual source. Nonetheless, there is no question that what the bishop wrote was oral poetry.

An Almanac of Proverbs

So far I have attempted to establish the diversity of oral poetry, outlining in brief format the tremendous variety of forms that it comprises.[24] Providing realistic breadth is one way of exposing the unexamined assumptions on the basis of which we text-consumers unthinkingly compromise our studies of oral poetry. Now I turn to another strategy, one that springs directly from oral tradition, in order to underline the diversity premise and to begin to move toward some perspectives on "reading" oral poetry. The strategy in question is the *proverb*, the small byte of wisdom that generically illuminates a host of different situations

---

24 For further examples, see Foley 2002: Seventh Word.

by alluding to something fundamental via a memorable phrase. In everyday English, we say "A stitch in time saves nine" not to comment on the arts of stitchery but to remind ourselves of the importance of preparation and deft timing. In South Slavic epic, the *guslari* say "San usnila, pa se prepanula" ("You've dreamed a dream, so you're frightened") not to delve into the dynamics of the unconscious but to indicate that a cataclysmic event lies on the horizon and, contrary to the speaker's dismissiveness, will soon bring tragedy. From another point of view, Odysseus's bowshot through the axe-handles also does what a proverb does: it reveals the underlying unity or alignment of disparate objects or situations.

That much said, let me admit that the proverbs cited below are entirely ungenuine and nontraditional. I have coined them in an effort to capture some complex and often slippery ideas in simple, memorable form. They employ some favorite proverbial techniques, such as wordplay, superficial contradiction, balanced clauses, and echoes of genuine proverbs. But they are nonetheless homemade, drawn not from a traditional word-hoard but from my own nontraditional composition. Here, then, are eleven maxims, each with a sentence or two of explanation (enough, I hope, to make them useful but not enough to compromise their proverbial function).

1. *Oral poetry works like language, only more so.* Oral poetry is not an object but an experience, even in texts; as such, it works like language, varying within limits. Oral poetry tends to be highly idiomatic (the "more so").

2. *Oralpoetry is a very plural noun.* As diverse as written literature has proven itself internationally and from ancient to modern times, it is dwarfed in size and diversity by oral poetry.

3. *Performance is the enabling event, tradition the context for that event.* Performance is part of the meaning (even when induced rhetorically in texts), and tradition fills out any single performance via implication.

4. *The art of oral poetry emerges* through *rather than* in spite of *its special language.* The often archaic, multidialectal, or otherwise specialized languages of oral poetry are not roadblocks but rather functional vehicles that actively promote traditional referentiality.

5. *The best companion for reading oral poetry is an* un*published dictionary.* Because oral poetry is highly idiomatic, conventional lexicons and dictionaries, intended as they are to gloss the narrower range of textual communications, are often insufficient to the task. We need to understand oral poetry on its own terms.

6. *The play's the thing (not the script).* Oral poetry exists in the exchange between performer/writer and audience/reader. No edition can truly capture an oral poem (though electronic media can bring us closer[25]).

7. *Repetition is the symptom, not the disease.* In those oral poetries where repetition (I prefer "recurrency") is common, it results not from iteration but from the inevitably recursive processes of idiomatic speech.

8. *Composition and reception are two sides of the same coin.* We cannot be content with explaining the "miracle" of oral composition; we need to pay at least equal attention to *how oral poetry means.*

9. *Read both behind and between the signs.* Oral poetry will usually contain both shared, idiomatic elements (traditional signs) and individual, situation-specific elements. We must be ready to appreciate both dimensions of the poetic landscape.

10. *True diversity demands diversity in frame of reference.* An awareness of variety in the forms of oral poetry must be paralleled by a pluralistic approach to interpreting oral poetry.

11. *Without a tradition there is no language; without a speaker there is only silence.* The age-old argument over the primacy of the tradition or the individual is nonsensical; to varying degrees depending on the particular tradition, both are crucially necessary.

Like any proverb, these byte-sized phrases are best pressed into service as the occasion and opportunity arise. Nonetheless, let me offer an example of how they work by applying a few of them to the ecosystem of oral poetry collected and examined by our fieldwork team in the Serbian village of Orašac. Hopefully, other fieldworkers and scholars will find other ways to use them in other contexts.

Proverb 1, which speaks to the idiomatic nature of oral poetries, bears on the epic narratives and lyric songs of this region of the former Yugoslavia. Names, stock phrases, typical scenes, and story-patterns all command a much larger and deeper field of reference than any literal analysis of the given poem can uncover. Only by becoming aware of the traditional context of such recurrent signs can we fully appreciate that "oral poetry works like language, only more so." But that is only part of

---

25 On the use of electronic editions to mirror oral traditional processes, see Foley 2001.

the story. Less "literary" genres—those that find no cognates in the world of literature—illustrate another dimension of this proverb. The "more so" of magical spells is their curative power, the "more so" of funeral laments is their therapeutic function for the individual and the community, the "more so" of genealogies is the maintenance of group identity in extended families, and so forth. These are crucial aspects of those genres of oral poetry, socially contributory aspects that we are likely to overlook unless we come to grips with what oral poetry can do in addition to what written poetry usually does for us.

The repertoire of speech-acts in a Serbian village certainly shows how "*oralpoetry* is a very plural noun" (proverb 2). From epic and lyric (itself highly heterogeneous) through magical spells (both curative and harmful) and funeral laments through folktales, recipes, and genealogies, it rapidly becomes apparent that no single definition or concept can ever pass muster. The verbal ecosystem consists of many different species. Meters change, registers or varieties of language shift, social embedding is always both idiosyncratic and determinative. Because of the reality of proverb 2, then, we also need to pay careful attention to proverb 10: "True diversity demands diversity in frame of reference." We must be ready to consult the whole range of possibilities and select the approach most suitable for each of these poetic types, whether it be a focus on performative aspects, on comparative analysis against the backdrop of other genres, or whatever.

Not seldom we may find that performers seem to repeat themselves on any number of levels. Perhaps the same phrase recurs or a description sounds familiar or an entire performance can be identified as following a pattern that allows for both stability and change (and, not incidentally, idiomatic implication). In such cases we would do well to recognize that "repetition is the symptom, not the disease," that the performer is working within a language whose traditional morphology—rather than simple iteration—is at the root of recurrency. Correspondingly, that recurrency is an important dimension at both ends of the overall communication, acting as a cue for the audience or reader: in other words, "composition and reception are two sides of the same coin." Important as such telltale signs are, however, we must also leave room for the poet's own molding of the utterance, for the inevitably personal, idiolectal features that mesh with traditional signs. As proverb 9 puts it, we must "read both behind and between the signs."

A Menu of Approaches

With these ideas about oral poetry's diversity and dynamics in hand, I turn now to a telegraphic suggestion of some methods for interpretation, specifically the approaches known as performance theory, ethnopoetics, and immanent art. Of course, this brief survey of three common approaches could be significantly lengthened,[26] just as we could devote all our attention to any single one of them. But what I aim at here is merely an illustration of diversity in frame of reference, a menu of approaches that collectively show how it will always be more fruitful to choose from a variety of tools than to insist upon always resorting to the same one. Not only will different methods yield different perspectives on different oral poetries, but more than one approach can provide multiple perspectives on the same oral poetry.

Performance theory derives from the fundamental observation that performance is part of the meaning. The very act of uttering an oral poem should alert us to its more-than-literal, more-than-textual sense, so goes the argument, to the reality that it is a developing and emergent experience that is only partially transferable to our usual medium of book and journal publication. Richard Bauman speaks of "keys to performance," including aspects such as special codes (of gesture and dress as well as speech) and appeal to tradition (as when a poet cites a traditional source or credits preceding bards).[27] These keys, always as idiosyncratic as the different languages, genres, and registers in which a performer composes, are coded signals to the audience to receive the communication on a particular wavelength. "Take what follows in a special way," these cues advise. Thus when a South Slavic Moslem epic singer says "Davno bilo, sad se spominjalo" ("Long ago it was, now it is being remembered"), he is asking his audience to place what follows in the mythological network animated by tales of wedding, battle, and return and populated by heroes such as Djerdjelez Alija, Mustajbey of the Lika, and Tale of Orašac. Such is the power of that key to performance.

To press this method into service, the investigator must first become as familiar as possible with the multifaceted language of performance. This entails not only close attention to the performer's words but also to all other circumstances of performance: the setting (ritual, quotidian, malleable?), the nonlinguistic aspects of the speech-act (melody or musical instrumentation, material accoutrements, etc.), the role of the audience (from the steady approbation of the West African Naamusayer to the raucous participation of the North American slam-poetry audience), and any other factors that bear on the expressivity of the oral poetry in question.

---

26 For more on these three approaches, see Foley 2002: Third Word (Performance Theory), Fourth Word (Ethnopoetics), and Fifth Word (Immanent Art). For a historical survey or "glossary" of approaches to oral tradition, see Zumwalt.

27 See esp. Bauman 1977, 1986; also Bauman and Braid.

Performance theory can also be applied to texts, to voices from the past or written oral poems, since some keys—such as formulaic language and appeal to tradition—can survive the translation from experience to object, though with inevitable semiotic change. Judiciously applied, this approach can illuminate a wide variety of oral poetries by bringing to light many of the poetic features we customarily submerge by regarding living entities as textual products.

With *ethnopoetics* we engage many of the same issues addressed by performance theory. Here, however, the program focuses on understanding oral poetries on their own terms and actively avoiding the reflex of defaulting to this or that set of external, extrinsic priorities. Thus Ethnopoetics asks first what makes an utterance "poetry." What constitutes a line or verse, for instance? In many traditions, the nature of this line-unit has absolutely nothing to do with such Greco-Roman features as syllabic regularity; Anglo-Saxon poetry operates on other criteria, for example. Perhaps an oral poetry signals its specialized way of speaking by rhyme, stress, intonation, or breath-group; the list of possibilities is extensive, and each tradition has its own modalities of expression at every level. Another common question posed by this approach concerns the larger units of poetry: stanza, strophe, scene, speech, narrative division, and the like. Which, if any, of these units is truly constitutive? But whatever the level of the inquiry, ethnopoetics concerns itself with discovering the poetics of the *ethnos*, the group who make and consume an oral poetry, and proactively guards against importing irrelevant measures and models, no matter how much success those measures and models have had elsewhere. In a sense this approach runs directly counter to textual colonialism, valuing above all else the indigenous reality of oral poetries.

Yet, not contradictorily, ethnopoetics aims at providing the reading audience a text. Of course, it is not just any text. What this approach attempts to provide is a libretto for reperformance, a guide for the reader to reconstitute an original performance on its own culture-specific terms—as far as that proves possible. Such texts contain not just the flattened, bleached-out words we inscribe and print but stage directions that bring the words to life. In Dennis Tedlock's brand of scores for reperformance, for example, one finds capital letters for loudness, smaller letters for whispering, curved arcs of words to indicate rising and falling intonation, and, most saliently of all, spaces to foreground silence. Voicing such libretti aloud brings a reader closer to how the oral poem means on its own terms.[28] Or consider Dell Hymes's version of the ethnopoetic credo,

---

[28] On this brand of ethnopoetics, see further Tedlock 1983, 1999; also DuBois 1998; Foley 1995:17–27 and 2002: Fourth Word.

which concentrates not so much on vocal as on rhetorical signals. From run-on prose he extracts verses, lines, stanzas, scenes, and acts, restoring relationships among phrases and ideas that prose characteristically hides away. Via this method Hymes has been able not only to score living performances but also to rescue performative reality from dictated texts taken down in writing many years before by other investigators.[29] Both Tedlock's and Hymes's versions of ethnopoetics, founded in Native American oral traditions, have now seen application in a wide variety of oral poetries, from oral performance through voices from the past.

The third item on our interpretive menu is *immanent art*, in some ways a development from the oral-formulaic theory inaugurated by Milman Parry and Albert Lord. Briefly stated, the difference is between structure and implication. On the one hand, oral-formulaic theory has concentrated on explaining the supposed "miracle" of preliterate epic storytelling.[30] For that reason it has focused on the structural features of oral poetries, most often on their formulaic phraseology, typical scenes, and narrative patterns, without much attention to their expressive content. Another way of saying the same thing is to observe that oral-formulaic theory has emphasized composition at the expense of reception. Immanent art, on the other hand, asks not just how the structures work (mechanistically) but how they mean (aesthetically). Instead of aiming solely or chiefly at a formal description of the specialized languages or registers of oral poetry, it tries to unearth their idiomatic meaning. Its goal is thus to establish, as far as possible, the traditional referentiality of these registers, to offer some insight into how "oral poetry works like language, only more so."[31]

Immanent art maintains that the "more so" is a function of fluency in the register, and further that even ancient and medieval texts—not to mention living oral poetry—preserve some echo of idiomatic meaning. Thus it is that Homer's oft-repeated (or often recurring) formula "green fear" (*chlōron deos*) can be shown to carry the unambiguous connotation of "supernaturally inspired fear," even though no lexicon will ever betray that sense of the composite phrase.[32] "The best companion for reading

---

29 On Hymes's version of ethnopoetics, see Hymes 1981, 1989, 1994; also Foley 1995: 17-27 and 2002: Fourth Word.

30 It has not been clearly enough recognized that oral-formulaic theory was founded on just one subgenre of European epic (Muslim South Slavic songs) and that therefore its premises were predisposed in certain ways. On this point, see further Foley 1990.

31 On the history of oral-formulaic theory, see Foley 1988; for bibliography, Foley 1985, with updates. On the approach from immanent art, see Foley 1991, 1995, 1999, 2002: Fifth Word; also Bradbury.

32 For discussion of this and other examples of traditional phraseology in Homer, see Foley 1999: 201-37.

oral poetry is an *un*published dictionary," cautions our proverb. Thus it is in *Iliad* 6 that Andromache vainly pleads with Hektor to remain with her and their son and to forgo battle by speaking through the traditional narrative pattern of lament; if we are alive to Homer's idiom, this pattern signals us that Hektor is as good as dead. Of course, we will not find lament in any published handbook or lexicon, but the six additional occurrences of the scene—in which various people mourn the killing of Hektor or Patroklos with speeches that follow the same schema—are evidence for the traditional referentiality of this narrative byte.[33] And thus it is that the *Odyssey* as a whole follows the well-worn track of the Indo-European Return Song, whose idiomatic sequence of events helps to explain problems as knotty as the nonchronological order of the poem, the (heroic) stubbornness and ambiguity of Penelope, and the riddle of where the epic actually ends.[34]

Like performance theory, immanent art seeks to discover keys to event-centered meaning, even in texts. And like ethnopoetics, it aims at portraying oral poetries on their own terms. All three methods address the "word-power" inherent in oral poetry; each one, in its particular way and from its particular perspective, can help us become a better audience or readership. Taken together, they offer a handy and effective set of procedures for "reading" oral poetry.

CODA

This essay began with two laments, those of the folklorist and of the literary scholar, that outlined some of the most basic problems we face in studying oral traditions. In response I have championed a wider, deeper, more inclusive idea of *oral poetry*, a perspective that appreciates diversity and interaction with writing and reading rather than tries to demarcate a tidy, one-dimensional field. With pluralism as the central credo, I then adduced a sequence of eleven proverbs as a (homemade) strategy for keeping track of some of the more elusive features of oral poetry, which "works like language, only more so." Finally, I have suggested that we need not one but an array of approaches to the study of oral traditions. If oral poetries dwarf their better-known, more high-profile literary cousins in both number and variety—and they most certainly do—then it is only responsible to learn to use not just one but a whole kit of interpretive

---

[33] On the idiomatic power of the scenes of lament and feast in Homer, see Foley 1999: 169–99.

[34] On the morphology of the Indo-European Return Song and its implications for the *Odyssey*, see ibid.: 115–67.

tools. Proverbially speaking, "True diversity demands diversity in frame of reference." By following the program very briefly and generally outlined here, and by adapting it as necessary to the wonderful heterogeneity we will meet at every turn, we can get beyond some of our unexamined assumptions about verbal art and give oral poetry its due. In the process we may even encounter some indigenous poems rather than limit ourselves to poring over their colonialist texts.

Cognition, Orality-Literacy, and Approaches to First-Century Writings

Pieter J. J. Botha
University of South Africa

1. Introduction

In his critique of rhetorical criticism—from a "socio-rational empiricist" standpoint—Bruce Malina queries the value of orality research with regard to the study of writings from the first century.

> For interpreters of ancient documents, the question of literacy and illiteracy in a given culture is not simply about the prevalence of the ability or lack thereof to read and write in a social group. The basic issue is whether a language document, whether an utterance, a speech, or a writing, was carefully composed and edited, or unprepared and extemporaneous, in the form we have it. The question of whether the document in question, to be performed or read aloud in any event, was written down or memorized is quite secondary to the point at issue, which is whether the document was carefully prepared or extemporaneous. Much that has been written on orality and literacy in the first-century Mediterranean world is rather beside the point. "[Sylvia] Scribner and [Michael] Cole's extensive research, published as *The Psychology of Literacy* (Cambridge, Mass.: Harvard University Press, 1981), reveals rather conclusively that being able to read and write has no great effect on cognition, certainly less than the experience of attending school and even less than whether or not one lives in an urban or agrarian community. [R]eading and writing, like any other activity, develop only those cognitive skills actually related to their use; that is, there is no reason to believe that a certain minimal mastery of literacy will result in profound changes in how people think or organize themselves." (Malina 1996:98, citing Tuman)

These assertions probably reflect much of the common opinion among New Testament scholars about orality studies, all worth commenting on. What, however, caught my attention especially is the reference to the research by Scribner and Cole (1981a) and the very distinct suggestion that reading and writing have a negligible effect on cognition and that consequently most studies on orality and literacy in the first-century Mediterranean world is "beside the point." That is, Scribner and Cole have shown ("conclusively") that the impact of "literacy" should not be of concern to New Testament scholars.

This may be true but, as I argue in this essay, should not be claimed on the basis of the research by Scribner and Cole. It may even be that what has been said about first-century literacy is beside the point, but that should not detract from the importance of analysis and historical understanding of first-century Mediterranean orality and literacy. These pursuits are *not* irrelevant, especially not when the aim is to *avoid ethnocentric presuppositions*.

The work by Scribner and Cole has become a major reference in studies relating to the effects of literacy. Its fame comes from the size and dimensions of the study, which are unmatched (to this day), conducted in Liberia in the 1970s, but probably also from the fact that many regard this study as the definitive empirical refutation of the various permutations of oral-literate theories. The conclusion by Scribner and Cole that their data show "unequivocally" that literacy does not have any of the general cognitive consequences attributed to it by the orality and literacy theorists has become the received wisdom in many discussions of the topic.[1]

---

[1] A noteworthy instance of the impact of the Scribner-Cole publication is the theorizing and analyses by David Olson—another important orality-literacy scholar. Olson grappled with the Scribner-Cole conclusions in most of his 1980s publications. Basic to Olson's views is the distinction between "utterance" (informal oral-language statements used in conversation, story-telling, verse, and song) and "text" (explicit written prose used in statements, arguments and essays). Utterances encapsulate knowledge in proverbs and aphorisms, and texts encapsulate knowledge in logical premises; meaning is "extrinsic" to utterances and "intrinsic" to texts (Olson 1977). There is a "transition from utterance to text both culturally and developmentally and ... this transition can be described as one of increasing explicitness, with language increasingly able to stand as an unambiguous or autonomous representation of meaning" (1977:258). The "ability to assign meaning to a sentence per se, independent of its nonlinguistic interpretive context, is achieved only well into the school years" (1977:275). It is only after children become literate that they can separate the literal meaning of a statement from what the speaker/writer means by it, by making the "said/ meant" distinction (Olson and Hildyard; Olson 1988a). That is, literacy has a distinct contribution to the development of the distinction between literal and intended meanings. Consequently, writing provides a model for understanding (1994:258, 273). After the publication of Scribner and Cole's findings, which seem to counter Olson's description of the cognitive effects of literacy, Olson reformulated his statements. "I now think this dichotomy [oral utterances versus written texts] is somewhat exaggerated .... That is, literacy may have more of an effect on a whole cultural tradition than upon the cognitive processes of individuals" (Olson 1980:187). The "simple theory relating the availability of an alphabet or the availability of the printing press to altered patterns of speech or thought is at best a conjecture and at worst simply false" (1994:16). An important development in his thought is that

Malina defends a historical approach to ancient texts, and he argues that one of the more serious obstacles to this approach is "ethnocentric presuppositions." It is in the context of accusing some scholars of working with *implicit* scenarios when interpreting texts (which is a bad way of doing things, over against the *explicit* use of models, which is good; see Malina 1982; 1991a; 1991b) that Malina suggests that when (New Testament) scholars write about first-century orality and literacy as of historical import, such assessments are burdened with ethnocentric presuppositions, referring to the article by Tuman as proof.

Tuman is criticizing Walter Ong (1982). Ong, as is well known, is partial toward orality and suggests that what is wrong with modern society, among other things, is the growing impact of literacy in communication. Tuman, in contrast, feels that it is precisely literacy that will help "us" to meaningfully "remake" ourselves and our worlds (Tuman: 779). In order to undermine Ong's claims about literacy as a causal factor in the development of thought and culture, Tuman (775–76) criticizes Ong's reliance on Jack Goody and refers to the work of Michael Cole and Sylvia Scribner, the argument that Malina cites.

In this essay I want to retrace these steps and place the conclusions of Cole and Scribner into perspective. I want to reiterate the importance of orality-literacy issues as *one of the factors* making up the first-century Mediterranean world.

2. Cultural Psychology and Speech and Writing

Linguistic research clearly leads to the conclusion that the distinction between *speech* and *writing* is quite real and extends across different cultures and languages. Speech and writing are characterized by distinct sets of attributes. These linguistic differences can be traced to the interactive, "evanescent" production and the use of prosody in speech that differ from the solitary, permanent, and planned nature of writing. These different attributes—it must be emphasized—are not exclusive. Some genres of writing may incorporate certain "oral" attributes, and some genres of speech clearly have certain "literate" characteristics.[2] More to the point is

---

"it is misleading to think of literacy in terms of consequences. What matters is what people do with literacy, not what literacy does to people" (Olson 1985:15). This is an important perspective, also promoted by Shirley Heath (1983). "Literacy's description is relative to particular practices and goals in particular societies" (Olson 1987:7).

2 A dichotomy can be maintained only at a high level of generality. Scholars emphasize the importance of referring to continua of habits and/or characteristics. See Akinnaso (1982; 1985); Bright; Finnegan (1974; 1988:175); Goody (1989:226–27); Tannen . To realize how complex things really are, one need only ask: What exactly is writing? Megaliths, property

to acknowledge the highly variable nature of spoken language. Depending on sociocultural conditions, speech reveals varying elements of "writtenness." It may be impossible to find a precise theoretical system with which to distinguish all spoken from all written genres, as Mulder (70–71) warns, but there are patterns of association between the modalities and different linguistic structures characterizing their relative autonomy. Interestingly, Mulder reminds us that a spoken language and its written counterpart are *not* obviously similar; the same language reveals extensive differences semiotically in its written and spoken forms.[3]

Perhaps the more significant blind spot of oral-literate theorists (with the exception of David Olson) is the neglect of the findings of cognitive psychology dealing with the processing of speech and writing. Of course the body of literature is enormous, and any brief review shows that we are still at the beginnings of understanding the processes and mechanisms that determine the cognitive handling of spoken and written discourse. What does emerge from this research clearly points to some cognitive differences relating to the two types of discourse. Analytical considerations, as well as experimental and clinical evidence, indicate that several distinct ways exist in the mind when dealing with the two language modalities.

Still, one may question the applicability of such data to historical analysis, and the anthropological fieldwork represented by cultural psychology seems to present more solid ground for developing interpretive models. Hence, I think, the appeal of the work by Scribner and Cole. They situate their research within psycholinguistic research focusing on the psychological functions relating to writing and speech.

2.1. Vygotskiĭ and Luria

The research by Lev Semenovich Vygotskiĭ (1896–1934) and Aleksandr Romanovich Luria (1902–77), done in the late 1920s and early

---

markers, African masks, tattoos, social symbols—are they not all instances of writing? Consequently, many "of the standard comparisons between oral and literate cultures are flawed because the role of writing is misrepresented" (Goody 1989:226). See further A. M. Davies; Goody (1987:3–54); R. Harris; Haynes; Kaplan; Schmandt-Besserat.

[3] "Spoken language and its written counterpart have a high degree of intertranslatability. This is probably due in part to the fact that they serve similar cultural purposes, but unless one has learned to read and write, there is for the native speaker no similarity at all between the two. It is therefore terribly wrong, as most people tend to do, to regard the two as mere variants of the same thing. [A sound basis] ... is to accept that spoken language and its written counterpart are two entirely different semiotic systems, which have to be described independently" (Mulder: 43).

1930s, represents prominent early efforts in this regard. Both these psychologists are deeply committed to understanding consciousness (and hence cognitive changes); Vygotskiĭ suggests that socially meaningful activity can be the explanatory principle for and generator of consciousness, and Luria examines the interrelationship of biology and experience on cognitive development.

Language and speech occupy a special place in Vygotskiĭ's psychological system: they are psychological tools that help form mental functions yet are also part of these functions. To Vygotskiĭ, human thought, having its roots in individual motivation and volition, takes form in an "inner speech" (12–57, 210–56). This "inner speech" is highly condensed, with each word carrying large amounts of meaning; it is the individualized reasoning-for-oneself. In inner speech, sense predominates over meaning (i.e., context over generalized concept), sentence over word, and context over sentence. It is not just an internal aspect of talking but a function in itself, thought connected to words. But the same meaning would require many more words to be expressed in outer speech. This verbal expansion from the inner to the outer speech occurs more in writing than in speaking. A writer elaborates and expands as one has to make up for the absence of intonation, facial expression, shared context, and so forth (Vygotskiĭ: 180–82).

Anticipating many of the linguistic distinctions between oral and literate discourse developed by later research (considered by, e.g., Ong 1982:36–56), Vygotskiĭ points out, among other things, that writing usually lacks a specific interlocutor and is detached from its situational context of composition (Vygotskiĭ: 239–43). This lack of context is the main reason for writing's need for expansion and elaboration, just as it is the main reason for the extreme brevity of the "inner speech" because the situation, the subject of thought, is always known to the thinker (243). "Inner speech works with semantics, not phonetics" (244). Writing also makes a person aware of the structure of language, as it requires deliberate analytical action and "deliberate structuring of the web of meaning" (182). "Inner speech," to interpretatively summarize Vygotskiĭ, is a paradigm for "orality."

In order to find empirical support for his theories, Vygotskiĭ, with the help of his junior colleague, Luria (who was actually instrumental in establishing Vygotskiĭ's academic career), planned a major field study in the remote parts of Soviet Central Asia. The actual study was carried out under the supervision of Luria, and its results were published in 1974 (English translation, Luria 1976). In this study, the responses of illiterate peasants in the mountain villages of Uzbekistan and Kirghizia were compared to the responses of literate (students studying at a teacher's college) or semiliterate individuals from the same communities. The study reveals the tendency of illiterate people not to think in "abstract," "logical" ways, regardless of how practically intelligent and shrewd they may be.

The illiterate participants were found unable to formulate abstract superordinate categories (such as "facial organs," "tools," or "weapons"). Instead, they would try to interpret images shown to them by means of practical (as opposed to categorical) relationships. They would contextualize concepts in experience, employing a "situational mode" in reasoning.[4]

The peasants found defining words difficult, preferring the dictates of practical situations for concept formation. When asked to explain what a tree is, a response would be, "Why should I? Everyone knows what a tree is, they don't need me telling them" (Luria 1976:86). Or when asked to explain what a car is, they would say: "Everyone knows what a car is, there are cars all over the world. There's so many cars it just can't be people have never seen them" (87). These illiterate participants also experienced difficulties with self-evaluation and self-analysis.

Remarkable among the findings of this study are those that deal with syllogistic reasoning. The peasants regularly refused to draw conclusions from the verbal premises they were given. Instead, they would base their conclusions on practical and personal considerations. The interviewer would ask: "Cotton can't grow where it is cold, and it's cold in England. Does cotton grow there or not?" The respondent would answer: "I don't know. I've heard of England, but I don't know if cotton grows there" (110). The researcher would say: "There are no camels in Germany. The city of B. is in Germany. Are there camels there or not?" The respondent would answer: "I don't know, I've never seen German villages" (112). These participants refused to solve verbal problems when the proposed premises contradicted their actual experience (127).

However, literate and semiliterate participants completed these tests within the expected parameters and were able to provide "conventional" answers, implying that they had greater facility for making use of abstract, theoretical terms.

Luria cites literacy as only *one* of the reasons for the difference— along with changes in "the basic forms of activity" and entering into a

---

4 Even when prompted by the researchers that, for example, "a hammer, a saw, and a hatchet are all tools," the illiterate peasants would still reply: "Yes, but even if we have tools, we still need wood—otherwise, we can't build anything" (Luria 1976:56). Or when told, "Look, here you have three adults and one child. Now clearly the child doesn't belong in this group," they would say: "Oh, but the boy must stay with the others. All three of them are working, you see, and if they have to keep running out to fetch things, they'll never get the job done, but the boy can do the running for them" (55).

"new stage of social and historical practice" (161). The data reported by Luria is generally understood as signifying the effects of literacy on cognitive operations.[5] According to Luria, writing influences thought by influencing the "inner speech" that structures thought (cf. Vocate: 132–33). Luria follows Vygotskiĭ in stating that writing is context-independent, is addressed to an unknown interlocutor, and uses longer sentences, more relative clauses, and fewer direct quotes; it also makes us conscious of language (Luria 1981:164–68).

2.2. Further Research

In a study exploring educational and subcultural language differences between groups (which, in her presentation, boils down to class differences), Patricia Greenfield refers to research she and her associates completed among schooled and unschooled Wolof-speaking children in Senegal (aimed at measuring the Piagetian stages of development in classificatory abilities). They found performance differences between the two groups with regard to object classification and other tasks dealing with differences in abstraction abilities.

Greenfield emphasizes that oral language is more context-dependent than written language and argues that "context-dependent speech is tied up with context-dependent thought, which in turn is the opposite of abstract thought" (Greenfield: 169); hence oral "thought" is more context dependent. Written cultures also tend to spread over larger geographic areas and cover more heterogeneous groups of speakers than oral languages. Consequently, among speakers of a written language "the assumption of a common frame of reference will often be invalid even where contact is face to face" (170).

In oral cultures education itself has a contextual nature, working through the situation in which it is to be used. Writing enhances the ability to abstract: written words represent the spoken words, which are, in turn, representations of their worldly referents. In traditional education a child typically learns through watching and imitation; teaching is by means of *demonstration* (in which the verbalization is *totally dependent* on the concrete physical situation). In technical societies with written languages instruction is based on telling *out* of context rather than *showing* in context (Greenfield: 170–71). There is an enforcing relation between context-dependent communication and egocentrism (absolutizing one

---

[5] Examples are Ong (1982:49–55); Havelock (1986:38–41); Goody (1996b:17; 1996a); Olson (1994:34–35; 1996:149–50). A more extensive exposition of Luria's work can be found in Vocate: 23–82.

point of view) and neglect of informational needs (170). Dominantly oral cognitive development entails a greater degree of egocentricity and an inability to shift perspective or context.

When compared to schooled children, the unschooled Wolof children seemed unskilled in the ability to distinguish between a statement about something and the thing itself; "the relativistic notion of multiple points of view was also absent to a greater degree" (Greenfield: 173). "Writing is practice in the use of linguistic contexts as independent of immediate reference" (174). Learning to embed a label in a total sentence structure through writing facilitates conceptualizing the label less to its situational context and more related to its linguistic context. "The implications of this fact for manipulability are great: linguistic contexts can be turned upside down more easily than real ones. Once thought is freed from the concrete situation, the way is clear for symbolic manipulation ... in which the real becomes but a sub-set of the possible" (175).

One should be wary of the use of generalities such as "Western" education, "lower-class," and "middle-class" and implicit suggestions that literacy is somehow "better" than traditional education. Contemporary literacy values are often interwoven with consumer capitalism, recalling a comment by Farrell (449) that while "there is good reason to take pride in both, the rub is that oral thinking patterns can be socially and economically limiting in our predominantly literate, highly technological society."

Yet if one reads Greenfield's study as *a way* of discussing cultural and educational differences, it is quite a useful contribution. The findings of this study correlate with the predictions of oral-literate theories, and, importantly, similar results have been replicated in several other cross-cultural studies utilizing measurements based on classification of objects or concepts by children and adults in different cultural contexts.[6]

With regard to differences between oral and literate cognition, these studies show that the more literate subjects tend to classify in terms of nominal (superordinate) categories by constructing abstract taxonomies such as "tools" or "vehicles." The less literate or illiterate participants have a greater tendency to use perceptual categories ("red things," "small things") or functional categories (classifying an ax with a tree rather than with other tools). The adjustment to nominal classification schemes with increased literacy is in line with the proposal of the oral-literate theorists, particularly Goody and Olson, that reading objictifies language and encourages abstract thought.

---

6 See, among many, Irwin and McLaughlin; Jahandarie; Lancy; Melkman and Deutsch; Melkman, Tversky, and Baratz.

Another approach that develops such theorizing is the investigation by Leonard Scinto. He reviews the research dealing with child development and written language acquisition, written language and social praxis, the acquisition and application of strategies for text construction, and how writing functions in relation to cognition. An extensive theoretical framework within which to analyze and evaluate such research is developed by him (Scinto: 5–66). Scinto criticizes the dominant formal structuralist tendencies in much of perspectives on language, which divorces language from its cultural context and reductively assumes "speech" (whose? which? where? when?) to be "real" language and other manifestations of human communication as secondary.

> Against this kind of mechanistic or perhaps electronic and computational structuralism we would argue that the determinants of the rational mind lie as much in [a person's] sociocultural experience and particularly in [one's] participation in the experience of language as in the experience and accretion of [one's] biological inheritance. (162)

The consequence is obvious: what the mind can do relates to the devices provided by one's culture.

> The nature of interaction with the world is never direct, except perhaps in the very early stages of development, but mediated. What mediates our interaction with the world is the representational system at our disposal. When a shift or change occurs in this representational system, the nature of interaction with the world changes. Such a shift in the nature of representational systems occurs when the child moves from an almost exclusive use of the oral norm to the use of the written norm. (160)

Scinto (165) notes that he is developing a grounding in linguistics for what Popper uses to illustrate human development: "instead of growing better eyes and ears, [a human] grows spectacles, microscopes, telescopes, telephones, and hearing aids ... instead of growing better memories and better brains, we grow paper, pens, pencils, typewriters, dictaphones, the printing press and libraries" (Popper: 238–39).

Noting that decontextualization and sequential construction—that is, the notion of establishing functional dependencies/relations between units (such as sentential propositions)—characterize "text operations" and not merely the arbitrary juxtaposition of such units in time and space as in speech operations, Scinto (139–60) suggests that the acquisition of such text operations leads to parallel changes in cognitive function during the period of acquisition. He acknowledges that his analysis stands in the line of theory developed by Vygotskiĭ and quotes the work of Olson (1977; Bruner and Olson) as well as Goody, Cole, and Scribner affirming that mastering writing affects the basic system underlying the nature of one's mental processes (Scinto: 167).

In a study dealing with the *contexts* of logical reasoning and reading comprehension, Bridget Franks finds that greater reading experience facilitated the drawing of logical conclusions from empirically false premises. "Skilled readers" show better adeptness at the ability to suspend their prior knowledge of the world and play along with make-believe premises. She argues that reading experience not only enhances reasoning but also helps children to construct their reasoning abilities, encouraging metalogical reasoning (Franks: 97). Comparable conclusions are evident from several research projects.[7]

In this context a brief reference to the views of the anthropologist Jack Goody is relevant. Goody has done research among the *LoDagaa* of Ghana but makes extensive use of historical data to develop his thesis that the oral-literate distinction should repace the conventional but ethnocentric dichotomies in use among anthropologists.[8] Of course we also find "the opposing tendency, adopted by many social scientists heavily committed to cultural relativism, which leads them to treat all societies as if their intellectual processes were essentially the same. Similar yes, the same no" (Goody 1977b:226–27). Goody correctly notes that the specification of difference is not enough in itself; one needs to point to mechanisms, to causal factors (227). "For some, at least, of the differences in intellectual processes that are indicated in a very general way by means of terms like 'open' and 'closed' can be related not so much to differences in 'mind' but to differences in systems of communication" (ibid.).

As an aside I would like to emphasize the importance of Goody's work to New Testament scholarship interested in the relationship between history and theology. He shows that writing creates an environment conducive to critical thinking. Contrasting oral and literate societies, Goody argues that

---

7 Relationships between exposure to print and certain cognitive abilities are shown by Stanovich and Cunningham; Echols, West, Stanovich, and Zehr; and Hedrick and Cunningham, among others.

8 Pragmatist philosophy and theory attacks reductionist and dualistic ontologies and epistemologies by utilizing the concept of *coordination*: human behaviour is ongoing, interconnected activities, which involves divisions of labor and functioning factors within a vast complex. Communication always depends on processes of reference and the circumstances of experience. It is in and through communication that human societies are created and maintained. Communication and the processing of information are not merely "aspects" of human societies; rather, societies would be totally impossible without communication in one form or another (Goody 1973; Maines).

the *essential* difference [is] the accumulation (or reproduction) of skepticism. Members of oral ... societies find it difficult to develop a line of sceptical thinking about, say, nature, or man's relationship to God simply because a continuing critical tradition can hardly exist when sceptical thoughts are *not* written down, *not* communicated across time and space, *not* made available for men to contemplate in privacy as well as to hear in performance. (Goody 1977a:43)

The religious systems of societies without writing lack the concept of a religion, "partly because magico-religious activities form part of most social action, not being the attribute of a separate organization, partly because of the identification with a people, as in 'Asante religion'" (Goody 1986:173). It follows that a society with a heavy oral residue will lack the experience of "religious conversion." Whereas a written tradition articulates beliefs and interests in a semipermanent form that can extend their influence independently of any particular political and cultural system, oral traditions are inextricably linked to their contexts, where one can only experience incorporation. "Conversion is a function of the boundaries the written word creates, or rather defines" (1986:10, 172).

Goody's analyses of the impact of writing on scientific thought, formalization, logic, expansion of laws, and profusion of lists and tables are substantiated (in varying degrees) by historical, cultural, and anthropological evidence. Although Goody is sometimes vilified by other anthropologists, the hostility is based more on (unwarranted) political suspicions than evidence. Goody's (1987) concept of "restricted literacy" is particularly relevant to historical approaches aware of making use of cross-cultural interpretive models.

3. Scribner and Cole: The Psychology of Literacy

Arguably the most famous among the cultural-psychological studies dealing with literacy is the research conducted by Sylvia Scribner and Michael Cole in the early 1970s in West Africa. Both are admirers of the work of Vygotskiĭ and Luria.[9] Accordingly, to Scribner and Cole, most cognitive abilities are very specific and narrow in their domain and are acquired from cultural practices and personal experiences that are also narrow and specific, and any generalizations about cognitive abilities are misguided.

---

9 Cole was, in fact, instrumental in introducing the English-speaking world to the views of these Russian psychologists.

Scribner and Cole (1981b:73) point out the problem of arguing for cognitive changes in *individuals* when analyzing *cultural* phenomena: there are limitations when relying "on cultural data as sole testimony to psychological processes." This is true, strictly speaking. However, cultural processes provide us with a *range of possibilities* for the historical individual and form a powerful resource in historical understanding. They also argue that even if certain cognitive skills have historically emerged as a consequence of literacy, there is no reason to believe that the causal relationship still holds: "There is no necessary connection between the modality in which new [cognitive] operations come into being and the modality in which they are perpetuated and transmitted in later historical epochs" (ibid.). They want to deny the relevance of historical generalizations to *current* educational policies and decisions. (This is a debatable point, but my interest *is* historical understanding). Cross-cultural studies are extremely useful to the historical imagination. Reference to the Scribner-Cole research should consider the context of *their* polemic.

To advance the discussion Scribner and Cole argue that attention should be given to psychological research that aims to measure cognitive differences between literates and nonliterates, that is, to gather "evidence that the consequences claimed for literacy can be found in comparisons of literate and nonliterate adults living in the same social milieu whose material and social conditions of life do not differ in any systematic way" (Scribner and Cole 1981b:74).

Since Plato a shift from a primarily oral-language use to a dominant written-language use has been seen as of consequence for forms of thought. In this vein, oral- and written-language use are contrasted as forms of language leading to either a *paralogical* form of thinking (oral culture) with heavily context-dependent communication or a linear, formal style of thinking (written language) with more context-free communication. The general hypothesis of the transforming effects of such a shift has been formulated by Goody and Watt. Goody (1977a; 1986; 1987), Havelock (1976; 1986), and Ong (1967; 1982; 1987) have explored aspects of these contrasts on the extended level of culture and society. Vygotskiĭ, Luria (1981), Greenfield, Bruner and Olson, and Olson (1977; 1988b) are examples of scholars who have analyzed and explored literacy and cognition issues relating to the individual psychological level.

Scribner and Cole (1981a) attack the proposition of the cognitive consequences of literacy head on, and a number of very important points are made by them. They warn that sweeping claims about the impact of literacy on the course of cognitive development should be substantiated by empirical work, and they problematize the notion of a monolithic concept of literacy.

Their main concern, however, is to assess the role that schooling and literacy are claimed to contribute to cognitive change. Scribner and Cole maintain that the differences observed by Greenfield between the schooled and unschooled African children are not due to abstraction abilities acquired through literacy but due to specific skills that children gain at school. They fault Greenfield for confusing literacy with schooling (Scribner and Cole 1981a:12–13). To them, literacy and schooling should be treated as *separable* variables: "In all research, literacy was confounded with schooling; yet students are engaged in many learning experiences in school besides learning how to read and write" (Scribner and Cole 1978:452). They argue that the social institution in which literacy is embedded underlies the actual causal mechanism with regard to different effects of writing. That is, one should think about literacy not in *developmental* terms, but in *functional* terms. This is an important facet of Scribner and Cole's contribution; many of the detractors of oral-literate theories read Scribner and Cole as if they deny that literacy contributes to or effects change. Scribner and Cole argue against the perspective that claims literacy results in the emergence of *general* mental capacities; they do *not* deny that literacy leads to *specific* skills. Their battle is with (contemporary) educational policies based on the assumption that (general) advancement of intellectual competencies *necessarily* follows from literate education.

Proper testing of the cognitive effects of literacy, without the "contaminating effects" of schooling, requires, according to Scribner and Cole, a community in which some people acquired their literacy without going to school. Liberia offered such a test case. The Vai people of Liberia had developed an indigenous script for their language: a syllabary that was normally learned in a nonschool setting from a relative or a friend. It seemed to fit the description of literacy without schooling. Since some of the Vai people also acquired schooled literacy in English and semi-schooled literacy in Arabic, it was possible to compare the schooled and unschooled literacies, thus, presumably, separating the effect of schooling from that of literacy per se. Scribner and Cole set out to measure certain cognitive abilities among the Vai and correlate them with their three literacies. Mindful of the effects of personality and lifestyle variables, they attempted to control the effects of factors such as modernity, urbanism, and multilingualism. The dependent variables—cognitive abilities—were measured by administering sorting tasks (involving geometrical figures), classification tasks (similar to those employed by Luria), recall tasks, logical reasoning tasks (not unlike the syllogistic reasoning tasks used by Luria), and language objectivity tasks (e.g., asking the participants what would happen if everyone in the world decided to call the sun the moon and vice versa). After completing some of these tasks, some participants were also asked to explain their reasons for sorting, classifying, or answering as they did.

To properly understand their contribution one should review their discussion of their experiments. An important conclusion stands out: "All our information points toward the specificity of literacy" (Scribner and Cole 1981a:107). Table 8.2 (118) summarizes the results of the tasks and measures that they used in their research. They categorize subjects according to nonliterate men, Vai script monoliterates, Arabic monoliterates, Vai-Arabic biliterates, (all) English-schooled subjects, English-schooled subjects with more than grade 10 level, and nonliterate women.

With the exception of "verbal explanation" by men with English schooling beyond grade 10, all these groups performed more like each other than unlike one another. With that one exception, *some* of the effects indicated could be statistically significant, although not particularly large.[10] The major conclusion must be that all these groups obviously belong to the same cultural background and operate with similar strategies in various cultural and social settings. A number of hypotheses can be framed for these conclusions. One, not considered by Scribner and Cole, is that the Vai-Arabic literacies are embedded in an oral-based culture, in other words, that the instances of the Vai writing are all interrelated and interacting with oral practices (on the oral-literate continuum). It is noteworthy that Scribner and Cole do not discuss "orality" and/or how orality pervades the cultural activities and social institutions of the Vai.

---

10 It emerges that literacy has some effects but mostly inconclusive results *based on the experiments attempted*. With regard to *abstraction*: "all three kinds of literacy enhanced the tendency to sort the cards according to form or number, an outcome consistent with the notion that literacy focuses attention on these aspects of graphic symbols" [rather than the nonrelevant attribute of color] (1981:121). To explain the principle of the abstraction adopted by the subjects, "only amount of schooling distinguished itself as a factor" (ibid.). Scribner and Cole note that "all groups, including nonliterates, could achieve at least one successful abstraction … and all were equally good or poor at breaking up one classification and achieving another" (ibid.). With regard to *taxonomic categorization* [constrained classification] "we failed to find an overall effect of schooling" (123) except for a "few subjects" who had high school background; and for "free classification" "only minimal school and no nonschool literacy-related differences were detectable" (ibid.). Scribner and Cole emphasize the "picture of little variation in scores" (ibid.) that emerges. "Overall, these results discourage conclusions about a strong influence of literacy on categorization and abstraction" and the "absence of strong effects of formal schooling (124). With regard to *memory*: "results have to be considered perplexing" (125). Only "biliterates" among the nonschooled literates performed slightly better (ibid.). With regard to *logic*: "logic problems proved the most predictable and demonstrated the strongest effects of schooling." "Schooling was the only background characteristic to improve performance" (127). The final task, testing for how writing objectifies language (*language objectivity*) found that, "No group responded in a particularly impressive fashion" (129).

It is also important to contextualize the literacies of the Vai. The Vai use these different scripts to write three different languages in fairly clearly delineated different contexts: the systems are complementary rather than alternatives. Arabic is the language of the Holy Book, English is the national tongue and Vai the maternal one. The three "writings" are not quite the same, and a method to compare groups and subtract variables supposedly leaving only the unmediated effect of writing must be misleading (a point emphasized by Goody in his critique of Scribner and Cole; see Goody 1987:219–57).

Against these comments as background it is interesting to see how Scribner and Cole themselves summarize their findings:

> The most impressive finding is that formal schooling with instruction in English increased ability to provide a verbal explanation of the principles involved in performing the various tasks.... neither syllabic Vai script literacy nor Arabic alphabetic literacy was associated with what are considered the higher-order intellectual skills. Neither literacy enhanced the use of taxonomic skills on any task designed to test categorization. Nor did either contribute to a shift toward syllogistic reasoning. Nor did the traditional literacies improve the adequacy of verbal explanations or foster greater use of category labels. (1981a:130–32)

They prefer to emphasize the impact of English schooling and underplay the effects of Vai and Arabic writing. The schooled participants did not perform any better than the unschooled participants on any of the tasks, except for their greater willingness to provide explanations for their responses. Those who were literate in any of the scripts, whether schooled or unschooled, exhibited the same level of performance on all the cognitive tasks. Rather than providing evidence that the enhanced cognitive abilities were due to schooling, these tests showed that there was hardly much cognitive enhancement at all. What little enhancement there was occurred independently of schooling. However, in their summary statement (that has been quoted verbatim by many others since), Scribner and Cole make it appear as if only the unschooled literacies failed to have an effect.[11]

Scribner and Cole completed a second set of more focused tests designed to measure metalinguistic abilities in particular. Oral-literate theories claim that literacy makes linguistic features explicit and causes readers to scrutinize their language, resulting in a greater consciousness

---

11 The authors repeat this conclusion in their other publications: "Vai script and Arabic literates were no different in average performance from nonliterates" (Scribner: 197). Literacies other than English "produced almost no changes" (Cole: 311).

of both the linguistic components (e.g., words, phonemes) and the logical relationships embedded in discourse. According to Scribner and Cole, the consequent set of tests, again, failed to pick up any consistent relationships between literacy of any kind and metalinguistic abilities.

> We can report at the outset that results of this work discourage the notion that metalinguistic knowledge, as exemplified in our tasks, can be considered a unitary phenomenon. If it were a unitary ability we would expect people who scored well on one task to score well on the others; performances would be correlated.... Some significant intertask correlations were obtained, but no more than we would expect by chance. (Scribner and Cole 1981a:138–39)

A closer look at the actual findings is quite instructive. First, there is no discussion of *orality*. For instance, during the initial survey testing for the objectification of language, they note that a "common reason for denying the possibility of exchanging names" was "practical consideration" (Scribner and Cole 1981a: 129). Rather than denying the influence of literacy, such data point to the influence of orality.

Second, the proper emphasis should be on the *inconclusivity* of the results—indirectly admitted by Scribner and Cole (the "unsatisfactory theoretical status" failing to construct meaningful hypotheses [159]). Interestingly, when the task involving the switching of the names of the sun and the moon from the first survey was repeated, it showed that all three literacies were instrumental in helping the participants separate the name from its referent. This is at variance with the earlier finding of no literacy effect in this same task. As the researchers asked the respondents to explain their answers, it became clear that even when the answer seemed to show a lack of distinction between the name and the referent (e.g., when the respondent said that it is not possible to switch the two names), it did not really mean that the distinction was not present in the respondent's mind, thus calling into question the very validity of the measure. Another task had the literate participants separate a text into its components to see if the Vai-script literates had the concept of "word," considering their script did not separate words from each other through spacing or other conventions—as do both English and Arabic scripts. The test failed because it became clear that there is no single term in the Vai language corresponding to the concept of "word," thus making it impossible to provide the necessary instructions for the task. The only test that seemed to provide valid data was a word-definition task in which the participants were asked to define words ranging from the more concrete (e.g., "chair") to the more abstract (e.g., "government"). The finding was that all the literate participants had much greater success in defining the concrete terms than the abstract terms, and those schooled in English were no better than those literate in Vai or Arabic.

All the literate groups were also equal in performing the syllogistic reasoning task while consistently scoring higher than the illiterate participants (Scribner and Cole 1981a:156, table 9.10). Still, Scribner and Cole summarize the latter findings as follows: "Taken together, these studies of logical-verbal problem solving cast doubt on hypotheses that implicate literacy directly in the acquisition of metalinguistic knowledge about the properties of propositions"—a conclusion not justified by the actual findings.

What Scribner and Cole are doing is to concentrate on particular skills that may result from the specific characteristics of each individual script and its uses. In the various stages of their research they looked for, and found, such specific effects. The Vai-script literates were much better than their illiterate counterparts at solving "rebus puzzles" (picture puzzles), implying their greater problem-solving and language-manipulation prowess. This was interpreted as a specific skill arising from learning the indigenous Vai script in which written symbols, each signifying a syllable, are strung together without word or sentence separators, turning the task of reading into a kind of trial-and-error problem solving. That interpretation, however, cannot explain the fact that the English literates, whose script is obviously unlike the Vai script in this respect, did just as well as the Vai literates, while Arabic literates, with a script falling somewhere between English and Vai in its ambiguity, actually did more poorly than the illiterates. In an ad hoc fashion the English literates' good performance is attributed to the effects of schooling, while the poor performance of the Arabic literates is conjectured to have something to do with their having to read the picture puzzles from left to right in opposition to the Arabic script,which is read from right to left. The ambiguity of the Vai script is cited as the reason for the Vai literates' good performance in an "auditory integration" task that required the participants to hold a number of meaningless syllables in their working memory until they were formed into meaningful sentences. The fact that the English literates did just as well as the Vai literates on the latter task is not allowed to enter into the conclusion that "ability to understand, remember, and reproduce sentences parsed into syllables reflects expertise in reading Vai script; no other literacy or non-literacy factor examined in our analyses appeared to offer an alternative route to these skills" (Scribner and Cole 1981a:183–84).

Similarly, when the Vai literates and English literates did equally well in a series of "communication" tasks (giving directions), the English literates' performance was attributed to the effects of schooling, while the Vai literates' performance was attributed to their greater penchant for writing letters. This amounts to giving different ad hoc explanations for similar findings and does not reflect consistent argumentation. Scribner and Cole try to explain away the lack of difference by invoking additional reasons for each group's performance (reasons that, as such, may be relevant but are at best to be regarded as hypotheses for further studies).

Though an important publication reporting on extensive surveys, some shortcomings are evident. Scribner and Cole tend to summarize their conclusions in ways not fully warranted by the actual findings and toward their belief that there are no real cognitive effects of literacy, except for limited effects associated with pertinent features of particular literate practices, specifically with schooling.

Some problems that relativize the value of their research have been indicated above. In addition, the composition of the sample studied is problematic. Since literacy in the Vai community is restricted mostly to men, the entire sample in this study consists of male participants. For practical reasons, the samples were not chosen at random but contained only those individuals who volunteered for the study. These limitations diminish the usefulness of the findings.[12]

Scribner and Cole should have attended more to the conceptualization and interpretation of "schooling." They attribute various outcomes to schooling as opposed to literacy. What, for example, is the role (and effect) of rote learning in these schools? Schooling, training, and socialization are all cultural activities tightly interwoven with each other. Furthermore, while English literacy and, to a large extent, Arabic literacy are acquired when the Vai children are generally under the age of ten, Scribner and Cole tell us that Vai-script literacy is usually acquired in adulthood. If, in fact, literacy does have cognitive consequences, they must be more pronounced if it is acquired in the formative childhood years than in the adult years. As such, one may expect a lesser impact of

---

12 With regard to metalinguistic skills, a causal variable often implicated in psycholinguistic research, along with literacy, is bilingualism. While by learning the Vai script the Vai participant is not learning a new language, the situation is very different when a Vai person learns the Arabic or English scripts. These scripts are not used to transcribe the Vai language; they are used to write and read Arabic and English languages, respectively. Most of those who learn the Arabic script use it only to recite the Qur'an without understanding the words. With the English literates, however, the script is learned in the context of learning the English language, which, as the official language of Liberia, is a major factor in advancing in their society. Aronsson (77) points out that Scribner and Cole focus on literacy "to the exclusion of other language practices of relevance for the visibility of language." Scribner and Cole are aware of this possibility and say that "multilingualism" was used as a control variable in their analysis—but do not explain how such control was actually implemented.

Vai literacy compared to the other two literacies, and it is misleading to say the difference is due to "schooling."

This distinction (literacy not to be confounded with schooling) clearly shows the complexity of the issues. *Any* schooling in a culture familiar with writing will involve "literacy." As Scribner and Cole themselves clearly note, it is extraordinarily difficult to advance our knowledge about cognitive effects when separating schooling and literacy. These are not actions and concepts in their own right with clear, distinct meanings and referents.[13] Aronsson (76–77) points to a related complication. The greater impact of English literacy may be due to its being learned through a more "extensive" process. Taking the language situation of Ethiopia as a point of departure, she discusses the characteristics and communicative consequences of multilingualism and multiliteracy. Restricted literacy, she argues, "may have purely marginal effects on cognitive development" (82). Language development is deeply embedded in a matrix of mutually influential forces.

Relating their research to the wider context of Liberian literacy is another gap in the research conducted by Scribner and Cole, that is, discussing the consequences (in a positive sense) of the low literacy rate as well as the limited social functions served by literacy. In their survey, only one-third of the adult respondents reported any degree of literacy in any of the scripts (Scribner and Cole 1981a:62). In the total population, the literacy rate was 19.1 percent and of the adult *male* population 28.4 percent (63). As Scribner and Cole point out (87), "With the exception of a small number of Arabic scholars and secondary English school literates, literacy rarely leads to acquisition of new bodies of knowledge." These literacies are used almost exclusively for practical purposes of writing letters and keeping records. As such, the Liberian test case does not seem to satisfy some of the requirements of a useful cross-cultural interpretive model. Nor, for that matter, does it provide a sound basis for a critique of oral-literate theories.

Goody (1987:225) argues that what Scribner and Cole were testing in this study was Vygotskiĭ's belief that writing has an "immediate" influence on restructuring thought rather than the hypothesis put forward by himself (and others) about the long-term effects of literacy. He points out that Scribner and Cole's account of how their findings contradict his views is simply "misleading." Similarly, Olson maintains that the syllabary structure of the Vai script and the absence of an archival literate

---

13 Incidentally, conceptualizing "schooling" is also a major problem in studies dealing with first-century education and literacy; see Botha 1999.

tradition among the Vai leaves the literacy theories "little touched" by Scribner and Cole's findings (Olson 1995:287).

Though the Scribner and Cole study is still the most ambitious and extensive cross-cultural study of the effects of literacy, it would be wise to deal circumspectly with their conclusions. A distinction should be made between what the study actually found and what the researchers construe from it. Their study shows that all types of literacy have certain cognitive effects. These effects are sometimes similar across the three literacies, substantiating the claims of generalized cognitive consequences made by oral-literate theories: literacy improves performance in categorization of forms, in writing with pictures, and in combining words into meaningful sentences. With other effects, the literacies were unlike each other, pointing to a need to consider their structural differences and the circumstances within which each particular literacy was learned and used. Scribner and Cole have a penchant for ascribing these interliteracy differences to the effects of schooling, dismissing other plausible explanations. They neither discuss nor analyze the oral culture within which these literacies function. These considerations should make us cautious of drawing any hard and fast conclusions from their study. It contains evidence for, against, and irrelevant to orality-literacy theories, depending on which specific research information is considered and in what perspective.

4. CONSEQUENT RESEARCH

An unfortunate result of the aura of definitiveness surrounding the Scribner and Cole study seems to have been a discouragement of further investigations.

4.1. Berry and Bennett

Berry and Bennett studied some of the cognitive correlates of literacy in an indigenous script among the Cree of Northern Canada. There are similarities between Cree literacy and Vai literacy (the Cree script is a syllabary, introduced in the early nineteenth century, and frequently learned outside school).

Many of the Cree are also literate in English, which is taught in modern schools. Like the Vai, the Cree use their syllabic script primarily for the practical purposes of letter writing and record keeping. They also use it to read the Bible and other religious texts, translated into the Cree language, but "they did not use it to create for themselves a body of 'literature'" (Berry and Bennett: 434), "and except for religious and some recent educational materials, there remains little for the Cree to read"

(439). As was the case among the Vai, the Cree culture remains mostly an oral culture where "the primary mode of expression remains the spoken and not the written word" (Bennett and Berry: 98). However, while the literacy rate among the Vai was very low, it is quite high among the Cree. In the four communities where the study was done, all the respondents were literate; one-third knew the syllabic script, one-third were literate in English, and one-third were literate in both.

A random sample of 148 Cree were administered several cognitive tests, and their linguistic ability was measured by vocabulary and reading tests in Cree and English. The findings of the study partly corroborate what Scribner and Cole found among the Vai with regard to English schooling. Literacy/schooling positively correlate with the spatial/figural abilities of the respondents but not between these abilities and the Cree syllabic literacy (especially when age or acculturation were controlled—Berry and Bennet define "schooling" as having spent five or more years in school).

4.2. Bain and Yu

An interesting article is Bain and Yu, reporting on a comparison of literate and nonliterate peasants from the same village in mainland China. They found that, on tasks of classification and verbal reasoning, the literate peasants provided more abstract and context-independent responses than the nonliterate peasants, whose responses were more concrete and context-dependent. Bain and Yu see these results as replicating those of Luria. In a consequent investigation, a story was presented to one nonliterate and two literate adult male peasants in rural China, and they were told that they would be asked to retell it immediately as well as three months later. The story was presented orally to the nonliterate participant and one of the literates, while the second literate participant received it in a written form. All three were allowed as much time as they desired with the tape or the text of the story until they felt they were ready to reproduce it faithfully. The three were found to be almost equal in their immediate recall, remembering virtually all the details of the story. In their delayed recall three months later, a dramatic difference had appeared between the nonliterate and the two literate participants. The nonliterate could still produce almost the entire story, while the two literate participants were able to reproduce less than half the details. Since the details deleted by the literates were not central to the story, Bain and Yu speculate that the literate participants had used their literacy-amplified abstractive and classificatory strategies to remember only the gist of the story, omitting the details that were not critical to the main story line. The nonliterate participant, however, not having the benefit of such strategies, had spent a greater deal of mental energy to retain the entire story with all the secondary details. This is an intriguing possibility, but case studies of this type cannot go beyond producing plausible conjectures. More extensive research is necessary to test the validity of such presumptions.[14]

4.3. Akinnaso

Another "case study" is the autobiographical account by F. Niyi Akinnaso (1991), who grew up in a village in southwestern Nigeria in a context of very limited literacy while learning to read and write himself.

Akinnaso carefully distinguishes between effects and functions of literacy as perceived by the villagers and by himself. To them, by and large, literacy had practical benefits, scribal functions that brought new patterns of social organization (1991:92). He emphasizes that it is "not only the literate whose consciousness is impacted by literacy. Nonliterates are also affected" (93).

> They have their own conceptions about literacy and they are aware of the impact of literacy on their lives and their environment. They sometimes change their conceptions and uses of literacy just as literacy changes the structure of knowledge and the patterns of social relations in their society. (ibid.)

To him, literacy made him engage in "thinking as a deliberate, planned activity" (1991:92). He notes that literacy "raises one's consciousness about language" (87). Literacy develops a critical attitude, something that had grave implications for the young Akinnaso (tension developed about the "usefulness" of literacy [89–90]). Although he questions the segmentation of experience (something encouraged by schooling and writing [85]), Akinnaso explains the impact of literacy on his consciousness with regard to language awareness, thought, religion and culture, and social organization. Although discontinuity between home and school language is a severe problem, "a keen sensitivity, especially on the part of the learner, to the differences between the nature and uses of speech and writing is very crucial to bridging the discontinuity" (87).

4.4. Denny

The cultural psychologist Peter Denny traces some of the consequences attributed to literacy by different theorists to the concept of

---

14 Though not a cross-cultural study, Painter's observations of the learning history of a child provide a few interesting comments about learning by means of written language.

"decontextualization." Denny attempts to reduce the cognitive effects of literacy claimed by various theories to a single determinant. His approach is based entirely on analytical arguments. Denny suggests that many purported attributes of the "literate" mind, as enumerated in oral-literate theories, are but different aspects of a tendency to decontextualize. "Decontextualizing is the handling of information in a way that either disconnects other information or backgrounds it" (Denny: 66). Denny argues that the main cause of decontextualization has been the growth of human societies to a size wherein one cannot assume any longer that others share the same background information. In small communities, where most individuals know each other and most interaction is face to face, there is little need for articulating the background cultural knowledge that forms the context of interaction. In larger communities, with thousands of individuals and many subgroups, the assumption of a shared background is more likely to be false, hence the need for stating the information in such a way as to be meaningful even if the recipient is unable to complement it with any contextual clues (72). Literacy, although not the main cause, is seen by Denny as a major "amplifier" of decontextualization (he cites the research by Luria and Greenfield as well as the research by Hutchins).

Denny criticizes an "overinterpretation" of the decontextualization tendency by Greenfield and others when they see their evidence as signaling other cognitive traits, such as greater abstraction abilities among the literates. Abstraction is the same as decontextualization if it is taken to mean "a separation of the thought unit from its context" (Denny: 76). But if literates are also considered to have a greater ability to use "general" and "insubstantial" concepts (other possible meanings of "abstraction"), then overinterpretation has occurred. Denny also treats the concepts of "subordinative," "analytic," "objectively distanced" and "abstract" that are used by Ong to describe the literate mindset as reducible to "decontextualized." He extends the same argument to Goody's emphasis on "list, formula, and table," Havelock's concept of "abstraction" (as attributed to the Greek thought), McLuhan's concepts of "hot," "fragmented," "aloof and dissociated," "private," "partial and specialized," and Chafe's concept of "detachment" (Denny: 78–80).

Denny's analysis shows, among other things, the need for definitions of greater clarity and specificity and more explicitness for the many terms that are used in this subject area. Most of all, he creates an awareness of how precariously small the actual "empirical" and comparative data base of anthropological and cross-cultural research actually is.

5. ORALITY, LITERACY, AND CULTURE

My interest in oral-literate theories is not to "provide a foundation for educational programs" or to devise model strategies for future research—against which Scribner and Cole correctly warn that oral-literate theories cannot be really helpful (1978:451)—but to understand cultural and historical *difference*.

From this perspective it is interesting to note that research on culture and cognition underwent a transformation during the 1980s from cross-cultural comparisons of psychological tasks to theory and research on people's thinking in sociocultural activities (Rogoff and Chavajay). The wide range of research that accumulated since the late 1970s clearly shows that cognitive development is intrinsically a cultural-historical process (ibid.: 869, 873).[15] Taking oral-literate dynamics into account allows one to be sensitive to cultural differences.[16]

Enculturation starts from birth. In an interesting cross-cultural study, Heath (1982) illustrates the effect of growing up in a worker society where literacy events and literate attitudes differ considerably from "mainstream" groups. As babies these children are encapsuled "in an almost totally human world, they are in the midst of constant human communication, verbal or nonverbal" (Heath 1982:64). Though skillful storytellers and adept at analogical reasoning, when they go to school "they face unfamiliar types of questions which ask for what-explanations" (69). By the time in their school career when reason-explanations and affective, creative comparisons are called for,

> it is too late for many Trackton children. They have not picked up along the way the composition and comprehension skills they need to translate their analogical skills into a channel teachers can accept. They seem not

---

15 For instance, the "conclusion from memory studies ... is that researchers cannot just assume, as we did before cross-cultural research, that a cognitive test reveals a general ability across tasks unrelated to people's experience. The cultural studies drew attention to the fact that it matters how researchers ask people to display their memory; if we ask them in a way that resembles what they do in school, of course the people who have more experience with schooling will do better" (Rogoff and Chavajay: 863).

16 "The sociological lesson of the history of literacy is not a celebration of the evolution of language functions or semiotic structures. In critical sociological terms, it is impossible to theorise or study empirically the social or intellectual 'function' of texts independent of the complex ideological forces, powers and struggles implicated in the social formation and organisation of technology and knowledge.... to understand and influence how literacy is tied up with social and cultural difference and conflict requires that we build a sociological model of how literacy education figures in (1) the differential organisation and distribution of power and capital; and (2) the normalisation and regulation of difference in literate populaces" (Luke: 310).

to know how to take meaning from reading; they do not observe the rules of linearity in writing, and their expression of themselves on paper is very limited. Orally taped stories are often much better, but these rarely count as much as written compositions. Thus, [they] ... continue to collect very low or failing grades, and many decide by the end of the sixth grade to stop trying and turn their attention to the heavy peer socialization which usually begins in these years. (Heath 1982:70)

Instead of simply *assuming* writing and speech to be unchanging or having little significant differences, we should be aware that our communicative activities are social constructs (see Street: 7). Like our other attempts at interpretation, understanding oral and literate traditions should not be ethnocentrist nor unhistorical.

Nowadays, in one way or another, voluntarily or involuntarily, we all participate more or less in oral and literate traditions. Adopting the perspective of oral-literate dynamics can contribute to critical and meaningful articulation of how communication echoes culture and how speech and writing manipulate the representation of reality. One can even expand this claim to the proposal that the concept *voice* provides a common ground for the social and human sciences.

Extending our consciousness in this sense allows self-criticism, putting literacy "in its place." As literates, we should heed what nonliterates have to say about our "bookishness" (as summarized by Gill: 136).

They note the tendency toward abstraction and depersonalization that may accompany writing. They point out that writing and reading may remove one from the immediacy of experience, particularly social experience. They point out that writing permits one the avoidance of responsibility, the false luxury of never having to learn, the possibility of detachment—all of which, from their point of view, amounts to a loss of meaning and a threat to existence.

6. Concluding Remarks

✦ The claim by Tuman, and from him by Malina, that orality-literacy research is of little relevance to historical understanding cannot be substantiated by appealing to Scribner and Cole. Certainly there is no justification for the widespread belief that their study has somehow debunked the oral-literate theories.

✦ Denying the importance of orality-literacy research would be to step neatly into the ethnocentric trap that Malina warns against.[17]

---

17 On a number of occasions I have tried to bring our contemporary, literate bias to attention: 1993a:746; 1993b:210; 1993c:410–13; 2001.

✦ What can be learned from cultural-psychological studies? Quite a lot, despite the various methodological and theoretical problems that surround many of the existing studies. Psycholinguistic and cross-cultural research do offer findings supportive of several assertions of the orai-literate theories, while also reporting evidence that reveals the complex nature of the relationships.

✦ Clearly, *particular* literacy—and its specific circumstances of acquisition and use—may give rise to its own set of cognitive predilections that may, or may not, accord with certain consequences. This is an important area of research, *especially with regard to first-century Mediterranean societies.*

✦ Approaching literacy as historically and culturally embedded is a perspective of immense importance. A great deal of the language of pre-literates and persons with poorly developed literacy, for instance, seems to be egocentric; that is, it does not have the function of communicating with others outside immediate experience[18] and lacks appreciation of what is involved in communicating with others by adapting their language to their listeners. It is not possible to pursue these topics further in this essay, but the relevance of these observations to understanding some peculiar facets of Greco-Roman writings, and particularly the New Testament writings, are obvious. Analysis of the orality of Hellenistic Roman culture can be a useful index to the worldviews and ways of thinking characteristic of inhabitants of that culture.

✦ The logic of writing extends to experienced reality on many levels. Religions familiar with writing "are clearly working on a more explicitly abstract (or generalized) base than those of purely oral societies (even centralized ones)" (Goody 1986:15). Goody reviews the evidence for the "flexible" nature of orally oriented religions. He notes that traditional African systems of belief are open-ended in a meaningful way, "encouraging the search, the quest after the truth," and that "African religions are more ... subject to change and absorption rather than to rejection and conversion" (8). This is an important hypothesis for understanding the diversity of Hellenistic religions as well as the scope of variety found in emergent Christianity. Various attitudes reflect different levels of involvement with writing.

✦ The insight that orality and textuality (as Kelber 1980:20 phrases it) are different remains a major challenge for New Testament scholarship. MacMullen has noted that we should not overestimate the impact and

---

18 For example: Akinnaso (1991:88–89) tells how he soon stopped telling stories from his books to a friend when he realized "that she could not respond. She knew neither Prospero nor Ariel and she could not relate to the story of Ali Baba and the forty thieves because their exploits did not happen in the village. Moreover, they were very different from the tortoise exploits and other folktales she knew."

influence of writings, even (or especially) when it comes to apologetic literature, apparently offered from within to an audience beyond the church but in reality serving chiefly for internal consumption. "And there was little enough reading of any sort, anyway. Three-quarters or more of the population were illiterate. Points of contact and media of communication that we take for granted in our world simply did not exist in antiquity" (MacMullen: 21). It is important to bear in mind that *even the "literates" were literate in a preprint culture.* Cultural-anthropological characteristics of speech (oral, nonwritten communication) and the social effects of illiteracy permeate even their "literate" communication (Botha 1991).

✦ It is remarkable that an awareness of the complexities of ancient literacy, orality, tradition, and communication came so belatedly to scholars. Although this is changing, a major problem with studies dealing with oral and written traditions in antiquity remains the assumption that writing/oral tradition can be conceptualized outside of specific functions, in other words, the assumption that because someone *wrote,* that activity is directly comparable to *our* writing today, hence differences can only lie in the content of writing. How, when, why, and what we write is determined by who we are, where we are, and what we believe ourselves to be.

Moving Beyond Colonialist Discourse: Understanding Oral Theory and Cultural Difference in the Context of Media Analysis

J. A. "Bobby" Loubser
University of Zululand, South Africa

Over the past centuries anthropologists have documented intriguing instances of cultural difference. Lucien Levy-Bruhl, for example, reports a letter carrier from (the previous) Bechuanaland as saying, "I will not carry letters any more. If this letter had talked to me on the way, I would have been so scared." Other letter carriers are known to have speared the letters they were carrying for fear that they would suddenly speak up.[1] A similar understanding (with a different approach) is reported of an American, nonliterate, Equiano who says, "I have often taken up a book, and have talked to it, and then put my ears to it, when alone, in hopes it would answer me; and I have been very much concerned when I found it remained silent."[2] In Buddhist monasteries of China and Tibet prayer drums with written prayers are used. It is believed that the prayers continue to be prayed as long as the drums are being turned around. To Western literates this practice seems perplexing. The same can be said of the icons of the saints in the Coptic churches of Egypt, which are believed to be alive and constantly praying for the faithful. Having been an object of study for a long time, cultural difference has presently entered the interdisciplinary scene. One of the pertinent questions asked is: How can one approach the issue of cultural difference without reverting to a colonialist discourse?

In this regard I wish to argue that unless we have an adequate theory for dealing with cultural difference we shall inevitably revert to a colonialist discourse. The contribution of this essay to such a theory is to explore the relationship between media and culture, especially between the oral medium and culture. For this we need a much wider definition of

---

1 See Olsen 1994:30–31 for quotation and references.
2 Referred to by Peters: 44.

the concept "medium" than merely taking it as referring to modern communication media such as newspapers, television, telephone, and radio. In this essay the term *medium* refers to any type of material (air waves, paper, laser beams, microchips) that is used to encode ideas and concepts. Thus, we can speak of an oral, manuscript, print, or electronic medium when any one of these materials is used as the physical medium for encoding semiotic signs. To this definition we shall return shortly.

In recent times the study of cultural difference has received a dramatic new impetus. For many centuries the academic world had been oblivious to the influence of communication media on culture. Until fairly recently there was little or no awareness of how media were influencing the shape of culture. A sign of this new development was UNESCO's expressed aim to eradicate illiteracy on the globe by the year 2000. Such an association of poverty and illiteracy is bound to be challenged but makes a powerful statement on the issue of media and culture. Recently historians have documented the development of communication media—from oral communication to scribal media, and from scribal media to different phases of manuscript culture, and from there through the printed media to the plethora of electronic media of today.[3] This new awareness of media did not necessarily involve an understanding of the properties of media and the constructive role they play in the development of culture.

Over the past century media-related issues manifested themselves in various forms and under different headings. The earliest such investigation is found in the nineteenth-century work of Wilhelm (1786–1859) and Jacob (1785–1863) Grimm on the German fairy tale.[4] This interest has generated a mighty stream of studies in folklore and oral narratives that have made an impact on many other disciplines.[5] The study of, for example, oral history, narrative ethics, narrative philosophy, and the like is evidence of this interest.[6] What the brothers Grimm and the theorists who succeeded them failed to realize were the reasons why the oral texts[7]

---

3 Such a description of the progression of communication media can easily support colonialist and racist arguments.

4 See the study on the impact of the brothers Grimm by Zipes.

5 An example of how the new knowledge was assimilated in other fields is the 1901 publication of a study by Herman Gunkel on the role of the folk tale in Genesis (Gunkel 1964).

6 A glance through the recently published anthology of Asante and Abarry will provide the reader with an impression of how wide this field has become. Though focused on the African heritage, such a volume of 828 pages would have been unthinkable without the massive interest aroused in the manifestations of oral culture in the Western academy.

7 The term "text" is used in this essay in a nonliterary sense. Etymologically it is derived from the Latin *texere*, "to weave"—an image that applies to the webs of meaning that are weaved into messages in whichever medium they are expressed.

exhibited peculiar characteristics. In other words, *they did not specifically focus on the media aspect of their subject matter.*

Another discipline with an interest in media-related issues was classical studies. In the 1920s Milman Parry and Albert Lord studied Slavic bards in an effort to understand Homer's epics.[8] Ground-breaking theories concerning the extensive memory spans of oral performers as well as their "rhapsodic" method of composition[9] prepared the way for further studies in orality in ancient Greece by Arnold van Gennep, Eric Havelock, and others. At the time of their studies there already were a number of scholars studying contemporary oral art forms (Vasilii Radlov, Friedrich Krauss, and Marcel Jousse).[10] Jousse identified mnemo-technical devices[11] and pointed to the profound difference between the "literary" products of oral and literate cultures. His work is of special interest because he was the first to propose theories to explain the "verbo-motor" lifestyle. Jousse can with some justification be called the father of contemporary media studies.[12]

One of the most active fields for media-related studies is theology. Many of the studies in folk tales and oral traditions were applied to a study of the world and culture of the Bible. Such studies have contributed to the understanding of cultural difference. The same can be said of the discipline of hermeneutics.[13] At present scholars using social-scientific, historical-rhetorical, and sociorhetorical methods to study the Bible are all contributing to our understanding of the cultural difference between the Near Eastern world of the first century C.E. and other cultures. A subdiscipline specifically directed at the medium of communication is that of textual criticism. This involves a study of all aspects of the production and transmission of the early biblical manuscripts. Because the Jewish and Christian traditions span three thousand years and involve a great diversity of cultures, these traditions will

---

8 See Parry; Lord 1960.

9 The "rhapsodic" method involves a "stitching together" (*raphis* is Greek for "needle") of epics consisting of twenty thousand lines out of stock formulae, stock characters, and a loose plot line with variant subplots. The bards make up the epic as they proceed, modifying their materials to suit the interests of the live audience. The mass of variant material from one rendition to another is estimated as 40 percent.

10 Mentioned in the review article by Peters: 29.

11 Devices developed for memorizing large bodies of information in oral cultures.

12 That Milman Parry studied with Jousse was brought to my attention by Prof. Edgar Sienaert of the Centre for Oral Studies at the University of Natal (Durban), who has undertaken the monumental task of translating Jousse's works from French into English (see Jousse 1990; 1997). See also my review of Sienaert's latest translation (Loubser 1999).

13 The German theologian Friedrich Schleiermacher (1768–1834) is generally acknowledged as the father of hermeneutics (see M. H. Smith).

remain some of the most important sources for scholars doing multicultural and media research.[14]

A last area where media issues came into focus is with the introduction of recent media technologies such as the modern printing press, radio, and television. Neo-Marxists were the first to point to the role of social class in media ownership and the interpretation of texts.[15] This generated some research and served to emphasize the decisive role that media control played in the production and dissemination of information.

A breakthrough on the theoretical side came from a somewhat different direction with the work of the Canadian theorist Marshal McLuhan (1911–80). McLuhan drew on his studies of social change during the transition from manuscript to printing culture in Western Europe to suggest a sweeping media theory epitomized in the slogan, "The medium is the message."[16] While the slogan suggests a deterministic point of view, this is not the case with McLuhan. He rather pioneered an understanding of the dialectical way in which media and society influence each other. With the advent of television as a mass medium the ground was cleared for widespread interest in the role of communication media in culture. The advent of the Internet, and the dramatic changes brought about by satellite telecommunication, has accelerated the interest in this field. Departments of communication science have mushroomed at universities around the world, populated by students eager to exploit the new technologies. It is probable that students of computer-enhanced media are now conducting most of the creative thinking on media and culture. Many media studies come from students with interests in journalism, though many unfortunately restrict their scope to the practical and technical aspects of contemporary media without developing a broader theoretical perspective.

The scholar who cast oral theory into a popular form was a Jesuit priest and professor in humanities, Walter Ong.[17] His *Orality and Literacy: The Technologizing of the Word* (1982), has been widely read, criticized, and applied to a great variety of study fields. Ong's most basic insight is that "writing restructures consciousness."[18] Though often criticized, along

---

[14] According to the 1997 *Yearbook of the Encyclopaedia Britannica*, 34 percent of the population on earth identify with the Christian tradition.

[15] See the informative article by Chandler.

[16] See esp. McLuhan 1994 and McLuhan and Fiore. His seminal work is *The Gutenberg Galaxy* (McLuhan 1962).

[17] See publications in Ong 1967; 1977a; 1982; 1982; Havelock 1982.

[18] See Ong 1982:78. This statement has been seriously challenged by Scribner and Cole. With the publication of their book, *The Psychology of Literacy* (1981a), they reported that they found that the introduction of script into traditional society produced no general cognitive

with Eric Havelock,[19] for positing a "great divide" between oral and literate cultures, he presented a clear and distinct typology with which scholars began to work. He has also contributed toward restoring the dignity of orality and enabling people coming from predominantly oral cultures to recover some of their heritage. In this sense Ong's studies and those of the scholars coming after him contribute toward a postcolonial scholarship.[20] Since Ong's first publications, a number of scholars have produced seminal works. Jan Vansina, who brought his experience in Central Africa to bear on the subject, published a noteworthy book, *Oral Tradition*, in 1965 and thoroughly revised it in 1985. Rosalind Thomas and Susan Niditch, reviewing the archaeological evidence in the light of the new theories, published monographs on orality and literacy, respectively, in ancient Greece and ancient Israel.[21] Ruth Finnegan, through numerous publications, refined the procedures for studying oral culture.[22]

The preceding discussion shows that a significant body of learning has been accumulated over the past century and especially during the latter quarter of the twentieth century. These studies focus mainly on the roles of orality and literacy in the shaping of societies and the texts[23] we find in those societies. The studies are seldom presented under the heading of "media" studies, and they are seldom integrated into a general theory of culture.[24] The question therefore has to be asked whether, and to what extent, studies on orality and literacy (i.e., media studies) can enhance our understanding of cultural difference. Can one understand more about the

---

effects such as the ability to memorize, to classify, or to draw logical inferences (Olson 1994: 20). Olson spends the major part of his book refuting this finding. My own critique of Scribner and Cole's finding is that the time span over which they conducted their research was too short. Shifts in consciousness patterns related to media usage usually occur over long periods of time.

19 Havelock's publications of 1982 and 1986 propose that Greek literacy, advanced by the unique intention of a complete alphabet, enabled the scientific and philosophical revolution of the classical era.

20 This is a point conceded in an essay by Hoogestraat (51). Her criticism of Ong for a male-chauvinist bias is, I believe, based on a misreading. Based on his remark to the effect that the male voice predisposed males for leadership in primal societies, she holds Ong responsible for the patriarchalism that he describes.

21 Such studies have been going on for more than a century, but what is new is that these scholars are reviewing the archaeological evidence in the light of recent theories of orality and literacy (see Thomas 1992; Niditch 1996).

22 See her publications in 1977, 1988, and 1992.

23 Texts are not only written or printed texts. Under *text* I understand a coherent set of ideas that have been encoded in any medium. It is therefore feasible to speak of oral texts.

24 It is noteworthy that Werner Kelber (1983) is criticized for failing to "ask what happens when the medium of communication becomes the bridge from the present to the past" (by Byrskog: 132). This remark clearly indicates the need for media theory.

difference between peoples and cultures by investigating the different media technologies in a given social context? What exactly is the relation between media and culture, and media and social reality? Is the time favorable for formulating theory of media and culture? How significant would a theory of media be to specific modes of interpretation, such as postcolonial readings, deconstruction, structuralism, and feminist readings?

Such questions are being raised. What, then, are the consequences of the development in media technologies for multicultural understanding? Two examples illustrate the challenges posed to students of media. The first concerns the recently restored Globe Theatre in London, which has the object to present Shakespearean plays in their original setting.[25] However, in spite of the efforts made it is realized that any reconstruction can only be partial. The arrangement of space, light, sound, and smell can be physically reproduced. However, there are issues more difficult to replicate. Elizabethan audiences were known to participate in a mode different from contemporary audiences. They would empathize with the characters onstage to a much larger extent than present audiences and would reply spontaneously to the "rhetorical" questions of the characters, sometimes holding the actors personally accountable for the misdemeanors of their characters. Thus the character of the theater as a medium has changed over time. This example illustrates just how difficult it is to reconstruct the way in which a text functioned in another medium.

A second example we can briefly examine is the e-mail message. Whereas the first e-mail messages resembled the form and shape of regular letters by mail, they soon developed their own rhythm. Because e-mail allows for a rapid exchange of information (press a button and it is delivered) writers are bound to compose cryptic and sharp notes. The author of this essay has witnessed more than one misunderstanding where a recipient, still expecting the mode of communication promoted by letters, was offended by the abrupt and seemingly impolite style of e-mail exchanges. Thus we are presently privileged to witness the birth of a new genre, the e-mail message, thanks to a change in media technology. Already this genre has subdivided into a spectrum of different types of e-mail messages, such as the chat-line, the memo, the commercial advertisement, birthday e-cards, the e-mail joke, and many others.[26] This raises a question: How much will the electronic media contribute to cultural divides between First and Third Worlds?

---

25 See the online article by Jean Cramer. This example was brought to my attention by Lucy Bregman.

26 See article by Murphy and Collins on the form and protocol of online instructions on the Internet.

These two examples concern differences in communication that arise when the media of communication change. In the above cases the changes are not as radical as, for example, a change from orality to a culture where electronic media are used (as is the case for some people in Africa, Latin America, and Asia today). When representatives from two extreme media cultures meet—such as rural African people (orality) with "Westernized" people (electronic media)—we are bound to witness tragic misunderstandings and conflicts of interest.[27] As translators have increasingly come to realize, it is not sufficient to translate propositional meanings from one language into another language if there is a large cultural divide. Paralinguistic features such as social organization and cultural and media practices play a significant role. This was one of Walter Ong's main interests (as also of Goody and Watt[28]) for working on orality and literacy.

Let us then consider a brief sketch of Ong's typology. According to him, words in oral cultures are dynamic, charged with power. Curses and blessings are efficacious. Those who can speak the best (and the loudest) are promoted to leadership positions (usually the adults and males). Orality induces a specific textual style. Concepts are arranged in additive rather than subordinate sequences. Oral communications employ redundancies to ensure the transmission of information. For the sake of clarity and definition, communications are often agonistically toned. Characters and situations are cast in terms of monumental stereotypes. Stories employ plots that are differently construed than in modern genres. Audiences are used to empathetic and participatory reception of oral materials. In oral societies memory is all-important for the preservation of information. This also has social and political consequences. The elders and shamans, who preserve the memory of the tribe, enjoy positions of power and privilege. Basic political units in primary oral societies are seldom larger than fifty persons. Oral societies are conservative and traditionalist.[29] Ong's main thesis is that the features mentioned above are directly related to the inherent advantages and limitations of the oral-aural medium, rendering this medium of communication one of the most significant factors in the formation of culture.

In contrast to the above, post-oral cultures still depend heavily on the spoken word and retain many of the features of orality (e.g., fairy tales are read to children from printed books or watched as animations on

---

[27] A case in point is the manner in which global markets, with the help of electronic media, from time to time challenges Third World currencies.

[28] See Goody and Watt; Goody 1977.

[29] The features mentioned in the paragraph are described in Ong 1982.

television). This is often called a "re-constituted" orality. Subsequent media integrate orality into new post-oral media contexts where its effects can linger for many centuries. Oral conventions may even influence the highest products of literate culture.[30] Post-oral societies exhibit a tendency toward innovative thinking because of the enormous amount and diversity of information that can be processed due to better techniques for recording, storing, retrieving, and disseminating data. Once this process has begun, more techniques follow. Two examples may suffice. At its height of influence the famous library in Alexandria (third century B.C.E.), which became the prototype of all libraries in the Greco-Roman world, housed between four hundred thousand and one million written book rolls. This way of managing information became the foundation for the sophisticated civilization of antiquity. However, when duplicates and the length of the scrolls are taken into account, it turns out that the information stored did not exceed the size of a contemporary village library with fifty thousand books.[31] Another example: it is calculated that before the invention of the movable type printing press by Gutenberg (fifteenth century C.E.) there were only forty-thousand manuscript titles in all the libraries of Europe. Within one century there were about 1.8 million. Together with an increasing ability for managing massive quantities of data, post-oral societies tend to develop different social structures (e.g., nuclear families, national states). Abstract notions of history, of nature, and of self are developed. An increased tendency for individual reflection leads to new levels of competition, capitalism, liberal democracy, and the rule of law. Religions become based on sacred scripture. Above all, increased ability to handle information leads to massive technological innovation that influences all aspects of life.

Any study of cultural difference has to deal with the above typology. This model is, however, general and abstract and can barely serve as a basis for refined and detailed observation, analysis, and description of cultural difference. Ong's sharp distinction between orality and literacy, if it has any use, would apply only to primal oral cultures where writing is completely absent.[32] It would be a serious methodological mistake to use this description to identify a set of "oral features" in a written document and then to assume that the documents are indicative of the conventions of a primary oral society. In the

---

[30] E.g., *Finnegan's Wake* by James Joyce has been studied for its reflection on orality and literacy.

[31] According to my own calculations.

[32] Contra Ong. He does not distinguish sufficiently between the many different types of orality. This could well be the most serious criticism leveled against his work.

words of James Barr, used in a different context, this amounts to "an illegitimate transfer of meaning."

To what extent can Ong's orality-literacy typology further an understanding of cultural difference? Let us consider an example. Although traditional African culture is rapidly dissolving in South Africa due to urbanization and universal schooling, all the above "oral" features can still be recognized among its "indigenous" population. Here we think of aspects such as the extended family (primary oral group), traditionalism (necessary to preserve information for survival), a communal and inclusive tribal ethic ("ubuntu"), the tendency for politics to be relationship driven instead of by the rule of law, a cyclical sense of history, emphasis on ritual, hereditary leadership, wisdom instead of an abstract view of history and nature, the experience of ancestral spirits, and myths. Many of these features have been branded to be "typically African"[33] but can be ascribed to the oral-aural culture that has until recently dominated in Africa south of the Sahara (except Ethiopia).

To some extent, then, Ong's typology assists us in noticing typical features in African culture. By pointing out universal aspects this approach defeats a narrow ethnocentrism that wishes to make these features unique to one race or continent. As already mentioned, it also fosters an awareness of oral culture and assists people to preserve their oral heritage. This is, however, where the usefulness of the typology ends. This is so because any student of a South African culture will know that there are hardly any communities left that participate in a "pure" oral culture. On the oral-literate continuum, the mass of people are gravitating toward the literate and semiliterate middle classes. Thus we can observe many different types of orality and literacy. One also has to deal with the fact that a simplistic distinction between "oral" and "literate" cultures often forms part of a colonialist discourse. Therefore, while scholars need to use abstract paradigms, we caution against this misuse. For the same reason we also have to emphasize (with Ong) that one culture is not superior or inferior to any other. People can live dignified and humane lives in any culture. This is especially important when we consider the contrast between a primary oral culture and cultures that have been shaped by post-oral media technologies (e.g., Western or Chinese/Japanese cultures, using writing, printing, and electronic media).

---

33 Although often associated with Africa, these features can be observed among primary oral cultures all over the world. Today in Africa there are large sections of the indigenous population that are no longer living in a primary oral society: e.g., the urban middle class in most cities, the Euro-African and Indian minorities, and the Arabic population north of the Sahara.

There are some urgent considerations before the scholar of cultural difference can proceed to move away from the usual generalizations. Let us therefore ask (again), To what extent is the use of specific media indicative of general cultural trends? There are good arguments for rejecting a deterministic position, that is, one that accepts media usage as the primary determining element of culture. Apart from media, factors such as climate, economic conditions, population density, natural resources, and the like all determine human culture. Remarkable, though, are the correspondences that can be noticed between similar cultures in different parts of the world. Let us briefly review some of these cultural types. In the most diverse climates and regions one finds small *hunter-gatherer societies* communicating with gesture and sound, using stone tools, ruled by family heads assisted by wise individuals.[34] The same applies to nomadic clans in different parts of the world.

They use primitive recording techniques, manufacture ceramics, and use animal transport, while they gather in larger federations and are ruled by patriarchs.[35] Another type of culture is found among those living in *agricultural settlements*. These are experimenting with more sophisticated sign symbols, melting metals, transporting goods with horses and carts, and being ruled by kings.[36] Writing first developed more than five millennia ago in the *small urban settlements* of Mesopotamia, Egypt, and China, where people developed irrigation systems, opened trade routes, and were ruled by feudal kings. Since the eighth century C.E. we see the gradual development of a manuscript culture in the ancient Near East, opening the way for the empires of antiquity with their improved communication systems and extensive governmental control. So one can multiply examples of transregional and transethnic cultural types that are found independently from one another. Does this mean that cultural change is *always* driven by new media technologies? It seems that communication media are integrally related to the dominant cultural paradigms. Theorists such as McLuhan and Ong point out that the rise of the *nation state* in Western Europe coincided with the invention of new printed media. At present the electronic media are enabling global communication to such an extent that national boundaries are no longer obstacles to stock markets. Transnational institutions are flourishing, heralding the formation of new social and political units. These examples show how

---

34 E.g., the San of Southern Africa, the Aborigines of Australia and Taiwan, and some tribes in the Amazon and Borneo.

35 Examples are the Khoi-Khoi peoples of South Africa in the seventeenth century.

36 Examples include Neolithic people of the Yellow River valley near Xi'an, China (2000 B.C.E.) and the people living presently among the upper reaches of the Nile Valley in Egypt.

media usage corresponds with and depends on the other elements of a cultural system and cannot be isolated from those other elements.

If we wish to conduct a detailed investigation of how media influence culture, we need a sustainable theory of culture. Among the multitude of definitions, there is the broad understanding that culture is a unique human product that is produced when humans modify nature. This modification of nature is the result of the unique human capacity for symbolization, that is, the capacity to represent information by means of symbolic systems.[37] Of all primates, only humans have the capacity for sophisticated symbolization. Culture is therefore unique to the human race.[38] This definition can serve to clarify the role of media with regard to *culture as the symbolic representation of concepts by means of media*. This is the widest possible definition of culture I can think of.

As an example of cultural production we can consider a table. The idea of a table as an "article of furniture supported by one or more vertical legs and having a flat horizontal surface"[39] cannot exist without being represented in a certain medium. When the idea is only an image in the mind, it is encoded in the neural network of the brain. This is then the primary medium (i.e., the electro-chemical reactions in the brain serve the same purpose as ink and paper, namely, to supply a material medium by means of which ideas are encoded). The concept of "table" can also be encoded in the oral medium by verbally describing it. Gestures can be used to enhance the oral description. It can further be represented as a drawing on paper. Above all, it can be represented in wood or some other material. This is the medium in which it becomes useful, but the latter is only one possible representation.[40] The use of media in such a

---

37 What is here called "symbolic representation" is sometimes also called "symboling" (see the article on "culture" in *Encyclopaedia Britannica Online*: http://www.eb.com:180/bol/topic?map id=51795000&map typ=dx [accessed 26 January 2001]).

38 Other primates are also known to make use of symbols, but the human capacity for symbolization is qualitatively different from those of any other animal. In California a gorilla, "Koko," is reported to have learned five hundred symbols of American sign language. It was found that she always understands words in the same way, regardless of their order. "Words" always have only one meaning. The capacity for polysemy is lacking (according to a program on the Discovery Channel on DSTV SA, 21 November 1999).

39 *The American Heritage Dictionary of the English Language*.

40 By this statement the distinction between a drawing of a table and a real table is suspended. I wish to contend that "real" tables are also symbolic representations, in this case not of ideal tables in a Platonic "realm of ideas" but of processes and objects perceived in reality. Thus, e.g., the abstract idea of a level surface fixed horizontally at a certain level can be seen as representative of what someone has perceived in nature. What makes it a cultural product is the fact that it could be symbolically represented and rationalized before being produced in a certain medium.

series of multiple symbolizations does not only apply to tables but to all cultural objects.

Since the medium, according to our definition, is an integral component in every process of symbolic representation, it follows that an analysis of media usage is profitable for the study of cultural difference. Usually the media are not the focus of attention in cultural activities, though there are specific occasions where they become that. This is when, in Roman Jakobson's terms, a certain aspect of a message is *overdetermined*. In the communication of messages, media overdetermination occurs when the sender of a message explicitly focuses on the medium, such as when the sender of an e-mail message includes some remark about the medium ("I hope you can open my attachments in your browser"). Usually the interpreter has to rely on implicit data to examine the "media texture" of a text (e.g., "Had I been present, I would have told her so myself"). Perhaps *Finnegan's Wake* by James Joyce is the best example of a text in which the medium is overdetermined. In this work the phonetic quality of the text usurps the conventional linguistic aspect, breaking up the expected semantic patterns and creating multiple levels of meaning and quasi-meaning. It is a play of the oral-aural medium with the visible, typographic medium.

The media aspect, however, does not need to be overdetermined to be the object of study. All texts exhibit a media texture. (Under media texture we understand *the network of signs in a text that relate to the management of the media used in the production of meaning.*[41]) The "poetics" of a text (i.e., the totality of features influencing the style and composition) usually reflect properties specific to the media used. Thus we find an *oral* texture even in written texts when these reflect the style and conventions related to oral communication. Over the past decade I have compiled a list of the general properties of media that influence various aspects of the communication process.[42] These can be used to analyze and describe the media texture of a text. As such, the media texture also points to the other textures of a text.[43]

---

41 This applies even to the most primitive of texts, namely, those that exist only as webs of concepts in the mind. In such a case the "neural" medium will determine features such as the durability of the text and the "density" of information.

42 See my articles in which some of the elements mentioned were developed (Loubser 1986; 1993; 1995; 1996). A fuller explanation will follow in a forthcoming monograph on orality and manuscript culture in the Bible.

43 For the concept of "texture" I am indebted to Prof. Vernon Robbins (1996a:18–43; 1996b:2–4). Robbins's sociorhetorical analysis consists in plotting the different textures in texts (inner texture and social, cultural, ideological, and sacred textures) as they interact with the contexts of sender and receiver. I wish to suggest "media texture" as a further element

Let us first examine those media properties that regulate the *production* of messages. The production of texts depends on the manipulability of the medium. One may ask, How easily can a text be produced and changed? In the oral-aural medium texts are produced instantaneously once the sender has learned how to use language. In contrast, printed messages require sophisticated technology and cannot be produced or altered without an investment of time and effort. Another factor influencing the production of messages is the total volume of signs/symbols that can be carried by a certain medium. If a politician prepares to address an audience, the length of his or her message will be adapted to the medium, whether it be a live address, a radio address, or a television interview. Whereas a live address may take, say, about forty minutes, a radio address might only allow for less time and the television interview for even less. When using different media (e.g., reading a book or watching television), the total volume of signs communicated will differ. Related to this, there is also the capacity of media to allow for a certain "infodensity," that is, the amount of information that can be transmitted *within a given time.* The infodensity of, for example, oral-aural communication is relatively low in comparison to high-speed electronic data transmission. The last property related to the production of messages is that of mass. This refers to the physical mass of the medium required. In the transmission of oral messages the physical mass of materials used is almost negligible. In contrast, stone tablets for monumental inscriptions have a considerable mass. As a rule, the more mass a medium requires, the more difficult it is to produce a text. In summary, we note that oral-aural messages are rapidly produced with very little effort and appear to have no mass. However, during oral-aural communication the volume of signs and information transmitted is relatively low in comparison with print and electronic media.

The *format* of messages also depends on media properties. Different media require the use of different codes that affect the format, that is, its form and style as well as the demarcation of units. The oral-aural medium, for example, requires the use of mnemonic devices such as repetitive formulae and a paratactic style. Stylistic devices such as rhyme, rhythm, and meter serve to optimize communication. The oral medium fosters the development of a range of genres, such as the folk tale or sung epics. Only with the advancement of writing could genres such as the historical essay, clear prose, and the modern detective story develop. Where

---

for consideration in sociorhetorical analysis. For this purpose, however, both the terms *media* and *text* as used in sociorhetorical analysis need to be expanded.

oral-aural communication depends on the management of sound, writing depends on the arrangement of visual marks on a two-dimensional surface. What sound and time is to orality, space is to writing.

Another media property that influences the format of messages is the capacity of the medium for synchronizing with other media (i.e., its multimedia capacity). The spectrum of media that can be incorporated has a direct bearing on the length and style of the message. Oral-aural communications allow for the use of gesture and intonation. Printing, however, could only begin using photographic pictures after the development of the technology in the 1840s. The importance of this for the format of the printed text can be observed in the contemporary glossy magazine, where much of the printed text serves to introduce and comment upon graphic images. Related to the multimedia aspect, but not the same, is the capacity of media for intertextuality (i.e., the incorporation of other texts using the same medium in a message). During oral-aural communication intertextual reference can come only from memory. Because memory is in a permanent state of flux, such references are usually adapted to the present needs of the audience to such an extent that the original context becomes obscured. Exact verbal citations do occur in oral cultures but are far less usual than free recontextualizations, reconfigurations, adaptations, and echoes of the texts to which they refer. Many of these intertextual modes are preserved in the manuscript culture of the first century.[44] Thus we see that the format of messages is strongly determined by the medium used.

A third aspect of messages that is influenced by media properties concerns the *distribution* of the messages. How far and wide messages are distributed depends on the durability, affordability, range of reception, copying, and storage capacity allowed for by the medium, as well as the type of censorship that is possible. Let us consider the distribution of oral-aural communications in a pure oral society in comparison to the manuscript culture. During oral communication only those within hearing range can participate. While being inexpensive,[45] the spoken word disappears as soon as it has been uttered.[46] This limits the range of messages to the immediate hearers and those among them who can remember

---

44 For a full list and description of intertextual insertion in New Testament manuscripts, see Robbins 1994, who refers to Theo. Robbins refers to the intertextual aspect as the oral-scribal intertexture (see Byrskog: 13).

45 Of course, this is not always the case. Since classical times rhetoricians charged their students for instruction in eloquence.

46 In fact, in primal societies people do not perceive words as separate units. Vansina begins his 1985 book on oral history by referring to the old saying: "Verba volent, scripta manent" (words fly, writings remain).

and transmit the message. Social structures are developed to support the preservation of memory. This involves the institution of elders (who preserve the memories of the tribe), the ritualization of myths, the development of a culture of bards and singers, and so forth. In predominantly oral societies gifted individuals specialize in memory.[47] By way of generalization one can say that the copying and storage of information in a oral culture remains volatile and evanescent when compared to writing. This puts a serious limitation on the range over which oral texts can be distributed. The distribution of written documents is also limited by their cost. The use of ink, papyrus, and parchment for producing manuscripts comes at a price. It is calculated, for example, that 350 sheep or goats were slaughtered to produce one of the fifty copies of the Bibles that Emperor Constantine ordered for the churches in Byzantium in the year 330 C.E.[48] Parchment manuscripts, especially codices, could be used for centuries and were distributed as far as transport routes went. Though such documents could never be copied with photographic precision, they represent a huge advance over oral communication. It was this medium that enabled the dissemination and standardization of scientific, religious, and philosophical information of the Arabic and European cultures during the Middle Ages. This type of manuscript culture was recently observed in Ethiopia by the author. These examples serve to show how media have a direct bearing on the distribution of the messages, but messages can also be suppressed. In an oral culture, use is made of taboos to prevent people from speaking about certain matters. To prevent information from spreading, it is often expedient to "kill the messenger." In manuscript and printing cultures the burning of books is the most efficient form of censure.

A last series of media properties that influence messages are those that have a bearing on the *reception* of the messages. Here properties such as accessibility, aesthetic impact, opportunities for reflection and feedback, and the level of distortion play a role. When examining a message the scholar has to ask, To how many people is this message accessible? The medium used, whether oral, written, or electronic, will make a considerable difference. Another question must seek to determine the nonverbal

---

[47] As an example there are the Tannaim in rabbinic Judaism, who served as "memory banks" for the rabbis and were often the object of ridicule because they memorized without understanding (see Gerhardsson). Such "human memory banks" could verbally recite large parts of the Torah, Mishnah, and Talmud—no small feat if taken into account that it comprised more than nineteen thousand modern printed pages. In contemporary Islamic communities youngsters are found who have memorized the complete Qur'an.

[48] Millard's estimate (45).

(illocutionary) aspects of the message. What aspects of the message cannot be encoded in the medium? In the first century the reading (or rather, performance) of literary works was often accompanied by sound, music, and gesture and elicited empathetic responses from participating audiences.[49] Today some of those manuscripts are extant, but their illocutionary force has been lost. When reading such manuscripts at contemporary academic institutions, scholars often fail to imagine such paralinguistic aspects (e.g., speed, tone) as presupposed by the author of the written text.[50] (Ancient texts are treated as having been produced by "disembodied brains."[51])

Another manner in which media influence the reception of messages is by the degree to which access and backtracking is allowed. The spoken word depends on linear, hierarchic, synchronous communication. No backtracking is possible except by breaking the live transmission of information. This fosters a sense of interiority, of emotional participation in a communicative event.[52] Whereas oral texts encourage communal participation, printed texts lead to silent and individual introspection—the extent to which this actually happens depends on the type of society at hand. Audiences tuned to oral-aural texts tend to dance and celebrate; silent readers of printed texts tend to reflect and think. Books allow direct access to information. Manuscript scrolls do not provide such access—the literary scroll of the Hellenistic age (often 10 meters long) had to be perused from beginning to end to find a specific reference. Books and codices (since 150 C.E.) can easily be paged through. The electronic word processor is only the latest technological advance in allowing direct access to the information contained in documents. The effect that such diverse media have on the receivers of messages can be observed in the time required to access information. Technical information takes much longer to be communicated orally. In printed form references can more

---

49 In a personal research of about 250 pictorial representations of writing on vases and reliefs in the Greco-Roman world, only a few instances were found where people were depicted with manuscripts without also the depiction of musical instruments, singers, or dancers.

50 This is especially true for Western documents. The ideograms of Chinese and Japanese writing allow for the communication of a register of connotative meanings that is not found in alphabetic script. It was pointed out to me that the Japanese "kanji," being a short poem written by means of ideograms, "evokes multiple associations, making reading an adventure in nuances, connotations and memories" (Lucy Bregman, Temple University, Philadelphia).

51 After a remark at a Society of Biblical Literature session by K. C. Hanson, with reference to the regular Pauline studies.

52 See Ong 1982:71–74.

easily be made. The media also determine the type of reaction required from the audience, whether it is immediate feedback (as in an oral dialogue) or a response over several weeks or months (as in the Hellenistic letter) or an immediate typed response (as per e-mail or chat-line).[53]

Lastly, we note the amount of distortion caused by the medium of communication. No medium allows for a perfect reproduction of signs. Speech is always heard somewhat differently from the way it is pronounced. There is always some "noise" that leads to misunderstanding. Over time, all media decay. In an ancient Near Eastern text there is an admonition to write the same text both on stone and on clay tablets. In case the world is destroyed by fire, the stone will crack but the clay will be baked hard. In case the world is destroyed by water, the clay will dissolve, but the stone will endure. In China we find a remarkable instance of how the distortion of sacred texts was kept to a minimum. Since the seventh century C.E. they developed the practice of making carbon rubbings on rice paper.[54] This practice is still in use. In contrast, we find that libraries have a problem with microfilm that decay faster than paper. Today scientists are worried about the medium and language to be used for instructions at sites for nuclear waste, because in ten millennia the waste will still be radioactive and no human message has endured for so long.[55]

In summary, then, the media texture of a message can be examined by considering the media properties that influence the production, format, distribution, and reception of the text. Studies that concentrate only on concepts (as all ancient studies) or codes (as is the case with structural and semiotic studies since De Saussure) are bound to miss this important aspect. Such studies tend to present a "docetic" view of reality, treating texts (and culture) as if they merely consist of some abstract system of ideas. This is bound to produce a distorted view also of cultural difference and to play in the hands of a colonialist discourse. It is thus in the interest of multicultural communication that the media aspects receive their due attention.

In this essay I have argued that the integral and constructive role of media should be considered in a theory of culture. This was illustrated by

---

53 For the latter, see the interesting article by Murphy and Collins on the protocols and conventions of instructional discussions on the Internet.

54 This is still practiced as observed by the author in the city of Xi'an. The Buddhist texts, brought to China in the seventh century, were translated and engraved on stelae. From these carbon copies were made. In the West no technique for exact copying existed before the printing press.

55 Mentioned by Kaku.

means of examples taken from a variety of cultures. It is now time to move forward from the simplistic categories of the past.[56] Studies over the past two decades have shown that we can no longer speak of a great divide between orality and literacy. Neither can we speak in a simplistic sense of "African" or "Western" culture. There are many different shades of orality and literacy and as many manifestations of the same cultural type in many places on the globe. We therefore need a theory of culture that allows for more sophisticated typologies.

Through the contributions of many scholars during the past decades the ground has now been prepared for media-critical studies in a variety of fields. We can only wish that scholars and students of literature, history, psychology, philosophy, theology, journalism, and other disciplines will make use of this opportunity to engage in this most recent and most rewarding field of investigation. A rich harvest can be expected. The most important result of such studies will be, as we have argued, an enhanced understanding of multicultural issues.

---

[56] Derrida's rejection of Levi-Strauss's lament over introduction of writing among the Nambikwara comes to mind. Derrida derides the latter for denying that the Nambikwara had writing at their disposal. He points out that they were using a great variety of signs like "dots and zigzags on their calabashes." It is a serious question whether Derrida, in his zeal to defend the dignity of a primary tribe, has given due cognizance to the role of media in the formation of culture. For a report on the issue, see Peters: 27–28.

WHY DID PLATO WRITE?

Jean-Luc Solère
Centre National de la Recherche Scientifique
(Paris)/ Université Libre de Bruxelles

For people today, philosophy is often represented by great works, voluminous books, such as those of Kant, Hegel, Descartes, and so on. It could even appear difficult to conceive of doing philosophy without writing, just as for mathematics or something like that.

However, everybody knows that the father of the Greek rational and critical thought, Socrates, never wrote a line of philosophy. Jesus and Socrates have often been compared. One of their common points is that we know only indirectly what they said. Others wrote their sayings down for them. Socrates preferred a "living" philosophy made of conversations with people he met in the street. He had no school and no books. For him, philosophy cannot be enclosed in formulas; it is a research made orally and in common.

Consequently, we must be aware that philosophy is not so evidently related to literacy. This is also the case for Socrates' best pupil, Plato.

1. THE CONDEMNATION OF WRITINGS

Plato has pointed out the dangers of written works. In his *Seventh Letter* he states that he never himself wrote in "the sublime questions of philosophy" (341B–D) and that no serious man will seriously write on serious problems, because he would so lay his thought open to the misunderstanding of the crowd (344B).

In the *Phaedrus* he tells a myth about the origin of writing. The Egyptian god Theuth is supposed to have discovered the art of fixing knowledge with signs, but the wise king Thamous criticizes his invention (274C–275B). Men, he contends, will lose their faculty of memory, and, moreover, they will be full of various knowledges, without having received a true teaching. They will know some things, but they will not be learned.

Further, in the same dialogue Socrates himself remarks that a written work is a child without father—it cannot protect itself (275E)—and that writing is deceptive like painting; the latter depicts beings that are falsely living and cannot answer questions; likewise, the former draws up books that can signify but one thing and are unable to provide explanations by themselves, shades of meaning, and so on (cf. *Protagoras* 329A). Moreover, the book escapes its creator's control; it soon becomes everybody's toy and is exposed to the danger of losing its true meaning.

Thus, for Plato, the oral discourse is better than the written one. It can be more accurately adapted to the person one talks to. One must not divulge anything to anyone (cf. *Tim.* 28C; *Theaet.* 180D). Plato had perhaps a personal reason to be suspicious about mass communication. Aristoxenes tells us that Plato once tried to hold a public conference on "the Good." People came to hear of wealth, health, happiness, and so on, but Plato spoke only of mathematical principles. His conference was a failure. From then on he decided to speak of those things with only a few select listeners.

Indeed, scholars have noticed that in Aristotle and some other works there are some indications of a teaching by Plato that does not look like the thoughts expressed in the written dialogues that we can read (see Robin). One believes, therefore, that in his school, the Academy, Plato taught the so-called *agrapha dogmata*, the nonwritten doctrines, to chosen pupils (this is the claim of the "school of Tübingen" [see Richard]). If this is true, they remained indeed only oral, and scholars today must try to reconstruct them from scattered allusions. The written dialogues are then presumed to be only a propedeutic, not Plato's real teaching.

It is not unlikely that Plato exposed his most important thoughts only *viva voce*. One must not forget, anyway, that in the ancient world written works were intended to be read aloud, for others or for oneself.[1] Saint Augustine was very surprised to see Saint Ambrosius reading "with the eyes only." The usual way of reading was to vocalize the text. This close relationship of literacy with orality can explain some peculiar characteristics of ancient works.

However, despite his condemnation of written works, Plato did write. Unless his dialogues are nothing more than advertising for his school, appetizers for the hidden doctrines, why did he do so? Is there another explanation, or is it a mere contradiction?

---

[1] See Hadot: 413: "la plupart des oeuvres, philosophiques, de l'Antiquité, étaient en étroite relation avec l'oralité, puisqu'elles étaient destinées à être lues à haute voix, souvent lors de séances de lecture publique. Cette étroite liason de l'écrit et de la parole peut expliquer certaines particularités déroutantes des écrits philosophiques." Cf. Svenbrö 1988; 1991.

2. THE JUSTIFICATION OF WRITINGS

2.1. The Principle of Imitation

Ancient Platonic commentators, of course, thought about this fact of the existence of Plato's written dialogues. An anonymous handbook, at the end of antiquity, the *Prolegomena to Plato's Philosophy*, answered as follows (3.13; Westerink, Gerrit, Trouillard, and Segonds: 20). Plato's main ethical rule of life was to imitate the divinity. Now, God has produced an invisible, spiritual cosmos but also a visible, material one. Thus, Plato wanted to produce visible works as well as invisible ones, which are the high thoughts inscribed in his pupils' souls. The pupils are nicely called by the handbook "living writings" (4.15; ibid.: 222), but Plato also had to draw up material works.

The same principle of imitation explains why Plato chose the literary form of the dialogue. A dialogue, with its various interlocutors, is a universe; conversely, the universe, according to Plato, produced dialogues. The dialogue is the most "living" literary form and is therefore an image of the life of the universe.

2.2. Palamedes and Orpheus

These explanations seem quite eloquent; nevertheless, in order to bring some other justifications for Plato's written works, we can also reexamine the texts where he speaks of the very fact of writing. It will perhaps appear that Plato did not condemn all writings but only a certain sort of writing.

I will first rehearse the conclusions of the French scholar Marcel Detienne, a specialist of ancient Greece, in his book on the origins of writing, which are, he says, twofold (Detienne: 101–15, 119). Two relevant mythical characters represent those origins: Palamedes and Orpheus. They are, on the one hand, opposed, and, on the other hand, complementary.

Palamedes is the inventive hero of the *Iliad* who discovers arithmetic and other arts. Writing is here one discovery among others, but it soon becomes noteworthy because of the multiplicity of its appropriations. Moreover, writing is always a matter of *logos*, according to the various meanings of the term: reason, calculation, discourse, and so on. So, the "palamedean" writing is a pedagogical utility; by this means, all other inventions are transmittable (see Cambiano: 251–73).

As T. Morvan points out, in Plato's *Phaedrus* Theuth has partly the same features as Palamedes. Surely Plato knew that his contemporary readers would identify the Egyptian god and the well-known Greek hero (Aeschylus, Sophocles, and Euripides each wrote a tragedy on Palamedes, and Gorgias an apology of the same character). Plato himself makes previous mention of Palamedes as a nickname for Zeno of Elea (261D), master in a higher art of speeches than the judiciary and political speeches. Now, the discovery of letters (*grammata*) by Theuth comes in the last place; previous inventions have been presented to king Thamous and appeared to be very valuable. Thamous settles an opposition between "dead" memory, set in *grammata*, and living memory (the *amamnesis*, main spring of thought). However, this opposition is provoked by Theuth's erroneous presentation of writing apart from the other discoveries. Writing is in fact justified because the use of *grammata* was necessary for arithmetic, geometry, and astronomy (see Detienne and Camassa: 22–26; Cambiano)—and those arts belong to the cursus of studies proposed in the seventh book of Plato's *Republic*. One must also mention, with J. M. Bertrand, the political importance of literacy; nonwritten laws are not laws but only customs, which can afterwards produce juridical rules; then literacy is "the properly political modality of language" (Bertrand: 65). It is a technique that correlates the sacral reality of origins with profane history (52).

Now, as regards Phaidros (the person in the dialogue who bears this name), he is presented by Plato as an enthusiastic but ingenuous lover of nice speeches. When he meets Socrates, he is carrying a copy of a discourse of Lysias that he has just heard. As T. Morvan again points out, one will find in him the same nearly automatic process of transcription of words that characterizes Orpheus according to Marcel Détienne. With Orpheus, the voice changes itself into writing. With Phaidros, any oral opinion gains the authority of a written thing, and he receives sayings of others in his soul without critical examination, passively as a writing tablet.

Further in the dialogue, it is Theuth who has now some features of Orpheus. Justifying his *grammata*, he contends that they are a remedy (*pharmakon*) for memory and learning (*sophia*). As Marcel Détienne points out, with Orpheus the book is represented as the deposit of a worthy message, secured from forgetting. The "orphic" writing is related to the problem of memory and as such is criticized by Thamous.

So the technical or "palamedean" writing is not condemned by Plato, only the orphic one. Or rather, it is the dissociation between the two writings that is condemned, inasmuch as the orphic communication of knowledge by written works does not take into account the requirements of the true art of writing.

3. The Right Art of Writing

Let us see now what is the right art of writing according to Plato. In the *Gorgias* he says that a good discourse intends to pour justice into the soul, just as a remedy intends to bring health to the body. The speech must have a wholesome effect on the listener's soul.

As the *Phaedrus* says, the good, philosophical rhetoric is a "psychagogy" (261A, 271 C; cf. Narcy). It must not only speak the truth but must be efficient; that is, it must be presented in such a way that the addressee can hear this truth. Then, the author has to know the addressees, that is, the different sorts of souls, and he must write accordingly to them (that is why the good rhetoric must be a philosophical one; it requires knowledge of the souls [271D]). Likewise, a good physician knows how to adapt his directions to the patient, and if he must leave on a journey he will give him a written prescription (*Pol.* 295C).

But how is this general principle consistent with the natural wandering of a text? Even if it is appropriate for a patient, it could be used by another, for whom it would be harmful. How can one avoid this danger? As Jacques Derrida (1972) reminds us, the Greek term *pharmakon* signifies both a remedy and a poison.

Plato's answer can be read in the *Seventh Letter*. He says that arguing on a serious topic is not a good thing, except for an elite who will find truth for themselves from "a few informations" (341E). Thus the written work must be conceived of as a test for the reader. The same text has to be silent for one reader and meaningful for another. It is selective; that is, it contains some indication that will be sufficient for its true addressees but meaningless for others. For a real understanding, one must pay close attention, and this is precisely the criterion that selects those who are able and worthy of understanding it. What is expressed in the surface is harmless. One must read between the lines, as Leo Strauss says in *The Persecution and the Art of Writing*. The quality of the reader makes the value of the text. Otherwise, writing is just a game, a hobby, like sowing "Adonis's gardens."

This could explain what Plato's real "esoteric teaching" is. It is not necessary to suppose an oral and secret doctrine. The "esoteric" is not outside the text, but inside it. The deep meaning remains hidden to those who do not know how to read with understanding, but all that is necessary is nevertheless said in the text (see Brague; Mattéi).

4. Some Rules for Writing

Plato left some indications about the rules of correct writing (see Solère-Queval 1988 and 1995). For instance, in the third book of his *Republic,* having exposed which poems must be read in the course of a proper education, after the *lekteon* (the contents) Socrates focuses on the *ôs lekteon,* how the contents must be expressed (392C). We can gather four rules.

4.1. The Rule of Organicity

Plato says in the *Phaedrus* that a text must be organized like a living being; it must have a body, a head, and feet (or a tail) that are connected (264C). Thus one must suppose that in Plato's dialogues there is a correspondence between the body of the conversation and its extremities, the prologue and the epilogue. These two pieces are not meaningless as regards the whole of the dialogue. They are not mere theatrical necessities.

4.2. The Rule of Beginning

The beginning has, according to Plato, a special importance. He says in the *Laws* that the beginning is more than the half of the action or that it is a god living among humans (6.753E, 775E). We can suppose, then, that there is something more here than the common-sense saying that one should begin at the beginning. The beginning is sacred because it is decisive for the growing of a living being. We must thus presume that the beginning of each Platonic dialogue offers precious indications of the meaning of the whole.

4.3. The Rule of Measure

There is no mechanical proportion between the parts of a text (*Pol.* 283B–287B). It is a matter of circumstance.

4.4. The Rule of Imitation

The form of the discourse must imitate the nature of its subject. "The demonstrations are akin, cognate [*sungeneis*], to what they prove," Plato says in the *Timaeus* (29B). For instance, strong, firm reasonings are required for firm and real beings (intelligible beings), while probable reasonings are appropriate to mutable beings (the sensible world).

As we have seen earlier, it is with this principle of imitation that the anonymous handbook, *Prolegomena to Plato's Philosophy*, justified the existence of Plato's dialogues. Strangely, however, it is with the same rule that Proclos legitimates a quite different form of writing.

5. Another Model: Neoplatonic Esotericism

Proclos, the most important and influential pagan and Neoplatonic philosopher in late antiquity (fifth century), based the method he used in his *Elements of Theology* on the principle of imitation, that is, by an analogy with Euclide's *Elements of Geometry*, the mathematical way of reasoning by deductions from axioms. This is rather surprising because this method seems to be contrary to the one that Plato recommended, a discussion with questions and answers (see Cambiano: 268–72).

Let us see first how Proclos justifies this new model. According to him, the main characteristic of mathematics is the perfect continuity between axioms and theorems. In this respect, the mathematical demonstration looks like the emanation of the universe from the supreme metaphysical principle, for Neoplatonists: the One. Further, in an axiom (or "element"), as in the One, all that will later be manifested is wrapped. Then, the axiomatic and deductive method is an exact image of the generation of things in reality itself. This is why, states Proclos, the mathematical order can be used in metaphysical works (Proclos, *Platonic Theology* 1.10 [1:46]).

However, as we noticed, this seems to be in opposition to Plato's preference for dialogue. Moreover, the axiomatic and deductive order is linear, so that it seems to be a perfect target for all the critiques that the *Phaedrus* levels against writing (275D), for it is unable to answer questions but will always repeat the same thing. It cannot adapt itself to the mind of the reader, so it is not relevant to a psychagogy and the like.

However, there could be an explanation for Proclos's choice. Perhaps he found in this mathematical method another means for preserving the platonic "esoterism," that is, not a secret teaching but a selective way of writing that can be understood only by those who are worthy of it. The mathematical order is selective because it was hermetic to the majority of readers in late antiquity, when the basis of the learned culture was exclusively rhetoric (cf. Mueller: 306–8). Saint Augustine is a good example of someone who had not the slightest mathematical formation.

This supposition receives a confirmation from Boethius, the last Roman Neoplatonist (in the early sixth century), who was also a Christian. When announcing the method of his treatise *On the Hebdomads*, he is quite aware of the opposition between rhetoric and mathematics. He writes to the friend who submitted a metaphysical problem to him (How can creatures be good without being identical to the supreme Good, God himself?): "I have therefore followed the example of the mathematical and cognate sciences, and laid down bounds and rules according to which I shall develop all that follows" (Boethius, *On the Hebdomads*: 40 lines 14–17).

He will then write *more geometrico*. He says that his rules or principles are "common conceptions of the mind," what we call axioms (40 lines 18–27). He intends therefore to solve a difficult metaphysical problem with the help of a mathematical method of deduction. Boethius calls his axioms "hebdomads" (we are going to see why), and he adds this warning:

> But I think over my hebdomads with myself, and I keep my speculations
> in my own memory rather than I share them with any of those pert and
> frivolous persons who will not tolerate an argument unless it is made
> amusing. Wherefore do not you take objection to obscurities consequent
> on brevity, which are the sure treasurehouse of secret doctrine and have
> the advantage that they speak only with those who are worthy. (38 lines
> 8–14)

I will make the following remarks: (1) Boethius says he prefers to
keep his speculations in his memory and is very suspicious regarding
their communication to all kinds of people. This is evidently an allusion
to Plato's attitude concerning writing (*Phaedr.* 275A–B, D–E, *Ep.* 7.341D–
342A, 344C).

(2) This method is a means for being understood only by those who
are worthy; its obscurity is quite intentional.

(3) The characteristic of this method, and the reason for its obscurity,
is its brevity. Boethius certainly knows very well that, on the contrary,
rhetoric, as Cicero said, is fond of "abundance."[2]

(4) The unusual term of "hebdomads" is an allusion that is so opaque
that it remained unexplained until our days. I have elsewhere proved, I
think, that this is an allusion to the proclusian symbolic meaning of the
number seven. According to Proclus, seven is the number of Athena and
so the number of philosophy. A hebdomad, he says, is an emanation of
the "intellective light" in us. When Boethius speaks of hebdomads, he is
referring himself to a certain doctrine, and he will be understood only by
some learned friends, in Rome, which is already remote from the Hellenic
culture. In his theological treatise *On the Holy Trinity*, Boethius also
appears to be mistrustful concerning the popularization of difficult ideas,
and he writes then to his addressee and own father-in-law:

> You can readily understand what I feel in this matter whenever I try to
> write down what I think, both from the actual difficulty of the topic and
> from the fact that I discuss it only with the few—I may say with no one
> but yourself.... So I purposely use brevity and wrap up the ideas I draw
> from the deep questionings of philosophy in new and unaccustomed
> words such as speak only to you and to myself.... The rest of the world
> I simply disregard since those who cannot understand seem unworthy
> even to read them. (Boethius, *On the Holy Trinity:* 2 lines 5–22)

Boethius clearly wants to write only for the happy few, and he
belongs to the Platonic tradition, which compensates for the dangers of

---

[2] *Or. Brut.* 14.46: "non ad philosophorum morem tenuiter disserendi, sed ad copiam
rhetorum." Cf. 32.113 and *De or.* 1.13.57.

writing with oral connivance and small indications in the texts. As
Boethius himself says about his hebdomads:

> These preliminaries are *enough* then for our purpose. The intelligent
> interpreter of the discussion will supply the arguments appropriate to
> each point. (*On the Hebdomads:* 42 1ines 53–55)

MITHRA'S CULT: AN EXAMPLE OF RELIGIOUS COLONIALISM IN ROMAN TIMES?

Baudouin Decharneux
Université Libre de Bruxelles

Until the end I bore on my shoulders the accomplishment of the divine commands. (Mithraic sentence of S. Prisca)[1]

INTRODUCTION

From the end of the first century B.C.E. we have evidence of a cult coming from the East and gradually and discretely conquering the Roman army and administration (Daniels). This god, previously unknown to the Romans, was called Mithra. Some historians believe (see Plutarch, *Pomp.* 24.7) that the notorious Cilician pirates defeated by Pompeius propagated this cult when deported in Calabria. We now believe that it was a late transformation of the god Mithra, the friendly protector of contracts (from the root *mei-, suggesting the idea of an agreement or settlement of human affairs, the Sanskrit word *mitra* signifying "friend" or "friendship," as in the Persian word *mihr*) and defender of true and just causes. Nevertheless, it shall be stated at once that these proposals, however appealing and interesting they may be, are no more than working hypotheses (see Meillet; Dumézil; and Turcan 1989, the latter an essential source).

We already have evidence of Mithraism in Asia Minor in 1380 B.C.E. in the form of an invocation of Mithra's name in an agreement between the Hittite king Subbiluliuma and the Mitannian king Mativaza. He is certainly a millenarian god, coming from India, whose cult became widespread throughout the Roman Empire. However, for want of more precise sources, we will only make mention of this fact, while emphasizing its plausible character, since we know how successful the god Mithra

---

1 For the S. Prisca inscription I follow the translation by R. Turcan, an indisputed reference for the mithraic cult.

was in the Parthian Empire. We must also stress that this god retained, in his manifestation in the Roman Empire, his essential characteristics of friend and guardian of contracts.[2]

To the specialists of early Christianity, the so-called "mystery religions" are little known. They are rather inappropriately called the cults of the *externa superstitio*, which, although very successful, were the object of political opposition in the Roman Empire. We do not wish here to study the reasons for this partial obliteration nor to do a complete survey of these cults; we rather wish to study a specific mystery cult (the cult of Mithra) that seems to be most interesting in the specific framework of this volume on the links between oral tradition and writing in the colonial perspective. It must be specified that taking the cult of Mithra out of the problematics of the mystery religions would be a methodological mistake, since a number of mythological and symbolical elements are shared between the members of mystery sects; however, we will stress the peculiar elements of this specific cult, and we refer readers to sources cited as far as the historical-social perspectives are concerned.

The cult of Mithra, seen by the Romans as a "religion of the enemy" (it was actually born in the Parthian Empire), spread first a bit shyly, then forcefully, throughout the Roman Empire, until it came into conflict with Christianity, which was politically emerging at the end of the third century and even more during the fourth century. Contrary to other religions of the same type, such as the cults of Isis and Osiris, Serapis, Dionysus (all well-known examples), Mithraicism eschewed any external manifestations and depended only on its initiatory nature to recruit its followers. Born in a "foreign" land, it gradually became a common faith for soldiers, civil servants, merchants, in short, to people circulating throughout the empire, very faithful to its structures and finding in its rites a way of identification. The members joined a spirituality of an initiatory type (a "constructed initiation"), shared with a large group of solar faiths—the cult of *Sol invictus*—that promised both a life near to the deity and a personal redemption.[3]

Therefore, due to its secrecy, Mithra's cult is not noted for subtle theological constructions. The rites of its followers have been mostly handed down to us by their Christian enemies, whose evidence should then be taken *"cum grano salis,"* in view of the fierceness of the detractors. We are

---

2 On the Avestic world, see Bidez and Cumont; Dupont-Sommer; Benvéniste; Gershevitch; and Widengren.

3 On the concept of "constructed initiation," see Decharneux and Nefontaine. On the propagation of Mithra in the Roman Empire, see Turcan 1989; Vermaseren; and Zotović. From the philosophical standpoint on the question of salvation, see Couloubaritsis.

otherwise informed, through the results of the archaeological digs, which provide us with important iconographical and epigraphical material and other scattered allusions, mostly of an esoteric kind. The scholar must reconstruct the cult, whose facets may have been various, relying on meager clues. This is a work of reconstruction that demands wariness and modesty. Our speculations on the doctrines professed by the members of the Mithraic circle are by no means sure.[4]

After stressing these points, we would like to divide our presentation into three topics: (1) we will describe in a general way the myth linked to Mithra's person, stressing its oriental connotations; (2) we will try to understand the oral specificity of this cult; and (3) we will study the reason for this cult's success in the Roman Empire.

1. The Myth

1.1. The Reconstituted Story

The origins of the Greek Mithra are common to the traditional theogony. Saturn emerged first from the original chaos; then came the sky and the earth, carried by Atlas. The three Parcae that tie and untie destinies were already at work, in a world where time marked out the rhythm of the astral revolutions. Zeus was born and received from his father the ultimate weapon, the formidable lightning. Using it wisely, he set humanity free from the Titans; these latter, according to the Mithraic tradition, were transformed into maleficent forces that wanted to rule the world. These evil forces, once at work, decided to destroy life by drought and thirst. One god stood against this dark project: his name was Mithra.

Mithra comes out of a rock (that is why the god is called "petrogenous") and undertakes the charge of master of the cosmos; with his bow and arrow he makes water flow, thus quenching the thirst of some shepherds. Nature regains its strength and force, trees bend under the weight of grapes and fruit, wheat covers the fields, the god harvests and gathers. When the order seemed to have come back, the lunar dampness is absorbed by a bull, thus depriving cosmos of its humid vitality. The animal flees from Mithra, who first sets fire to a house in which he sought refuge, in order to make him run away; then he captures him, makes him

---

4 We could apply to Mithra's cult an idea proposed by Jeanmaire. He emphasized that the cult of Dionysus was not theologically developed. It is the same for Mithra, probably because of the law of secrecy or perhaps because of the social status of the followers.

bend under his knee, then kills him, probably accomplishing the orders of the superior gods, transmitted by a crow (Turcan 1981). The bull is wounded in the shoulder, his blood spills, while a scorpion, a crab, and a dog attack the bull's genitals. Vegetation grows around the dead animal, as if generated by his blood, and a lion comes to drink. A ray of sun strikes the scene as if to confirm the complicity of the sun.

Between the sun and the god Mithra there is a somewhat militaristic hierarchical relation. Mithra rides his chariot, the sun shares with the god the sacrificial bull during a banquet. He holds in his hand the god's right hand and seems to occupy the same place in the center of the cosmos. The moon, the winds, the planets, the constellations of the zodiac participate in the scene so as to attest the grateful cosmic unity for this order reestablished by the savior god. Next to Mithra we often find two characters, one holding an upward torch and the other holding a downward torch. They are the "dadophora": Cautes and Cautopates, who symbolize the rise of the sun and its descent (Beck). The savior god here represents the cosmic harmony. Robert Turcan, following Plutarch, emphasizes the fact that Mithra often appears as a god of midday or of the middle, accomplishing a function of "Mesites" between two worlds (Turcan 1989:219). The providential action of the god seems to be proven by his actions, which make him king of the cosmos and a way of redemption for his followers. The dimension of the god is here cosmic, as we can see from an abundant iconography that represents him standing, with a snake coiling around him, and sometimes with a lion's face, spitting fire (Duchesne-Guillemin 1960). He holds torches, a key, or a scepter, attesting his cosmic royalty, both eternal (*aiōn*) and providential (*pronoia*), which he conquered after a fierce fight with the bull.

1.2. Between Salvation and Order

1.2.1. Salvation

> Thou hast saved us by spilling the eternal blood. (Mithraeum of S. Prisca)

We must now situate Mithra in the specific context of the reconstructed initiatory societies and consequently measure the intensity of the relations existing between the myths, the symbols, and the rites within this kind of structure. As often happens in the initiatory structures, the praxis is fundamental, as shown by the material in our possession. We are therefore obliged to reconstruct the mythology around which the rites and the symbols were articulated. Consequently, the leading thread between them is not well known and can be reconstituted only by conjectures. For instance, the different phases of the story (birth of the god,

creation of the spring, announcement by the crow, search for the bull, sacrifice of the bull in the cavern, solar symbolism, etc.) seem to be directly
linked to the Mithraic stairway that led the adept, through seven steps, to
knowledge of the superior mysteries. This progression, in a rhythm of
seven initiations, sets a series of symbols that correspond to the same
number of episodes of the founding myth: the adept passes through the
stages of Crow, Nymph, Soldier, Lion, Persian, Heliodrome (i.e., Sun
Messenger), and, finally, Father. Unfortunately, in view of the lack of
information, we cannot analyze this progression any further.[5]

The myth nevertheless gives a central position to the cosmic harmony, as shown by the correspondence between initiatory stages,
planets, and metals. The solar year followed the rhythm of the equinoc-
tial and solsticial feasts, thus creating a feeling of rebirth in the rhythm
of time.

On the night of 25 December the most important feast of the year
took place. This was the date when Mithra was said to have come out of
the rock.[6] This solar symbolism, which aimed, on the shortest night of
the year, to revive the solar cycle by a rite of hope, shows the importance
of the cosmos and its cyclic harmony in these rites. From a theological-
philosophical point of view, this cosmic symbolism ought not to be
surprising, because it is a common ground with Middle Platonism,
which instituted the themes of providence and of salvation as central
doctrinal stakes.[7]

The greatest concern of the people at that time was without doubt
personal salvation. During the first centuries of our era, a philosophical
form of subjectivity appears that asserts the possibility of an afterlife and
of an improvement of humans during their subsequent existence, or
existences. The polytheistic world moved significantly toward henothe-
ism and adopted doctrines or ideas such as metempsychosis and

---

5 The mosaic of Felicissimus at Ostia gives us an example of this well-known initiatory
scale that we should interpret in four dimensions, circling the figure of the human soul,
which in antiquity was believed to be able to attain a new life (reincarnation, metempsychosis).

6 It is the theme of Mythra " petrogenous."

7 See note 2. It is important to separate the concepts of social devotion from the philosophical ideas, since the areas and times of enunciation and of reception are not the same.
In addition, the characters in a certain context take different positions that amaze us with
distance and time (for instance, in antiquity). We will must be careful to notice that, in the
liturgical context, the teacher in theology is no different from that of antiquity. His social
position will vary without him noticing the difference due to the context and not necessarily to his personal strategy. Lévi-Strauss studied thoroughly this topic in his famous book
The Savage Mind. Thus the permeability to philosophical ideas is a reality, but their percep-
tion is different.

reincarnation, in order to reassure the believers about their postmortem future. Jews and Christians, on the other hand, opted for the thesis of a resurrection, accompanied by theories on eternal life, more or less tinged with millenarianism. The philosophers promised a "godlike life," asserting the divinity of *nous* (intellect) and its eternal character. At the end of antiquity they would affirm the possibility of the reception of the divine by humans: this process was called "theurgy." The Christian theologians affirmed that, after death, one or many judgments would reward the just, and more and more destruction or of eternal punishment was supposed to strike the wicked, who were consigned to an eternity of torment.

These kind of affirmations cannot be conceived of on a strictly intellectual basis; we can also argue that theological rationalization of these ideas came *a posteriori*, as they seem to correspond to a spiritual need that affects all social strata. The phenomenon of magic, which begins now to be more systematically explored, shows well the search for a personal relation with the Invisible (Graf). The evolution of divination apparently follows the same path. In the early Christian literature, some apocryphal texts, particularly the so-called Childhood Gospels, are also a part of this spiritual trend.[8]

Mithra appears therefore as the god who, halfway between the intelligible and sensible words, ensures the cosmic order, by taking care of the celestial revolutions and the perpetuation of the Whole.

In their longing for immortality, the followers of Mithra, like many of their contemporaries, conceived their salvation through a personal initiatory search or through a search reserved to a small group of believers compelled to silence. Mithra was of course the god of everyone; in fact, he had saved the whole universe thanks to the sacrifice of the bull, and, moreover, as *Sol Invictus*, he was shining for everyone. A god of a cosmic contract between gods and humans, a god of a personal contract between himself and his followers, Mithra is also a god of secret attributes, keeping for his followers the mysteries of eternal life.[9]

---

[8] In their excellent book, *Whoever Hears You, Hears Me: Prophets, Performance and Tradition in Q*, R. A. Horsley and J. A. Draper show well the pervasiveness of orality in a context where writing is not the dominant feature. The question of integration of magical practices in the written texts (at first as magical "recipes," then as part of a more complex story), seems to relate to the same evolution, that, starting from the oral structures, slides to writing that can become very complex, under the effect of theological rationalization. See also Nasta for the rites of immortality.

[9] We know that one of the great claims of the late antiquity was on the polytheist side to "become like the gods." See Liefferinge, who reviews the subject very well.

1.2.2. Order

Here also the goat runs ahead and in a strict order. (verse from the Mithraeum of S. Prisca)

If we insisted on the themes of unity and cosmic harmony, it is precisely in order to show that one of the major theological attributes of Mithra is that of keeper of the order and coherence of the universe. Mithra, a helpful god and a warden of contracts, stands on the side of life. His symbolism shows an image of power in the midst of time, a kind of mediator between eternity (unity) and time (multiplicity). These philosophical considerations are not surprising; they were a part of Middle Platonism, a philosophical trend we have already mentioned, which affects the religious tendencies of the time.

The order of cosmos is represented by a complex symbolism that makes use of the celestial vault, the planets, the zodiac signs, as an iconographical and initiatory medium. We must stress that this cosmic order of which the god is the guarantee, and the initiatory order that he proposes, are closely linked in a common symbolism. The adept gradually discovers these hidden "truths" throughout his initiation. The visible order of the external world was therefore completed by an invisible order that the believer kept secret. From this point of view Mithra is a demanding god, summoned in secret and refusing the ostentatious ceremony of the "profane." His followers did not open the doors of their sanctuary but practiced their rites inside their own initiatory society, thus proving the double nature of the order of the cosmos: the one exterior and visible, the other internal and invisible. After all, is there not a fundamental tension between the sacrifice of the bull in the crypt and the circuit of the solar chariot?

Nevertheless, the followers of Mithra saw themselves as members of another order equally important to them, that of the Roman Empire. As Turcan stressed, *a priori*, these small groups came together to celebrate the mysteries of a "foreign" god that did not seem to have any political aim. Nevertheless, we would be mistaken to think that the followers of Mithra were organized as philosophical communities, grouped as theological "elites" concerned with the same speculations. This is probably a point of difference between the cult of Mithra and the Pythagorean movement, which was mainly theoretical. We believe that the theological-cosmological preoccupations are the result of a ritual *praxis* that induces these kinds of metaphysical interrogations.

The adepts of Mithra were recruited from different social strata, as the sociological study of the sources in our possession has shown. In the first century, some imperial freedmen, as well as some legionaries of the *limites* of the Danube and of the Rhine, were members. Covering the structures of the empire, the cult reached also the kind of people (e.g., traders, merchants, craftsmen, civil servants, physicians) who followed the legions due to their occupations. The movement of the legions due to the military needs propagated the cult from the regions of Asia Minor to the West. After the second century we find treasury officers, farmers, salt and iron-mine workmen, weapon makers, but also city councillors, magistrates, freedmen, and legionaries. The inscriptions show us well that this is not a world of philosophers looking for speculations, but a fraternity offering its followers a way to discover, through its rites, the link to the deity.

Mithra probably won over even the imperial house. We are wary about the well-known initiation of the emperor Nero to the mysteries of the Magi through Tiridates (see Turcan 1989:237). However, it seems that the emperor Commodus (192) was an unworthy adept of the mysteries, because he was suspected of having killed a fellow-adept during a ceremony simulating a ritual sacrifice. The imperial house had a much worthier adept in Diocletian and his colleagues of the Tetrarchy: Galerius and Licinius. The god is then called the *fautor imperii sui*, the "protector of the imperial power" (Inscription of Carnuntum in 307).

These few examples show that the cult of Mithra was an important piece on the imperial political chessboard. His followers certainly did not have any coherent political aim, and their desire to influence the emperors is not confirmed at all. On the other hand, on the social level people learned, in the "Persic Cavern," to respect the contract linking the human being to the cosmos and to the gods, and then, at least in an implicit way, to respect the emperors, who were divine beings, as intermediaries between the sky and the earth. The faithfulness to a vivifying cosmic order was thus accompanied by faithfulness to the one representing this order on earth. It is not surprising, then, that Mithra was invoked as Jupiter Dolichenus for the salvation of the emperor. In time, a cult ascribed to the enemies gets mixed up with the worship of the protecting gods of Rome!

2. MITHRA BETWEEN ORAL AND WRITTEN TRADITION

As we all know, the Mithraic cult developed in a period when philosophy and letters were not confined to a restricted circle. To be sure, the number of people having access to study was small, but the philosophical influences largely outpaced the schools because of the philosophical militancy of the latter.[10] The worshipers who crowded the Cavern of the god

---

[10] The philosophical militancy is often largely ignored by the commentators because of the ever-present image of our own system of education. We should notice that missionary

were neither "elites" nor "plebians" but, as briefly explained before, people coming from different social backgrounds of the urban environment. The question of the lack of written documents arises directly in the case of the initiatory groups, whose vocation was to transmit the rites.

Many hypotheses are possible, and it is not necessary to choose between them. First, as is the case for every initiatory society and philosophical school, we describe a wreck. The paucity of the documents that have reached us must not make us forget the dimension of the phenomena. For instance, in the city of Rome alone the mithraea are believed to have numbered over a hundred. This shows the importance and diffusion of the cult. Still, it must be stressed that many archaeological, iconographical, and epigraphical documents survive, while literary texts are only allusive (Turcan 1998).

Second, we can think of a voluntary obliteration of the cult, which was strongly persecuted and intimidated after the advent of Christian hegemony (see Chuvin; Lane Fox; P. Brown). Thus, a number of mithraea were devastated, burned down, and also set up with a "pedagogic" aim, as in Sarrebourg. The invocations against this "satanic" cult were the cause of the destruction of both the texts and the shrines.

Third, the secret and the silence were initiatory obligations common to all personal religions. The cult of Mithra, because its practices were strictly confined to its members, did not practice "small mysteries," open to outside persons who benefited from the god's favors. The rites were strictly secret, and these secret societies absolutely forbade the writing down of the rites. Mithraism has often been compared to freemasonry. This transposing of an antique religion out of its context goes perhaps a little too far, but as far as writing is concerned, however, this parallelism is not completely groundless. There are many studies on this topic, but no more than two decades ago there was still a ban on written rites in some American lodges. This example gives a measure of the gap that can exist between an initiatory society and its time.

However, the religion of the Persic Cavern is silent and discreet. It transmits its secrets exclusively orally in an initiation ceremony, thus creating a screen between the adepts and the profanes. Orality in mystery societies seems to be a real value, overturning the superiority of written over oral records that society tries to impose. This is part of the initiation process but also part of an initiatory strategy (since this is a "constructed initiation") rather than a social initiatory datum. Indeed, the circles in

---

philosophers and theologians are attested in many of the beliefs of antiquity. We therefore have to associate, for example, the image of Paul the missionary with that of the Stoic philosophers who preached the benefits of the philosophical life.

which the rites were developed and the members assisting the assemblies probably had access to written documents.[11]

This overthrow of writing in favor of orality can be interpreted in different ways. Once more, it is very difficult to choose. Probably a decisive factor is the law of silence that unites the members of an "interior" fraternity. The adepts overturn the laws of society and then, somehow, of the established order because the initiatory progression is not necessarily linked to social status. Secrecy is seen as a rampart between the outside world and the Mithraeum: it reinforces the value of its internal laws, while the adepts are still respectful of the laws of the outside world.

Another deciding factor would be the explicit or implicit theological interdiction. We can here make a parallel with the cult of Dionysus.[12] The initiatory process seizes the adept by the power of the ritual: in a first moment the symbolic speculation and the mythical message are put into the background. The initiation is transmitted by the power of the ritual; its intrinsic value (which often is not understood by the initiand but which is believed to work in him without his knowledge) links him to the group. The constructed initiation is in the first place an overturn, a way of deconstruction that, throughout the rites, is supposed to gradually restructure the adept.[13] The coherence of the theological ideas, the force and quality of the speculations, do not have the same value in all of the groups. In the Mithraic cult, apparently, the great importance of the rite, of the *praxis*, led the adepts to propagate the message orally. The mythological and symbolical ideas were supposed to go back as far as prewriting times. This was supposed to be a proof of the "great antiquity" of their rites.

3. A "COLONIAL" TOOL SERVING THE EMPIRE?

First, we must stress that "colonialism" does not have the same pattern in the Roman Empire as in modern and contemporary times. The differences are numerous, because the ideas of state, nation, ethnic group had different social and political meanings. The absence of a

---

11 Either by reading or by writing. Both kinds of learning were not necessarily combined in antiquity.

12 Jeanmaire proposed this hypothesis for the cult of Dionysus. We think that the same applies to the cult of Mithra, but it should be remembered that the theological interdiction can be integrated in the context of the law of silence. Thus, a religious assembly, even if partly composed by scholars, could not produce a single theological text, because of an internal interdiction of the spreading of the secrets of the group.

13 The idea of progression (initiatory steps) symbolized by the mystic scale probably follows this principle.

political philosophy in imperial times has long been discussed, or rather the sort of consensus around one single model, which gradually imposed itself as "universal" inside the philosophical schools. It must be noted that the message of the initiatory schools was not at all revolutionary. Since the Hellenistic period, politics were not a great issue for ancient people

These remarks, even if correct according to philosophical politics, show us only part of the mentality of the time. The emperor, a real intermediary between heaven and earth, has both a political and religious role, hence his divine character. In accordance with this, he is the *Pontifex Maximus* and participates de facto in every form of cult aiming to ensure the safety and the prosperity of the empire. A conflict arose on this point between the fathers of the church and the imperial authority. Mithra, an intermediary god, savior and warden of contracts, has on a cosmic level the same authority as the emperor. His "adventures" in the company of the solar god directly echo the importance of the *Sol Invictus* cult, a polytheistic but also Christian success, since the emperor Constantine.

Since the conquest of Alexander the Great, the will to gather everything under a single ruler and in a single harmony developed first in the Hellenized empires, then in the Roman Empire. This project, specially influenced by the oriental monarchies, was reinforced by the obsession for unity that characterized ancient thinking. The need for the government of one ruler, tempered by fair laws, was by its own nature an appealing political project in a world whose proportions, in view of the nature of communications and management tools, were not compatible any longer with the political representation seen in certain cities in antiquity.

The imperial power had to be sure of the fidelity of "new men" who were supposed to ensure the defense and the organization of this gigantic structure in which one quarter of the world's population now lived. The city or family rites were no longer sufficient for these people, who were supposed to travel, to settle down, and then to leave again in the service of the empire. A cult such as that of Mithra played a key role in that project, and it is not very surprising that he was favored. It blended very well with the political structures whose essential values it defended indirectly through its practical oral theology.

We know that the Romans paid particular attention to control the integration of the new deities brought inside their pantheon by conquest. In order to succeed in their conquest of, and consequently their hegemony over, the whole of the Mediterranean, they had to accept (despite their initial reluctance), the integration of the gods of their allies and even of certain gods of their enemies. This integration was not painless: remember the famous affair of the Bacchanals under the Republic or the strange "Paulina" affair under the rule of Tiberius.

In order to have a new god accepted as a part of the Roman pan-theon—this was a great privilege—its cult had to be examined by fifteen men (*quindecemviri sacris faciundis*) concerning its specificities and its com-patibility with the "Sibylline oracles," which foretold the future of Rome. The name of the god could be "translated" in Latin by the *interpretatio romana* procedure, which Latinized all that was alien. To integrate a deity who was an enemy to Rome, a ritual of *evocatio* could be performed in order to force the enemy god to join the pantheon.

It is quite striking to notice that, throughout the expansion of the Roman Empire, enemy gods were integrated. This was *perhaps* the case for Mithra, the god of the Cilician pirates, supposed to protect them by his invincibility against the thunderbolts of Rome, who became a faithful servant of those he was supposed to fight.[14] This god to whom Darius III prayed before a decisive battle against the Macedonian invader, this powerful god of armies and justice, was thus annexed by new believers in a new world. The first mention we have of the Mithraic cult in the Roman Orient is in Tarsus (Cilicia), the home of a number of Stoic philosophers and of the worshiping of Herakles Sandan, the bull-killer, and also the place where Saul of Tarsus started his strange path.

4. Open Conclusions

If we cannot speak of a "colonial strategy" *stricto sensu,* the Mithraic cult contributed, according to the ideology of the ancients, to the prosper-ity of the empire by developing loyalty among the adepts, by promising a better life to the soldiers, and by implying that the imperial construction was in accordance with the economy of the cosmos. The ancients thought that, in order to better colonize people, they should enlist their con-science. An important element of the colonization strategy of the ancients was played out by the oral tradition in the silence of the Mithraic circles. We nevertheless distinguish, however imprecisely, the real impact of this policy, which was not intended as part of a planned strategy. It was more a way of sensitization to politics and religion, closely linked in imperial times, which varied according to the important groups sharing power.

In the face of the Parthian Empire, Mithra was then a both an ancient and new god who loudly displayed Roman superiority, ensur-ing finally the cohesion and the unity of those who fought his ancient adepts. His time passed with the emergence of Christianity, but, before

---

[14] This reading is of course a hypothesis, as are many of the philosophical interpreta-tions linked to a cult lacking doctrines.

disappearing, he transmitted to it an original and rich symbolism that greatly influenced the apocryphal literature. The god himself had warned its worshipers by saying:

> We have to pass through difficult times with devotion.

THE ORIGINS OF THE HEBREW SCRIPTURES
IN IMPERIAL RELATIONS

Richard A. Horsley
University of Massachusetts Boston

A central feature of the standard picture of ancient "Judaism" at the time of Hillel and Jesus has been an already well-defined canon of Scripture, the Hebrew Bible, consisting of Torah, Prophets, and Writings. This Scripture, moreover, was supposedly being read by a highly literate Jewish people educated in ubiquitous schools who possessed scrolls of the Bible (Hengel: 78–83; Safrai: esp. 952, 954). Even recently, scholars who otherwise acknowledge that literacy was limited in Greco-Roman antiquity still take at face value Luke's portrayal (4:16–20) of Jesus in the Nazareth synagogue reading from the scroll of the prophet Isaiah. This view, like much of the rest of the modern understanding of life in ancient Judea and Galilee, involved heavy projection of later Jewish and Christian assumptions into a time when literacy was extremely limited and the Judean Scriptures had not yet developed into what later became the Hebrew Bible. Three recent recognitions in particular require the deconstruction of this standard view.

First, some pioneering scholars pointed out that oral communications were predominant in ancient Judean and other ancient Mediterranean societies (Botha 1992; W. V. Harris; Kelber 1983; and see now Hezser 2001). Literacy was limited mainly to a scribal elite. The vast majority of people, peasant villagers and urban poor whose lives did not require literacy, would have been unable to read. Moreover, scrolls were both cumbersome and prohibitively expensive (Botha 1992:201), and until late antiquity Judean and Galilean villages had not begun to construct synagogue buildings in which to house such scrolls (Horsley 1995:222–27).

Second, even though the Pharisees and other scribes/sages in Second Temple Judea may have had access to scrolls of scriptural books, they engaged primarily in oral communication. The Pharisees, say both Josephus and the Christian Gospels, promulgated for the people a whole set of oral rulings (the "traditions of the elders," *Ant.* 13.296–298; Mark 7:1–13) in addition to those written in the Torah of Moses. Their successors, the highly educated, literate rabbis, learned and debated thousands of issues of halakah (legal rulings) orally both before and after they were codified in written form in the Mishnah (after 200 C.E.). The later compilers of earlier rabbinic traditions "were pedagogically and ideologically committed to the *oral* mastery of the traditions.... Written texts were preserved.... Yet their use in instruction was discouraged. Rather, the exposition of Sages' teachings took place in a highly ritualized setting designed to recreate and represent an original imparting of oral tradition from Moses to his disciples" (Jaffee 1994a:143–44; see now 2001). Even Scripture was cultivated primarily in oral recitation by the Pharisees—including the famous renegade, Paul—as well as the rabbis. "Neither Paul nor the Sages had writings before them as they composed their discourses" (Jaffee 1994b:70–71). They were working from Scripture committed to memory, not from a scholarly study lined with scrolls.

Third, in what will probably be most threatening (but ultimately most convincing) for Jewish and Christian Scripture-scholars wedded to the assumptions of print culture, close study of the actual scrolls of scriptural books discovered among the Dead Sea Scrolls at Qumran is now demonstrating that there was a remarkable textual plurality even among literate circles in late Second Temple Judea (Tov; Ulrich). The diversity of scrolls discovered in the Judean wilderness indicates that there were different versions of the scriptural books, varying textual traditions, not simply textual variations in a common textual tradition. It is becoming clear, therefore, that we can no longer speak of a Hebrew Bible as a canon of authoritative books with a standardized textual tradition prior to at least the second century C.E.

Rather, literate Judean communities such as that at Qumran (and presumably others in Jerusalem) had a number of scriptural scrolls in the sense of revered and/or authoritative writings, many of them in two or three versions. The number and sequence of books in the Torah was standard, but versions of particular books such as Exodus and Deuteronomy varied. There was a collection of "prophets," but the particular prophets included and their sequence were not standardized, and some prophetic books, especially Jeremiah, existed in very different versions. Most suggestive of all is that different editions or versions of many scriptural books coexisted, in some cases resembling the Septuagint versions, in some cases resembling the later Masoretic Text versions, and in others resembling the so-called Samaritan Pentateuch, which apparently was based on an earlier textual tradition current in late Second Temple Judea. The scrolls of various versions of these "books" thus appear to represent literature that was revered and authoritative, that is, Scripture. But those scriptural books were still pluriform, not yet standardized in Judea. Moreover, the variation among the versions suggests that the same process that characterized the composition of these books from their beginnings (i.e., of additions and revisions as well as editing) continued all the way through the Second Temple period (Ulrich).

This situation—where we find revered authoritative texts in various versions in a society, but the vast majority of people removed from their use as well as composition and further development, and even from their scribal cultivation in memory and oral discourse in scribal circles— invites further investigation into their origin, development, and function. The first step would appear to be to break with the kind of Christian theological essentialism represented in the standard construction of the Scripture or "Hebrew Bible." That is, we must pointedly cease thinking in terms of "Judaism," that is, a modern construction of a "religion" that did not yet exist. Instead, we must begin thinking in terms of a concrete historical world of political-economic-religious power relations that structured societal life and determined the dynamics of cultural developments in ancient Judea.

TEMPLE AND TORAH AND IMPERIAL RULE

The formation of the temple-state in Jerusalem and a compilation or composition of Judean law were both sponsored by imperial regimes as instruments of imperial rule, starting with the Persian regime. This is coming increasingly to scholarly recognition, in contrast to the earlier construal of Judea as virtually autonomous, politically and religiously. Indeed, the situation was at least somewhat comparable in certain ways to modern European colonization in Africa and Asia.

Prior to the Babylonian conquest in 587/6 B.C.E. the people of Judah had been ruled by the Davidic monarchy, which in turn sponsored the temple in Jerusalem as part of its divine legitimation. After destroying the city and its temple, the Babylonian imperial regime took the Jerusalem ruling class, the royal family and their ranking retainers, including leading priestly and scribal families, into "exile" in Babylon (2 Kgs 24–25). Fifty years later, however, when the Persians took over Babylon and its empire, they reversed the policy of deporting local ruling elites and restored them to their positions of power and privilege as instruments of imperial control. Among the early Persian emperors, Darius in particular pursued the policy of rebuilding temples (i.e., restoring temple-states) throughout the empire as extensions of the imperial administration. He thus gained the goodwill of the various priesthoods in the provinces and posed as a beneficent ruler who restored the cultures of subjected peoples. Conveniently for maintenance of the imperial order, a temple served a variety of functions simultaneously: along with a restoration of a local elite's (and people's?) service of their own deity(ies), a temple constituted a local financial administration for the imperial regime's revenues, the point of establishing an empire in the first place (Berquist: 52–57, 63; Schaper). Not only did the Persian imperial regime encourage the exiled Judean elite to return to Jerusalem, but it virtually mandated the rebuilding of the temple, indeed financed the project out of the imperial treasury, as indicated in biblical traditions (Ezra-Nehemiah; Blenkinsopp 1991:51).

The restored Judean elite and the rebuilt temple in Jerusalem thus constituted a virtual colony of the Persian regime in Judea, with many of the power relations associated with colonialism. The Babylonians had deported only the Jerusalem ruling class, while leaving the Judean peasantry on the land. During the seventy or so years between the Babylonian destruction of Jerusalem and the Persian-sponsored rebuilding of the temple, local leadership would have emerged in Judea, including perhaps ordinary priestly groups and Levites who had not been among the deportees. The deported Jerusalem elite had meanwhile become dependents of empire and now owed their restoration to Persian imperial sponsorship. To complicate matters further, after their return to Jerusalem the restored Judean elite began to intermarry with powerful families elsewhere in Palestine, such as the priestly aristocracy in Samaria immediately to the north. Nor did the restored Jerusalem elite's dominance over the people who had remained on the land go unchallenged. Indeed, the multiple conflicts within early Second Temple Judea, whether between factions competing for power in the temple-state or between the people and the restored ruling elite, emerged within the first generations of the restoration, as evident in Haggai, Malachi, and Isa 56–66. Indeed, they became sufficiently severe that the Persian regime was forced to intervene by the mid-fifth century.

The successive missions of Nehemiah and Ezra just after the mid-fifth century attempted to "reform" the situation that was threatening to dissolve into severe conflict, as evident in the "memoirs" that offer somewhat confusing accounts of the circumstances and events. Almost certainly connected with the struggle for power among the wealthy and powerful, the "nobles and officials" of Judah had been severely exploiting the peasants economically, charging them interest (against Judean custom), forcing them into debt and loss of their ancestral lands (Neh 5:1–6). The Persians, of course, had a vested interest in a viable provincial peasantry, which served as their own as well as the provincial elite's tax base. The Achaemenid regime thus found it necessary to reimpose order in Judah from above through a military governor. It is significant surely that the three governors mentioned in our sources all had either a Babylonian name (Zerubbabel) or explicit roots in the Persian court (Ezra and Nehemiah; Berquist: 136) Although all three apparently had ties with the exiled Judahite elite in Babylon, they were all clearly taking orders from the Persian imperial court.

Although Nehemiah is traditionally understood as a Judahite hero of the restoration, it is clear from his "memoirs" (the later book of Nehemiah) that he was sent by the Persian court as governor, escorted by Persian officers and mounted troops—which he needed, given the strong opposition from various wealthy and powerful figures competing for power in Judah (Neh 2:9). Besides his commission to rebuild the walls of Jerusalem, he was clearly also responsible for regularizing the revenues of the imperial regime and the Jerusalem temple alike. Not only did Nehemiah expropriate payments in kind (allotments of grain, wine, and silver) from the populace (Neh 5:14–15) and see that "the king's tax" on cultivated land was collected (5:4), but he also regularized the contributions of goods and funds to the central storage area of the temple for the support of the priestly families (10:26–29, 40; Gottwald: 110). In what is surely a mark of the previous irregularities he confronted, he established a regular supervision of collections and disbursements by a panel consisting of one priest, two representatives of the lower clergy, and a certain Zadok, who was apparently his own representative (Neh 13:13; cf. 2 Macc 3:5–6, 10–12; Josephus, *War* 6.282; *Ant.* 14.10–13). It is also clear that Pethahiah the overseer was an imperial appointee (Blenkinsopp 1991:49). We can thus discern from the reform of Nehemiah that the Jerusalem temple-state was supposed to serve simultaneously as a largely self-governing body (under minimal imperial supervision) and a branch of the imperial fiscal administration. Under imperial supervision, the officers of the temple were evidently to operate both the imperial and the local tax systems, that is, the collection and payment of the tribute, a poll tax, and a land tax to the emperor (Ezra 4:13, 20; 6:8; 7:24; Neh 5:4) and the collection of the firstfruits or *teruma* for the temple revenues (Neh 10:26–29, 40; Schaper).

The mission of Ezra has proven less susceptible of historical verification, but the account in the book of Ezra portrays it as an implementation of Persian policy and directed by the imperial regime. Even more sharply than Nehemiah's reform, Ezra's aimed to consolidate the position of the previously exiled elite in Judah. Indeed, virtually by definition in these reforms, the *Yehudim* were identical with the returned (*golah*) community. In repeatedly reinforcing the power of the returned Judahite elite, the Persians were backing a ruling class with both roots in traditions of the Davidic dynasty and Jerusalem temple and strong cultural ties with and understandable allegiance to their Persian "liberators" (Berquist: 136). However, this colonialist policy either excluded the indigenous "people of the land" or subordinated them to the temple-state as second-rate or lesser-status people (Blenkinsopp 1991:44–47, drawing somewhat on the work of Weinberg; cf. the response in Horsley 1991; Carter: 297–306). To reinforce the severe exclusivity of the returned *Yehud* community, intermarriage was strictly forbidden. To retain their positions of power, priestly aristocrats were supposedly forced to dissolve their alliances with other, non-Yehudite families of prominence in the region. Thus the very exclusive definition of who belonged to Judah, while presumably strengthening the dominant group, would have alienated rather than integrated the people of the land in Judah itself and other powerful families in the region from the dominant faction that controlled the temple-state.

Besides restoring temples and their administrations throughout the empire, the Persian regime "promoted the codification and implementation of local traditional law as a closely related instrument of the *pax Persica* throughout the empire." (Blenkinsopp 1987; 1991:24; Berquist: 51; and the broader discussion in Watts). It remains unclear whether the Jerusalem elite restored to power in the late sixth century brought with them some sort of law or law book. In any caṣe, Ezra, who was a priest and "a scribe skilled in the law of Moses that the God of Israel had given," became the great symbol of the "restoration" of the law. According to the (at least extensively edited) "copy" of the official "letter," Ezra was commissioned by the Persian emperor Artaxerxes to enforce obedience to "the law of your God and the law of the king" on "all the people in the province Beyond the River who know the laws of your God." He was to do this by appointing (apparently Persian) judges and magistrates who would enforce "the laws of your God" under threat of confiscation of goods, banishment, imprisonment, or death (Ezra 7:25–26). Obedience to "the law of your God" is also obedience to "the law of the king," which is probably a reference to the transcendent Law/Justice by which the king established Order in the empire (Fried). The principal account of the establishment of "the law of God" in Judah thus clearly presents it as authorized, imposed, and enforced by the Persian imperial regime.

Although we can infer certain contents of Ezra's law book from the text of Ezra and Nehemiah (e.g., Neh 10:20–39), we have insufficient basis for identifying it with any bodies of law now included in the Hebrew Bible. Although some of the allusions to and citations of laws in Ezra and Nehemiah bear some relationship to Deuteronomic laws and others some relationship to the Priestly laws, some of the references (e.g., Ezra 9:11, 12) do not appear in what we know as the Pentateuch (Blenkinsopp 2001:57; Gottwald: 102, 109). It thus seems unlikely that "the law of God" or "the law of Moses" that Ezra supposedly enforced was an early form of what we know as the Pentateuch. But the law enforced by Ezra clearly reflected the interest of the priestly aristocracy that it legitimated and gave full imperial authority and enforcement. Moreover, in sponsoring a written composition of Judean law, the Persian imperial regime also in effect imposed a particular story that "defined what Yehud was, rhetorically limited Yehud's own self-understanding, and kept it within certain ideological confines" (Berquist: 138). What the Persians sponsored as the normative law in Judah, enforced by the imperial regime, however, would have been only one or two forms of Judah's legal legacy, which derived from the exiled and then restored Jerusalem ruling class, to the subordination or exclusion of rival versions of Judean law. Yehud, like Babylon and Egypt, had its own law, under the umbrella of Persian imperial rule. But it would have been contested among the population of Yehud itself that still operated according to its own, alternative versions of Judean tradition. The defining story, self-understanding, and ideology imposed by the Persian regime would have taken a long time to "filter down" and "sink in," if it ever did so effectively. In sum, we need do no more than read the "memoirs" of the imperial "reformers" Nehemiah and Ezra to discern that the written law book of the temple-state in Yehud was sponsored by the Persian imperial regime as an instrument of imperial policy.

That Ezra's law book served as a constituting authority of the Jerusalem temple-state (as part of the imperial order) is also evident in the kind of literacy it exhibits. Ezra's law book was both composed and presented as sacred-magical writing. This can be seen clearly in his reading of the law before a grand assembly of the (returned/ restored) Judahites (Neh 8).

Ezra's ceremonial reading of the written law book may be modeled after an earlier ceremonial reading of a Mosaic law book apparently written to authorize a previous centralization of power in Jerusalem, under King Josiah. The story of the "book of the law" that was "found" in the temple such that it both required and then authorized Josiah's "reform" (2 Kgs 22–23) illustrates that a written law book was unusual, perhaps unprecedented even at the center of power in the Davidic court and Jerusalem temple. This suddenly discovered scroll was certainly not simply a dusty old copy of the law that had somehow gotten displaced (or suppressed by a previous regime) from the temple library, where it would previously have been read by priests in regular study or teaching of the people, or from the royal "archives" where such law books would supposedly have been regularly consulted by royal scribes or other officials. Communications in the royal court and in the temple were basically oral. The "book of the law" discovered during repairs to the temple had obviously been composed for the purpose of mandating and authorizing the centralization of political-religious power in Jerusalem. This is similar to the function of "found book" traditions in other societies that legitimate innovation in highly traditional societies (Speyer). This worked only because writing was not a familiar aspect of life that was simply taken for granted, as in modern print culture. Only because a writing in general was utterly unusual in ancient Judah did the discovery of a written law book "work," evoking the awe of the people. Like the covenant tablets supposedly written by God given to Moses on Mount Sinai, this suddenly "found" *sepher* was endowed with aura and mystery. "It validates reform not only because it is written and true, but because it is unusual, mysterious, and divinely sent" (Niditch 1996:104). In authorizing the centralization of power, the scroll, inscribed with the sacred words of God, whose contents and authority was managed by the royal scribes and priests all the way, was read aloud, "in the hearing" of all the people.

The story of Ezra's reading in Neh 8 portrays "the book of the law of Moses" as a numinous sacred object (Niditch 1996:105–6). Ezra reads, or rather proclaims, from the book to the assembly of the Judahites supposedly just returned to Jerusalem from exile in an unprecedented founding ceremony on the first day of Tishre, the first month of the New Year. Ezra was "standing above all the people" on a platform made specially for the occasion. "And Ezra opened the scroll in the sight of all the people … and when he opened it, all the people stood up. Then Ezra blessed the Lord, the great God, and all the people answered, 'Amen, Amen,' lifting up their hands" (8:4–6). That the formal public reading of the sacred writing must be "interpreted" or "translated" for the people, who probably spoke Aramaic, indicates that it was (probably) written in Hebrew, to authenticate its hoary antiquity as a/the law of Moses. That the "citations" concerning the Festival of Booths (8:14–15) "found written in the law which the Lord had commanded by Moses" do not appear in the older material contained in the Pentateuch, however, indicates that Ezra's "book of the law of Moses" was written to authorize a new foundation, that of the temple-state under the Persians. Ezra's law book was written to serve as the numinous sacred law, proclaimed before a founding ceremonial assembly to authorize the (new) temple-state as the imperially constituted political-economic-religious order over Judah.

Having been established under Persian imperial sponsorship, the temple-state and its written law continued under the Ptolemaic and Seleucid Empires, even if as less purposeful instruments of imperial policy. Although they indeed founded new cities with Greek language and constitution, the respective successors of Alexander the Great's imperium over Egypt and the territories from Syria to Bactria both continued the Persian practice of recognizing and working through temple-states as instruments of their control and economic exploitation of indigenous peoples. The complex of intrigue and negotiation between rival factions among the Jerusalem elite and rival Ptolemaic and Seleucid imperial regimes for control of Judea, particularly from the mid-third to mid-second century, provides a vivid illustration that the principal concern of the imperial regimes was to secure and maximize their revenue. In the mid-third century when the Tobiad Joseph outbid the incumbent Oniad high priest for the contract to collect taxes from Judea for the Ptolemies, it presumably weakened the position of the high priesthood. When the Oniad high-priestly party then changed their loyalty to the Seleucids just as the latter finally succeeded in taking control of Palestine, the power of the high priesthood, its role in tax collection restored, was presumably strengthened. Ironically, it became an attractive plum for rival elite factions who miscalculated the strength and importance of Judean/Israelite tradition among the indigenous priests, scribes, and peasantry.

We catch glimpses of the close association of the (now presumably written) sacred law with the high priesthood at the beginning of both the Ptolemaic and the Seleucid rule over Judea. A fragment from Hecataeus of Abdera, writing at the beginning of Ptolemaic period (i.e., late fourth or early third century) observes that

> The Judeans believe that the high priest acts as a messenger to them of god's commandments. It is he who in their assemblies and other gatherings announces what is ordained, and the Judeans are so docile in such matters that straightway they fall to the ground and do reverence to the high priest when he expounds the commandments to them. (Diodorus Siculus 40.3.5–6).

It is difficult to tell whether this refers to the high priest's proclamation of the law from the sacred scroll kept in the temple or to his pronouncement of rulings with his own august authority backed by the divine writing of the law housed in the temple. About a century later, as the longest and central section in the scribe/sage Jesus ben Sira's sustained paean of praise of the great ancestral rulers that grounds the authority of the current high-priestly regime is a glorious adulation of Aaron and his descendants, who received from God an "everlasting covenant" to be the (high) priesthood over the people and were also ordained by Moses as teachers of the law. "In his (Moses'? God's?) commandments, he gave him (Aaron) authority and statutes and judgments, to teach Jacob the testimonies, and to enlighten Israel with his law" (Sir 45:17).

Ben Sira's references to the law, and even more his lack of references to specific laws, enable us to discern also that, similar to its function evident in Ezra's reading, the (written) law of Moses apparently provided authorization for the Jerusalem temple and high priesthood as an almost ethereal entity, while apparently not applied to particular issues by scribal interpreters (Horsley 2001b). While Ben Sira emphasizes that "the fear of the Lord" is the beginning of wisdom, he does not refer to the law very often, contrary to common scholarly assertion. Virtually the only passage where he explicitly identifies wisdom with the law of Moses is in interpretation of the famous hymn of self-praise by the heavenly figure Wisdom in Sir 24. Thus, when he declares that "all this (i.e., Wisdom) is the book of the covenant of the Most High God, the law that Moses commanded us" (24:23), he thereby locates the latter in the temple: "In the holy tent I ministered before him, and so I was established in Zion.... In the beloved city he gave me a resting place, and in Jerusalem was my domain" (24:10–11). That is, the law is under the custody of, while lending its divine authority to, the high priesthood in the temple. Ben Sira's lack of references to specific laws or other passages in the Torah, however, indicates that, in contrast to later "rabbinic Judaism," the law / Torah was surely not under the custody of the scribes/sages as its interpreters. Judging from the anthology of his teachings, Ben Sira is devoted to the law, calls his students to obedience to the law, and claims once to study the law of the Most High. However, he does not interpret or apply the laws.

While Ben Sira belonged to a circle of scribes that ardently supported the incumbent high priest as well as the high priesthood as an institution (while conveniently ignoring its sponsorship by the imperial regime), other scribal circles attacked the incumbent high-priestly rulers and/or even rejected the institution(s) of temple and its high priesthood (Horsley and Tiller). Enoch literature more or less contemporary with Ben Sira pronounces God's condemnation of the wealthy and powerful (apparently the incumbent priestly rulers), declares the whole period of the restored temple to be "a perverse generation," and envisions a future kingdom of God without this ruling apparatus (1 En. 92–105; 90:28–38; Horsley 2000). The active priestly, scribal, and popular opposition to the incumbent high priesthood that erupted after 175 B.C.E. had plenty of background and preparation in the various earlier priestly or scribal circles that had periodically contested the incumbent high-priestly rule backed by the imperial regime since the restoration in the late sixth century. Pertinent to the role of the written law in the Jerusalem temple-state is the question of how to interpret the downplaying or utter absence of the law in some of the same early Enoch literature that is obsessed with finding other sources of revelation (1 En. 89:36–38; 1–36; 83–90). Did some circles of scribes/sages, by the end of the third century, reject and/or look for alternatives to the law that, housed in the temple, provided its divine authorization (Horsley 2001b)?

To complete this sketchy history of the written law as an instrument of the political-economic order sponsored by the regnant empire, we should take two further steps. First, although evidence is lacking (e.g., for Ezra's "book of the law of Moses" and Ben Sira's "law of Moses/the Most High") to establish when and how, at some point in late Second Temple times the officially recognized law took on more or less the contours we recognize as the Pentateuch. The scrolls of various scriptural books found at Qumran indicate that, while the Torah still existed in variant versions of the proto-MT, the proto-Samaritan Pentateuch, and so on, it had assumed the basic form we recognize as the Pentateuch (from the MT) at least by the first century B.C.E., perhaps earlier. Prominent scribal factions in the temple-state known from extant sources such as Josephus and now certain Dead Sea Scrolls, to wit, the Pharisees and Sadducees, and at least one dissident group alienated from the incumbent regime, namely, the Qumran community, recognized more or less the same law of Moses as authoritative. Rather than produce different law codes, they now argued over the necessity and kind of interpretation that the law should receive (Horsley 2001b). The Sadducees took their law straight; the Pharisees interpreted the law liberally and, says Josephus, most acutely/accurately; the Qumranites were rigorist interpreters, viewing the Pharisees as "smooth interpreters." Nevertheless, other forms of Torah/law codes/law books were being cultivated and promulgated. For example, the Pharisees continued to promulgate rulings in their "traditions of the elders" that were recognized as official state law under John Hyrcanus and again apparently under Alexandra Salome. The book of *Jubilees* evidently contains a law code alternative to the Pentateuch, and the discovery of the *Temple Scroll* and 4QMMT now gives us examples of relatively extensive law books evidently intended as alternatives to the Pentateuch recognized by the incumbent temple authorities. These alternative books of law indicate that, while the Pentateuch had become dominant, perhaps by weight of the length of time it had held official sacred status in the temple, by no means did all Judeans recognize the same law as authoritative.

Second, when the Romans finally took direct control over the eastern Mediterranean, they continued the imperial sponsorship of the temple-state and its law. Indeed, when they installed Herod as their client king over greater Judea (resulting from earlier Hasmonean expansion), he not only retained the temple-state but aggressively reshaped the temple and the high priesthood as instruments of his pro-Roman rule. Indeed, he completely rebuilt the temple as one of wonders of the world and the pilgrimage center of a worldwide Jewry as a subset of the Roman Empire with himself as its royal patron. The law was evidently retained as part of this whole ensemble, liberally interpreted by leading Pharisees, of course, whom he maintained at court (Josephus, *Ant.* 14.176; 15.3–4, 368–371; 17.41–42).

Caught in Mediating Power Relations: The Ambiguous Role of Scribal Orality and Literacy

In the very structure of the imperial order established in the Jerusalem temple-state, scribes became "caught in the middle" of the power relations. In the ancient Near East scribes had traditionally served as intellectual "retainers" in priestly, royal, and imperial regimes (Horsley and Tiller). Their possession of reading and writing skills provided the basis for their many functions in service of the rulers, such as record keeping, diplomatic correspondence, astronomy and calendrical construction, divination and dream interpretation, and the political-religious self-presentation of the regime. If the books of Chronicles can be used as sources for the early Second Temple period, then scribes were already important from the time of Nehemiah and Ezra. It is significant that Antiochus III's charter for Judea at the beginning of the second century lists "scribes of the temple" (along with the *gerousia*, the priests, and the temple singers) among the principal officers and staff of the temple-state. Ben Sira provides a firsthand source for the social location, roles, and ambiguities of Jerusalem scribes/sages.

Ben Sira portrays the scribe/sage as deploying his literacy as well as his predominantly oral communication in service of the ruling aristocracy in general and the incumbent high priest in particular. Much of the "wisdom" in his book is clearly professional advice to other, younger scribes/sages (-in-training). Such scribes/sages, however, apparently found greatest satisfaction in their service among the rulers, particularly in their assemblies. As indicated above, moreover, scribes such as Ben Sira also "underwrote" the high-priestly regime with supportive ideology such as the sustained hymn of praise that grounds the temple-state and the Oniad incumbency in the hoary cultural tradition of Israel's past leaders and rulers. Such advice, public discourse, and hymnic performance, of course, were oral. However, as is evident in the very existence of Ben Sira's book and his grandson's translation into Greek, his wisdom and high-priestly propaganda also took written form, through which it had influence far beyond the frontiers of Judea itself and the career of Ben Sira.

The prominent Jerusalem scribe/sage, however, also points to the awkward potential circumstances in which scribes might come to oppose ruling aristocrats. While he encourages payment of tithes and offerings to the priests, he warns scribes about the dangers of their own vulnerability to wealth and powerful patrons. He also indicates that scribes/sages had not only developed a loyalty to the law that they supposedly studied but also had developed a sense of their own authority independent of their "employment" by the priestly aristocrats (Horsley 2001b).

While Ben Sira gives little indication of being an interpreter of the law and early Enoch literature downplays or ignores the law, documents found at Qumran from a few generations later indicate that close study and interpretation of the law had been developing in other scribal-priestly circles at least during the early second century. In the text

4QMMT ("Some of the legal rulings of [pertaining to] the Torah") some proto-Essenes or proto-Qumranites evidently prior to the decisive leadership exercised by the Teacher of Righteousness wrote a letter to the Jerusalem high priest explaining why their dissident group differs with the establishment on several issues focused on sacrificial law, priestly gifts, and ritual purity (Schiffman). They quote Deut 31:29 and 30:1–2 in particular and appeal to the heads of the incumbent high priesthood to "investigate the words of the Book of Moses, the Prophets, and David," evidently the scriptural books recognized by both the writers and the addressees. The body of the letter discusses some twenty issues of (Mosaic) law. In several other documents of Qumran literature, moreover, the scribal-priestly authors engage in extensive discussion about laws, many from the Pentateuch-in-development. Occasionally in the course of the discussion they explicitly criticize the "smooth interpreters" for their lax interpretation, as noted above. The *pesharim* on the prophets also found at Qumran might be explained as having originated in the very crisis by which the community went out to the wilderness in self-imposed exile as a new exodus. But these other documents displaying precise and almost systematic reflection upon and interpretation of laws from the Pentateuch/Torah, including polemics against other interpreters, indicate that such scribal-priestly interpretation of the Torah had been developing for some time—despite the failure of such interpretation to appear in the book of Sirach.

The close study and interpretation of the Book of Moses/Torah evident in such documents represents a relationship, a close identification and working with Scripture, that goes well beyond the adoration of and submission to the Scripture as the numenous embodiment of divine authority in sacred writing housed in the temple and proclaimed at ceremonial assemblies. Some priestly-scribal circles, at least, do not so much submit to the authority of the scriptural law as they identify with it as the basis of their own roles and prerogatives. Priestly-scribal groups, moreover, are now using their literacy actively in the factional struggle for position and power within the temple-state. Written (but still orally recited) Torah and its written (but still orally recited) interpretation even become the basis on which one group withdraws from the temple-state, albeit in the hope of their position or perhaps even leadership being accepted by the establishment. This is not resistance to the incumbent high priesthood, let alone a challenge to the institution of the temple-state (much less the sponsoring empire). However, the possibility of future developments precisely on the basis of the (written) Torah can be discerned in these texts. Scribal-priestly circles could potentially use their literacy (along with their orality) in resistance to the temple-state and imperial order on the basis of the written Torah with which they identify as their sacred writing but which developed/stemmed from written Torah that was originally imposed by empire.

What touched off widespread scribal, priestly, and even popular resistance to the incumbent high priesthood and its imperial sponsors was a series of successful maneuvers by aristocratic factions to change not the basic structure of the imperial relations but the long-standing recognition of the developing law of Moses as the authoritative and authorizing writing by which Jerusalem was constituted as the ruling body in Judea. The Seleucid Empire included *poleis* with constitutions patterned after Greek city-states, as well as temple-states. The priestly elite in Jerusalem who had acquired a taste for Hellenistic culture, led first by Menelaus and then by Jason, offered the ever-needy imperial regime greater sums of tribute for the privilege and power of the high priesthood and transformed Jerusalem into a *polis* with a Greek-style constitution. That move, however left the ordinary priests and scribal circles without "income," as well as alienated from their traditional roles in the temple-state. Thus it should not be surprising that scribal circles might resist their displacement in whatever ways available, including an alternative use of their literacy.

It seems too risky as historical method to use the book of 1 Maccabees as an example of the resistance to the imperial order on the basis of scriptural Torah, despite the theme of "zeal for the law" that supposedly fired the rebellion against the repressive military forces of Antiochus Epiphanes, since 1 Maccabees is so clearly the propaganda of the Hasmonean regime that resulted from the leaders of the revolt maneuvering themselves into power as the new high priests in the same imperial system. Thus the Hasmoneans themselves needed as well as desired legitimation as the defenders of the temple-state's Torah, with its authority as the glorious and ancient Israelite tradition. A better illustration of a scribal circle using its literacy in resistance to imperial domination would be the book of Daniel, or rather the series of visions in the archaic language of Hebrew in chapters 7, 8, 9, 10–12. Daniel 9 even takes the form of an interpretation of Scripture, specifically of a prophecy from the scroll of Jeremiah. These visions-plus-interpretation are also genuinely anti-imperial, and at least their authors, the *maskilim*, are not active advocates of a restored temple-state in the future deliverance from imperial rule and restoration of the people. One detects a similar stance in the Dream Visions in 1 *Enoch*, which must have been composed and transcribed onto scrolls right around the same time as Daniel, against the "reforms" of the priestly elite factions led by Jason and the emperor Antiochus Epiphanes' attempts to suppress opposition (Collins).

As noted above, the Hasmoneans moved from leaders of rebellion against the Hellenizing aristocracy and their imperial backers to insinuate themselves as the new rulers of the Jerusalem temple-state. Once in power, they took a leaf from the imperial notebook and expanded their domination over rest of Palestine, first Samaria, then Idumea, and finally Galilee and some of the Greek cities, and increasingly patterned their regime after Hellenistic models. And after the Romans took over the area, they soon replaced the Hasmoneans with Herod as their client king. The scribal faction of the Pharisees periodically led serious resistance to the most blatantly expansionist Hasmonean, Alexander Jannai (Josephus, *Ant.* 13.372–383). In opposition to Herod's collaboration with the Rome, they mounted no more than a refusal to sign a loyalty oath (*Ant.* 17.41–46). More comprehensive ideologically, while utterly ineffectual politically, were the scribes and priests in self-styled exile in the wilderness at Qumran as a renewal of the Mosaic covenant of Israel and its law. They not only condemned the Wicked Priest for his utterly misguided ways in several of their literary products but rehearsed fantasies of a final battle of cosmic dimensions against the Romans, who were the imperial embodiment of demonic forces opposed to God and God's people, as recorded in the "War Rule" of the Qumran community (see esp. 1QpHab 8–12; 1QM 1–2). Like Enoch literature or Daniel, such Qumran literature was apparently intended only for a tiny in-group. All these documents, moreover, are written copies of what were also ceremonial performances or revelatory dream-visions. Modern scholars of such literature should perhaps problematize such documents a bit, for why would scribal circles commit the narrative of the Animal Apocalypse or the visions in Daniel or the ritual warfare evident in *War Scroll* to writing? Was writing an *aide memoire* or a way of inscribing their visions and ritual more permanently in sacral aura or a means of recording for wider dissemination to other literate circles?

More serious resistance to Roman rule was offered by the scribal(-led) group that Josephus calls "the Fourth Philosophy." Josephus's accounts make it clear that the basis of their organization of resistance to the Roman tribute was the Mosaic covenant (*Ant.* 18.4–6, 23–25; Horsley 1987:77–89), which was otherwise central to the developing Pentateuch/Torah. The first principle of the covenant was that Israel was to have no Lord and Master other than its God. For the scribal teachers and Pharisees who led the Fourth Philosophy, this meant that—once Rome imposed direct rule in Judea—Judeans could not render up tribute to Caesar since it entailed service of another Lord and Master. The Roman imperial regime, of course, viewed failure to render tribute as tantamount to rebellion. It would seem that this more radical faction among the scribal retainers of the temple-state who, as its professional guardians and interpreters, took the content of their Torah most seriously found revolutionary implications in the Mosaic covenant as they faced newly imposed circumstances under Roman rule. However, although their resistance to the tribute was rooted in the Mosaic covenant, which was a central component of the scriptural Torah, there is no indication that the scribal leaders of the Fourth Philosophy used writing in any way in their resistance.

In sum, for the relationship between the scriptural Torah of the temple-state and its supportive or dissident circles of scribes/sages we can draw the following generalizations.

One particular version of Israelite/Judean law and tradition—or perhaps rather a compromise composite of Priestly Torah that legimated the centrality of the Zadokite high priesthood and Deuteronomic materials tied to the Levitical priesthood—was installed as the official founding history-and-law book that provided divine authorization of the temple-state in sacred writing (much of which was dictated by God). Other versions continued and/or developed among subordinated priestly-scribal or other groups, and some scribal circles apparently rejected the incumbent high priesthood and its official Torah and/or developed alternative Torah.

By the first century, perhaps by sheer weight of its domination for centuries, a Torah standardized in all but particular variations in different versions became authoritative and accepted by the principal players in Judean politics, including the Sadducees, the Pharisees, and the dissident priestly-scribal community at Qumran/the Essenes. Under the Roman regime, at the latest, the Torah had for some apparently been associated with (if not identified with) the sacred tradition of Judeans over against the empire and its clients in the high priesthood.

Scribal circles played a special role. As the professional literates, scribes serving directly under the regime that sponsored the composition of a law book as "Scripture" were necessarily involved in its composition and perpetuation. It is understandable that those scribes would develop a sense of their own authority associated directly with the official Scripture or associated with alternative revered traditions (and the divine), authority independent of their aristocratic rulers-patrons. As the cultivators of Judean sacred traditions, whether those in the official "Scripture" or others, scribal circles also understandably would have seen those sacred traditions as the authorizing basis of Judean interests, especially in situations of conflict with the imperial regime. On those or other bases, certain scribal circles in Jerusalem came to oppose the incumbent high priesthood from the late third century and on into the first century C.E. And certain scribal circles appealed to the sacred Judean traditions, apparently including the written Torah, as the basis of their opposition to empire, particularly the Fourth Philosophy in its active opposition to the tribute when direct Roman rule was imposed in 6 C.E.

POPULAR OPPOSITION TO THE IMPERIAL ORDER—
ON THE BASIS OF THE ORAL "LITTLE TRADITION"

The vast majority of people in any ancient agrarian society, of course, were peasants. And because Judean peasants were nonliterate, they not only had no role in the production of the Judean Scriptures but also could not have read the Scriptures. The assumption by modern Scripture scholars that the Judean people used the Judean Scripture has generated a great deal of false knowledge as well as blocked discernment of the power relations and dynamics between imperial and Jerusalem ruling circles and the Judean peasantry. That the peasants were nonliterate, however, does not mean that they had no knowledge of their cultural traditions or that they acquiesced in the arrangement of Judean cultural traditions by the priestly and scribal elite. Since nonliterate ancient peasants left no literature, of course, we have no written sources for their culture and actions. Modern anthropological and other studies, however, have discerned some significant aspects of popular culture and behavior that not only can but must be projected onto ancient counterparts.

The distinction that anthropologists and others make between the "great tradition" and the "little tradition" in agrarian societies may help us understand the difference and dynamics between the Torah of Moses as it developed in Jerusalem and the popular cultural traditions and customs cultivated and practiced in the village communities of Judea and Galilee. In James C. Scott's comparative study, the "little tradition" is "the distinctive patterns of belief and behavior that are valued by the peasantry." The "great tradition" is the corresponding patterns among the ruling elite and their retainers, often existing partly in written form (Scott 1977:2–5). The great and little traditions usually function along parallel lines, with some interaction according to particular circumstances. The developing Torah of Moses, for example, took over the tradition of Israel's originating liberation from bondage in Egypt and from subjection to the kings of Canaan but ironically framed them in a larger story that led to the reestablishment of monarchy and temple in Jerusalem. In both the book of Deuteronomy that developed from the "reform" carried out under King Josiah and the "Holiness Code" in the book of Leviticus, Mosaic covenantal law that had apparently been cultivated among Israelite villagers for centuries was adapted into monarchic and then temple-state law. The oracles of the prophets Isaiah and Jeremiah, on the other hand, originating in Jerusalem and preserved in Jerusalem circles and/or on written scrolls, would have become known among Judean villagers only by way of direct or indirect contacts with representatives of the Jerusalem-based great tradition.

The great and little traditions, however, are not simply variations on the same culture. Rather "each represents a *distinct* pattern of belief and practice." In the absence of integrating factors such as the mass media in modern urban industrial society, the popular tradition in the ancient Judean villages would have differed considerably from the Jerusalem great tradition (Scott 1977:7). The cultural differences can be seen in matters such as residence, income, consumption, language, religious practice, education, juridical status, and ethnicity (9). The priestly elite lived in mansions and enjoyed the finest cuts of meat and breads and wines, while the peasants languished in debts and hunger under obligations for tithes, offerings, and interest payment on loans (see Neh 5:1–5; 10:32–39; 13:5). The great tradition in Jerusalem was to a degree composed and cultivated in the archaic language of Hebrew, while the Judean people spoke some local dialect of Aramaic (as illustrated in the necessity of "interpretation/translation" at Ezra's ceremonial reading of the law before the great assembly [Neh 8:8]). While scribal circles engaged in formal instruction of their younger successors (see much of the material in Sirach), Israelite/Judean popular traditions and customs would have been cultivated in the course of local communication and practice. Such differences indicate a considerable gulf between the great tradition in Jerusalem and the little tradition cultivated in Judean village communities. The differences between the Jerusalem great tradition and the popular Israelite tradition in Galilee would have been even greater, since only after the Hasmonean regime took over the region in 104 B.C.E. and subjected the people to "the laws of the Judeans" would the official Torah have been introduced (Horsley 1995:147–57).

We have no information whatever regarding the Judean peasants' traditions and customs and their interaction with the Jerusalem high priesthood and great tradition for most of the Second Temple period. Insofar as peasants as well as ordinary priests and some scribal circles participated in the Maccabean revolt in 167–164, we can surmise that they shared the Maccabean leadership's sense that the "reforming" high-priestly faction and their sponsor Antiochus Epiphanes were violating the covenant at the center of the law of Moses. Only under Roman domination, for which we have Josephus's accounts of popular movements that caused a great deal of trouble for both Jerusalem and Roman rulers, do we have a sense of how the popular tradition informed popular actions of resistance, rebellion, and renewal. It seems clear from Josephus's accounts of the popular messianic movements of rebellion against the imperial-royal-high priestly order at the death of Herod and the similar movement during the great revolt of 66–70 that they modeled themselves after the Israelite movements against oppressive foreign rulers led by popularly acclaimed ("messiahed") kings such as the young David (Horsley 1984). Moreover, the popular prophetic movements led by Theudas, the "Egyptian" Jewish prophet, and others at the mid-first century were clearly patterned after the exodus and entry into the land led by Moses and Joshua (Horsley 1985).

It is extremely rare that we have any sources whatever from peasant movements. This makes all the more valuable the sources produced in the Jesus movements that emerged in Galilee in the mid-first century C.E. Because these movements originated in Galilee, which had regional history different from that of Judea and Jerusalem, they may not be typical for possible earlier popular attitudes and movements in Judea. But at least we have these examples of popular rejection of the temple-state and imperial order that involve explicit interaction with the Scripture of the Jerusalemite great tradition. In both the Gospel of Mark and Jesus' speeches that appear closely parallel (many verbatim) in Matthew and Luke, but not in Mark, known as Q (for *Quelle*, "source"), we have written transcripts of what must have been repeated oral performances (Kelber 1983; Botha 1992; Horsley and Draper; Horsley 2001a; the latter two heavily dependent on Foley 1995). Both Mark's story and the Q speeches represent Jesus as working out of and defending Israelite popular tradition (Horsley and Draper; Horsley 2001a). In the Gospel of Mark, Jesus spearheads a renewal of Israel in village communities over against both the Jerusalem temple-state and Roman imperial rule. He performs a prophetic demonstration in condemnation of the temple, proclaims a prophetic parable announcing that the high priests stand under God's judgment, and even declares that the people "lawfully" are not obligated to pay tribute to Caesar ("render to God the things that are God's [everything] and to Caesar the things that are Caesar [nothing]"; Mark 11:15–17; 12:1–8; and 12:13–17; Horsley 1987:306–17). In Q, the dominant theme of which is also the renewal of Israel, Jesus pronounces prophetic condemnations of the Jerusalem ruling house (Q/Luke 13:28–29, 34–35; Horsley and Draper: 277–85).

These "Synoptic Gospel" materials, both Mark and Q, make many allusions to Israelite traditions that have previously been taken as quotations from Scripture. Treatment of these references to Israelite traditions as quotations from the "Old Testament" (an utter anachronism in Christian scholarly discourse), however, predates the recent recognition of Mark and Q as oral performance and the even more recent recognition that we must allow the reality of popular, little tradition. I have argued recently that Mark and Q present virtually no evidence of the use of written texts of scripture (Horsley and Draper: 98–104; Horsley 2001a:156–61, 232–34). In any case, caution should have been used in claiming such use for the "original" Mark, since our only manuscripts are from generations later, and references could have been conformed to the Septuagint (Greek Jewish Bible) text by copyists familiar with the latter (the Bible of many developing Greek-speaking churches). The fact that the references to supposedly "scriptural" passages were not conformed to the Septuagint text is all the more suggestive, either that the written textual wording was not an issue or that Mark's story and Jesus' speeches in Q became more or less set in revered Greek form such that copyists would not have changed the revered story and speeches of Jesus. In Q three of the four possible biblical "quotations," all supposedly from Deuteronomy, are from the same passage, the testing of Jesus the prophet by the devil (Luke/Q 4:1–13). The first, "humankind does not live by bread alone" (Deut 8:3), had surely become a common proverb. The second does not follow either Deut 6:13/10:20 or 5:9 closely, hence seems some variation on the basic principle enunciated in all of those texts. The third is closest to the Septuagint text (of Deut 6:16) but so short and simple a commandment as to have become standard in Israelite culture. In the fourth supposed "explicit quotation" in Q (7:27) it is unclear exactly what passages and what textual traditions are referred to.

Survey of ostensible cases of quotation in Mark leads to doubts about whether written texts of Scripture were involved in its composition (Horsley 2001a:231–35). Some references that scholars take as scriptural quotations are words uttered by characters in the story (e.g., "Hosanna..." in 11:9–10, which varies considerably from Ps 118:25–26—but could simply have been a reference to a familiar festival psalm sung by pilgrims to Passover celebration! Cf. 10:4; 12:36). Some of Mark's supposed scriptural quotations are of the most fundamental principles and memorable statements of the earliest Israelite covenant tradition (hence in the popular tradition; 7:9–10; 10:22) or passages from Scripture that would be well known (10:6, 8). Sometimes Mark simply alludes to Israelite traditions, as in the messianic entry into Jerusalem on a colt (11:2–8) and the passion narrative, which is replete with allusions but not precise quotations. Other "quotations" in Mark are composites of poetic couplets that would have been written in different scrolls, such as the combination from Isaiah and Malachi in Mark 1:2–3. Many of these references were surely contained in the popular tradition. The references that indicate interaction with the great tradition, such as the combination of prophetic couplets, would appear to have been borrowed from the great tradition and adapted and/ or combined in the oral popular tradition.

Most telling surely are the appearances of "it is written..." and "scripture" (*gegraptai* and *graphe*, respectively). These have often been taken as indications of textual quotations or references to actual written passages. But this now requires reconsideration in light of our dawning awareness of the function of sacred writing, such as the Torah that was written on scrolls kept in the temple and read aloud on ceremonial occasions but not literally read/used/studied as texts even by priests and scribes, who rather recited memorized scripture (Jaffee 2001; Hezser

2001). The reference to "according to the Scriptures" in the early creed Paul cites in 1 Cor 15:3–5 is not to particular passages but to the authority of Scripture. Analogously, references to "the gospel" in the *Didache* (8:2; 11:3; 15:3–4) are probably not to a particular written text but to the authority of the gospel, not its written text (Henderson: 292). Similarly, "it is written" in Mark and Q signal an appeal to the authority of the scripture (yes, of the written *great* tradition) by the popular movement that produced these oral-derived "texts."

In that sense we can discern the thrust of some Markan references, several of which are explicitly marked with "as it is written" or "Scripture." The references in 9:12–13 are an appeal to the general authority of Scripture (with no specific texts) over against the scribal authorities on Scripture. More sharply, when Jesus cites Isaiah against the scribes and Pharisees in 7:6 and Jeremiah and a festival psalm against the rulers of the temple in 11:17 and 12:10 with "it is written," he throws back at the literate elite the very authority they themselves claim as legitimating their own power. In 10:3–5 he throws a quotation of Moses back into the faces of the Pharisees, the experts on Moses, from whom they derive their authority. Thus in Mark Jesus cites Scripture pointedly against the rulers and their scribal representatives who depend on it as the authorization of their positions of privilege and their power over the people.

Only in the passion narrative does Mark appeal to the general or particular authority of Scripture as explaining events that were difficult to accept or understand, such as the betrayal, arrest, and crucifixion of Jesus and the desertion of the disciples (14:21, 27, 49). This is similar to the way in which the creed Paul cites in 1 Cor 15:3–5 appeals to the general authority of Scripture to authorize Christ's crucifixion and resurrection. But that also means in the broad "plot" of Mark's story that the Scripture is again being used against the elite that keeps possession and control of it, since the betrayal to the high priests, their arrest of Jesus, and his crucifixion by the Roman governor are all events in the overall opposition to and condemnation of the oppressive domestic and imperial rulers. Thus in most of its appeal to the authority of "Scripture" Mark is opposing the Jerusalem rulers and their representatives who, as its sponsors, custodians, and interpreters, depended on it for their own authorization.

Mark also, furthermore, portrays Jesus as challenging the oppressive practices of the ruling elite as based in and authorized by their great tradition, which was partly written (scriptural) and partly oral, on the basis of Israelite popular tradition. This can be seen in several episodes often called "controversy stories" or "pronouncement stories," usually set up by the Pharisees challenging Jesus on a particular issue of law (Horsley 2001a:161–76). To gain fresh perspective on these episodes we must remove the old scholarly glasses colored with Christian theological concepts and replace them with lenses that can discern the dynamics of an imperial/colonial situation of confrontations between representatives of the Jerusalem temple-state as an institution of the Roman imperial order and a spokesperson representing the peasantry of Galilee, which had been controlled by the temple-state in a variation on "internal colonialism."

The opening of the episode in Mark 7:1-13 immediately signals the power relations inherent in a situation of internal colonialism. The narrator brings onto the stage the surveillance officers of the temple-state, the Pharisees and scribes "who had come down from Jerusalem," the capital. They accuse Jesus and his disciples of not observing purity codes and other "traditions of the elders," that is, the oral rulings promulgated by the Pharisaic party among the scribal retainers of the temple-state, which they presented as deriving from Moses on Sinai, of equal authority with the written Torah of Moses given on Sinai. These Pharisaic rulings were not simply the preferred practices of a "sect" but had, off and on, functioned as part of the official law of the temple-state, according to Josephus's accounts (*Ant.* 13.293–296, 408–410). English translations still impose the essentialist, orientalist Christian concept of "Jews" and "Judaism" as the hopelessly legalistic religion that Jesus supposedly rejects precisely in this episode. To outsiders such as the Romans, all inhabitants of Palestine appeared to be "Judeans," since they had been ruled at one point by the Rome-installed Herod, "king of the Judeans." To Israelite insiders, however, the term *ioudaioi* in Mark 7:3 was a regional-ethnic reference to "Judeans" in the immediate area around Jerusalem, as distinct from Idumeans to the south and Galileans and Samarians to the north. Thus in Mark's narrative itself, when the Roman governor Pilate or his soldiers are speaking, Jesus is charged and crucified as "the king of the Judeans." But the episode of 7:1–13 is making an exaggerated parenthetical explanation (probably a caricature) to the hearers of the story that "the Pharisees and (indeed) all the Judeans" up there around Jerusalem are super-meticulous in observance of purity codes that pertain only to priests regularly serving in or lay people making occasional forays into the sacred precincts of the temple. In this connection we should also note that the comment about declaring all foods clean in 7:19b is almost certainly a later insertion or gloss. This episode thus begins by sketching the conflictual structure of the situation in which the representatives of the temple-state in Jerusalem are attempting to dictate behavior in the outlying district of Galilee. Indeed, during Jesus' lifetime and on into the first decade of the Jesus movements, Galilee was not even under the official jurisdiction of Jerusalem but that of Herod Antipas. Nothing in the episode suggests a conflict between an old legalistic religion (Judaism) and a nascent ethical-universalistic religion (Christianity).

In reply Jesus first attacks the Pharisees' and scribes' obsession with their oral "traditions of the elders" on the basis of their own written Scriptures, throwing a version of Isa 29:13 in their face. With that entry, he quickly drives a wedge between their "traditions of the elders" and the basic "commandment of God" and decisively changes the subject from purity codes to the deployment of the limited economic resources available to peasant families. He pointedly chooses as an example of the commandment of God, by which he clearly means the Decalogue of the Mosaic covenant, "honor your father and mother." He thus focuses attention on an issue that would form the most sacred and fundamental of duties in any agrarian society, people's care for their aging parents. The scribes and Pharisees, says Jesus, prevent the people from honoring their parents, effectively rejecting or making void the basic Mosaic covenantal commandment of God, the basis of Israel's common life. This they do by urging peasants to devote (*korban*) a portion of their crops or the produce of part of their land to (the support of) the temple. However, that means that those resources could then not be used in support of parents who have become nonproductive in their older years. A report by the early Christian writer Origen illustrates the ominously binding economic implications of "dedicating" something to the temple: his Jewish informant mentioned that, in revenge against debtors who could not repay their loans, creditors would declare that what was owed was *korban*, thus foregoing repayment themselves but leaving the debtors still obligated to pay their debts, now to the temple treasury (Horsley 2001a:170, 277 n 39). In their imperial "management" of Palestine, the Romans had proliferated layers of rulers with a claim on the produce of peasantry: on top of the original tithes and offerings due to the priests and temple-state came taxes to Herodian "kings" and the tribute to Rome (not to mention the interest on debts accrued in order to pay the tithes, taxes, and tribute). Perhaps precisely because after the Romans placed Antipas as tetrarch over Galilee and Perea, apparently leaving the Jerusalem high priesthood with jurisdiction over only part of its former tithe-paying peasantry, the temple-state had all the more reason to promulgate "traditions of the elders" that encouraged peasants to "devote" resources to the support of the temple. One suspects throughout, particularly from the focus of attention first on "the basic commandment of God" before introducing the focal issue of honoring parents, that the latter is a focal instance in a general charge against the representatives of the temple-state that in their economic exploitation of the people they are making it impossible for them to live according to the traditional Mosaic covenant, the core of Israelite tradition, particularly Israelite popular tradition.

In another episode, 10:2–9, the Pharisees ask Jesus pointedly, "Is it lawful for a man to divorce his wife?" (Horsley 2001a:172–76). But in what way could the Pharisees thus have been "testing" Jesus? If we simply remember back several episodes in the overall story of Mark's Gospel, the prophet John the Baptist, who had announced that Jesus was the "stronger one" coming to baptize with the Holy Spirit, had been arrested and then lost his head for pronouncing that "it was not lawful" for Herod Antipas "to have his brother's wife." He made this pronouncement on the assumption that remarriage after divorce was adultery, precisely what Jesus is about to declare in this episode. Why was divorce such a "loaded" issue, such that prophets were executed for condemning it and tested about whether it was lawful? Divorce would surely not have been frequent among peasant families, for it would break up the fundamental family unit of production, which was barely viable yet essential for subsistence under normal circumstances. Among elite families, however, marriage, divorce, and remarriage were common as instruments of rearranging and consolidating political-economic power. Antipas did not evoke John's condemnation simply because of his personal morality. Besides his divorce of the Arab king Aretas's daughter having international political fall-out, his remarriage to Herodias, the last remaining member of the Hasmonean family, presumably had ominous implications for further Herodian consolidation of power in Palestine. Bad enough that Antipas had (re-)built two capital cities in the tiny district of Galilee on the backs of rigorously collected taxes from the peasantry. What if he attempted to out-do his father Herod in massive new building programs and lavish munificence to foreign Greek cities and imperial family members? After all, for a client king to become a major player in the new world order, he had to "strut his stuff," displaying development projects at home and with lavish grants to imperial family and Hellenistic cities abroad.

"Liberal" divorce laws were thus important to enable the ruling families and their ambitious underlings to maneuver for position and power via marriage and remarriage. This had ominous implications for the peasantry in at least two principal respects. Peasants indebted to Herodian officers could be caught in the middle of such manipulations. Such "liberal" maneuvering, moreover, provided a unwelcome paradigm for ambitious villagers who might be tempted to take advantage of the disintegrations of their neighbor families resulting from the tightening economic pressure of multiple layers of tax demands on their limited productivity.

Jesus' dispute with the Pharisees on divorce focuses on references to central parts of Israelite tradition, "great" and "little," written and oral. Jesus' initial response to their question is not "What did Moses say/ write" in general or "What did Moses write for us" (i.e., in the Scripture), in order to establish common ground with his challengers. Rather, he pointedly asks "What *to you* did Moses *command*? With this (Markan) formulation Jesus distances himself and the people for whom he speaks from the Pharisees, and he makes far more of what Moses said to *them* than they do. It is standardly understood that what they say Moses "allowed" alludes, in a brief summary, to the teaching on divorce and remarriage in Deut 24:1–4. Certainly the text of Deut 24:1 does not lend itself to characterization as a command. Moreover, Jesus's immediate retort to the Pharisees' recitation of "Moses'" permissiveness both mocks their attribution of authority to *their* law of Moses and, in effect, attacks their written law as the virtual opposite of the will of God. "To promote/ incite your hardness of heart he [Moses] wrote you this command." Contrary to the usual interpretation, Jesus is here not saying that Moses gave the command as an antidote to *humanity's* or *Israel's* hardness of heart (in general). That would weaken the contrast with God's will that immediately follows in Jesus' argument ("But from the beginning of creation... "). Rather, Moses "wrote" it to exacerbate the *Pharisees'* hardness of heart. Apparently Mark's Jesus has in mind the disintegrating effects on popular life, in its families and village communities, of their advocating such permissive laws that allow license to the wealthy and powerful (e.g., probably in manipulating property arrangements, as implied in Jesus' dispute with the Sadducees about Levirate marriage, in Mark 12:18–27).

If Mark 7:1–13 shows Jesus condemning Jerusalem's great tradition in its oral formulation, the Pharisees' traditions of the elders, as exploitative of the people, Mark 10:2–9 shows Jesus rejecting Jerusalem's great tradition in its written form, the supposedly scriptural Torah of Moses, as a threat to the people's fundamental social forms (family and village community). In both cases, the people had for centuries cultivated the Mosaic covenantal commandments, both the Decalogue and a wider range of Israelite "common law," orally in village communities. Both of these cases in fact revolve around one of the Ten Commandments, the most fundamental principles of social interaction in Israelite communities. In the case of Galilee, the Jerusalem-developed scriptural Torah had been introduced at the earliest after the Hasmoneans took over the area in 104 B.C.E., which had not left much time for those scribes and Pharisees to "resocialize" the villagers into the officially promoted "laws of the Judeans." There is therefore no reason to imagine that Jesus and his movement, as evident in Mark's Gospel, viewed Deuteronomy as authoritative law. Once we recognize the common reality and operation of the little tradition among peasantries, in fact, we can entertain the possibility that as likely as not the Galilean peasants would have rejected or kept at arms' length the officially promulgated law. It did not represent their interests but those of their Jerusalem rulers. One suspects that Judean peasants would have felt similarly, even though they had been subject to the developing official Torah for many more centuries than the Galileans.

A final case of Mark's Jesus' disputes with representatives of the imperially installed rulers and the official twisting of Israelite tradition on the basis of common or at least popular Israelite tradition brings us around full circle to the fundamental purpose and force of imperial rule: the empire's extraction of resources from subject peoples. As a key episode in his climactic face-off with the Jerusalem rulers, Mark's Jesus is challenged by a coalition of Pharisees and Herodians aiming to entrap him. "Is it lawful to give tribute to Caesar?" As we know from covenantal principles ("No other gods... ") and from the Fourth Philosophy's resistance to the tribute on that basis a generation earlier, the Pharisees and Herodians knew very well that imperial tribute was not lawful and that Jesus, solidly rooted in the stricter popular tradition, surely opposed the tribute. The high priestly and Herodian rulers, along with their representatives the Pharisees and Herodians, however, had acquiesced in the imperial arrangement and even functioned as the collectors of the tribute (as we know from Josephus). Here they try to force Jesus into a public declaration of what would be tantamount to rebellion and grounds to arrest and execute him. He not only skillfully slips out of the trap they have set but clearly reaffirms the basic covenantal principle of the sole kingship of God in his reply. In the popular Israelite tradition at the very least, and perhaps in the common Israelite tradition, the audience understands very well that everything belongs to God and nothing to Caesar.

This dispute between Jesus and the Pharisees and Herodians dramatically displays both the very structure of the imperial situation of Judea and Galilee under Roman rule and the operation of literacy and orality in that situation. The Roman-imposed high priestly and Herodian rulers, as well as their representatives, the Pharisees (for the Jerusalem high priests) and the Herodians (for Herod Antipas in Galilee, etc.), as mediators of the imperial order, had to collaborate in its operation, in this case by collecting the tribute for Caesar. The indigenous Israelite tradition, however, includes fundamental covenantal principles that exclude the payment of tribute to an imperial regime, particularly one headed by a king who also pretends to divinity. Ironically, those covenantal principles had been included in the sacred writing of the law of Moses that had been originally sponsored by the Persian Empire and, over the centuries, developed into a more or less standard form accepted at least by the principal priestly and scribal factions of the Jerusalem temple-state. When the written (or oral) form of the rulers' "great" tradition turned out not to represent the interest of the elite or required "clarification," the recognized guardians and interpreters of the written Torah could take either or both of two forms of interpretation and adaptation: promulgation of oral law, as in the Pharisees' "traditions of the elders," or less "codified" practice that simply ignored the pertinent Israelite traditions, oral or written (as in the case of the first commandment). The Galilean peasantry, however, and probably the Judean villagers as well, orally cultivated their own (popular) Israelite tradition of covenantal law, which represented their interests, and while influenced by the great tradition and its interpretation (which could be enforced by power) were not utterly dependent on or completely subjected to it. Rooted solidly in the Israelite tradition as it had been cultivated for generations in village communities, the Galilean and Judean peasantry repeatedly generated movements of resistance against the rulers and beneficiaries of the imperial order.

Concluding Reflections on Orality, Literacy, and Imperialism in Ancient Judea

One of the principal factors, perhaps the principal factor, leading to written scrolls of Israelite/Judahite law and other cultural traditions was the Persian imperial practice of sponsoring the writing of indigenous legal traditions as a device to strengthen and legitimate (the restoration of) native/local elites as the governing infrastructure of the empire.

Insofar as the early written Judean law was deposited in the Jerusalem temple and read in ceremonial performance before a public assembly of the temple-community, it functioned as magical writing, serving to authorize the imperially established political-economic-religious order in Judea. Writing and oral performance went hand in hand with the consolidation of power in the temple-state.

The writing of Judean law involved a selection from a wider range of Judahite/Israelite law and tradition. Other versions of Israelite tradition continued to be cultivated orally, certainly among the peasantry and apparently even among (rival) priestly and scribal circles.

Scribes and scribal circles who were responsible for cultivating Judean cultural traditions, including the written law, even though they were economically dependent on the high-priestly rulers, developed a sense of their own independent authority as interpreters of the tradition, written and/or oral. Scribal authority in interpretation of Israelite tradition thus became a factor in the potential structural conflict of the imperial order. That is, if the Jerusalem priestly rulers collaborated with their imperial patrons in ways that violated Israelite cultural tradition, such as the law, the scribal guardians of the law might well oppose the rulers on whom they were economically dependent in order to remain faithful to their revered traditions.

There is no record of any Judean interpretation of particular laws in (what became the text of) the Torah prior to the earliest documents from

Qumran, such as 4QMMT. Thus it may well have been the conflict between a scribal-priestly circle and the dominant high-priestly aristocracy who were collaborating closely with imperial regime that led to the focus on particular laws and passages in the struggle to legitimate dissent on the basis of the Torah. While the sacred scrolls of the Torah stored in the temple functioned as magical writing authorizing the temple-state, it may well be that the written text itself was first studied and claimed as an authority by dissident groups of scribes and priests attempting to justify their dissent from the imperial/colonial order.

Attempts to understand the relation between orality, textuality, and imperialism, in ancient Judea and Galilee, at least, must include attention to the fundamental (class) division in the society between rulers and ruled, between the local Herodians and high priests and their imperial patrons and the peasant villagers. Far from being educated readers of Scripture, the latter cultivated orally their own popular Israelite tradition that varied in emphasis from the "great tradition" cultivated both orally and in written form in Jerusalem.

Popular movements of resistance to or rebellion against the imperial order and its local representatives, in their social form and purpose, arose directly out of Israelite popular tradition.

One of those movements, as evident in its earliest "oral-derived texts" (Mark and Q), clearly aware of the function of the "great tradition," both oral ("traditions of the elders") and written (the "Scripture"), in authorizing the imperially backed local rulers' expropriation of local resources, appealed to their own popular tradition against the officially promulgated tradition. And in one instance, where the written and oral "great tradition" overlapped and confirmed the popular tradition, this popular movement appealed (albeit in disguised form) to the common Israelite tradition against the rulers' and scribes' compromising avoidance of its implication.

Of course, it is only because the orally performed Gospel stories and speeches were given written form and, however much they continued in oral performance, were eventually preserved and read as texts that we have access to their historical oral function in resistance to empire.

ROMAN IMPERIALISM AND
EARLY CHRISTIAN SCRIBALITY

Werner H. Kelber
Rice University

In the ancient world, including the Mediterranean civilization of late antiquity, the scribal medium was the prerogative of the political and intellectual elite who administered it in the interest of its national, memorial objectives. As a rule, those in positions of power shared a vested interest in advancing the cause of scribality because control over the medium allowed them to govern the public discourse. More often than not, colonial masters in antiquity—and throughout world history—promoted, shaped, and employed literacy as an instrument of imperial domination, even of oppression. Most frequently and influentially, scribality was applied for the purpose of recording the people's stories and history. And in producing and controlling the record of the past, those who were in charge of the scribal medium decisively determined how people would remember the past, how they thought of their identity—past, present and future—and how they acted in accordance with it. In this way, scribality, literacy, identity formation, and cultural memory constituted a syndrome that could well serve the self-legitimating interests of religious-political powers (Assmann).

The upper class's cultivation of the craft of scribality as an instrument of controlling public consciousness, setting the political agenda, and constructing collective memories is only one possible alliance of social power and scribal medium. It by no means exhausts the uses of scribality. In antiquity—and throughout world history—dissenting groups likewise seized upon the scribal medium to construct their identity vis-à-vis dominant power structures. The Jewish community at Khirbet Qumran, living in self-imposed exile on a high plateau at the northwest corner of the Dead Sea, constitutes a case in point. Originating in the priestly power structure of Jerusalem, the community, once settled down in self-imposed exile, took full advantage of its scribal legacy. Fiercely dedicated to scribal culture, the Qumran dissenters pursued the copying and composing of manuscripts largely in the interest of defining their religious and social identity vis-à-vis both the priestly establishment of Jerusalem and Roman imperialism.

In antiquity, considerations of the media cannot be limited to scribality. Orality, by far the predominant mode of communication and one that is generally more impervious to public control than the scribal medium, needs to be taken into account as well. So also must the oral-scribal interfaces and conflicts that characterize the medium landscape of antiquity. As far as the oral-scribal dynamics are concerned, what comes to mind is the historic struggle between the Pharisees and the Sadducees (Wellhausen; Rivkin; Neusner 1972; Stemberger 1995b). Like the Qumran community, the Pharisees posed a challenge to the priestly establishment of Jerusalem, but unlike Qumran they designed their strategies largely from within the city's power relations. For the most part, they stayed in Jerusalem and worked within the system, so to speak, while developing beliefs and activities that—by implication at least—threatened to erode and displace the Sadducean establishment.

To begin with, the Pharisees were known for their interest in and cultivation of the written word. In that respect, they hardly differed from the Qumran dissenters or even the Sadducees. But there is more to it than meets the eye, for the Pharisees infused the scroll with a sense of sacrality that exalted it to a point where it was viewed as something like a portable temple or even the promised land. When, therefore, in 70 C.E. the center of the temple went up in flames and the Pharisees—along with the Jesus people—turned out to be the principal survivors among the dissenting groups, they were already conditioned to conduct their religious and civic life apart from the temple and in intense devotion to the new center of the sacred texts. In retrospect, therefore, we can see how the Pharisaic cultivation of the written word unwittingly prepared the people for a diasporic existence in the absence of the physical center.

In contrast, and indeed opposition, to the Sadducees, the Pharisees additionally cultivated the spoken word, or the Oral Torah, as they called it. As far as the Sadduccees were concerned, they insisted on the religious validity of a limited body of manuscripts. For the most part it consisted of the Pentateuch with many of the other writings still being undetermined as to their canonical status. The will of God was thus assumed to be incorporated in a number of scrolls that were both identifiable and controllable. In contrast to the Sadducean concept of the chirographically rooted will of Yahweh, the Pharisaic embrace of the Oral Torah implied that divinity was not to be limited to a narrowly confined body of manuscripts. Hence, not only what was written down, but memorable sayings, ethical instructions, and notable stories enjoyed authoritative validity as they were placed on the same footing with a select group of scrolls. From the perspective of the Pharisees, therefore, the Oral Torah signified an ongoing revelation apart from and in addition to the scribal medium. From the perspective of the Sadducees, on the other hand, the privileging of oral tradition violated the Written Torah and, significantly, placed revelation outside of their control. In thus viewing ancient history as media history, we see how the seemingly esoteric quibble over the Oral Torah among Pharisees and Sadducees in effect constituted a power struggle over the control of the media. What was at stake was the nature and scope of revelation that was to govern Israel.

Viewing the ancient media of orality and scribality as instruments of identity formation, control, and domination used both by the elite and by marginalized groups invites questions about the motives of early Christians in their use of the scribal medium. Ostensibly, early Christianity will have seized upon the scribal medium for purposes of shaping and constructing its identity, consciousness, and history. This is all the more obvious since early Christian appropriation of scribality coincided with a time in ancient Mediterranean, and especially Israelite, history that was marked with a steady oppression by Roman military forces, excessively punitive taxation, growing discontent and recurrent protests, mass crucifixions as political deterrent, and frequent resistance and renewal movements. How did early Christian writers compete with Greco-Roman powers on the marketplace of scribal communication? Specifically, how did they negotiate their message that was politically fraught with danger because Jesus was generally known to have been executed by the Romans on charges that were likely to have been political and, yet, the message by and about him was in the view of many believers designed for public consumption? With these perspectives in mind, this essay will discuss three early Christian documents, the Gospel of Mark, the Gospel of Luke, and the Apocalypse of John, and examine ways in which these three texts entrust their message to the scribal medium in view of Roman imperialism.

THE GOSPEL OF MARK: AN ALTERNATIVE TO ROMAN POWER

The pivotal metaphor in the Markan narrative is the kingdom of God. Unlike the role it plays in the Fourth Gospel (John 18:36), it is in fact of this world, involving individual and communal life, and constituted to revamp the structure of society as it presently exists. Announced to people, it is intended both to enlist people and to serve them. Undoubtedly, the kingdom does have sociopolitical implications, though it is an entity in the process of actualization whose final objective still remains to be fulfilled. While fermenting the social body by way of confrontation with evil and renewal, it moves irresistibly toward its historical self-realization.

Recently Horsley (2001a) has written on the sociopolitical dimensions of Mark's Gospel and developed its oppositional features to Roman rule. The interpretation given here differs in suggesting that the kingdom's mission in Mark to revalorize society is at most by implication opposed to Rome and careful to disguise any pronounced opposition to Roman imperial power. While established in this world and designed to transform this world, the kingdom is neither identical with nor in explicit opposition to the powers of this world. In fact, what gives it its distinct qualification is that it is God's kingdom (Mark 1:14-15) and hence neither the Herodians' kingdom nor Caesar's kingdom. In and through the person of Jesus, the kingdom of God is presented as the grand alternative to all other imperial hegemonies.

The Gospel's plot is driven by a great urgency for deliverance that in the first part of the narrative is executed by Jesus' extravagant deeds of power. Both his exorcisms and healings involve him in a severe power struggle with spiritual forces who disclose themselves as representatives of the satanic power structure. Mark clearly narrates a confrontation between the kingdom of God and the kingdom of Satan, and the Romans are, with one exception, not identical with the latter. In short, Jesus' battle with Beelzebul is not perceived in terms of a political confrontation.

One may nonetheless ask whether the Gospel's considerable preoccupation with demon possession and its emplotment of a global confrontation with superhuman forces represents on Mark's part a transposition of political-economic pressures onto a spiritual plane. By both personalizing and globalizing the problem of imperial violence, the exorcism stories would draw attention away from direct confrontation with the Roman oppressors while making sure that the violence that was affecting society was decisively challenged at the highest possible level. It is not inconceivable that Mark's preoccupation with healings and especially exorcisms is not unrelated to the violence inflicted by the Roman occupation and on a subliminal level represent a projection of social suffering and pent-up resentments on demonic forces. However, it is doubtful whether an ancient audience was in a position to hear the exorcism stories with what are after all the anthropological and psychological insights of modernity. While on the micro-level Mark's exorcisms and healings function to liberate individuals from physical suffering and to restore them to the fullness of life, they form on the macro-level part of a cosmic strategy to tie up the strong man Satan and to plunder his house (Mark 3:27). It would be difficult to read a political subtext into this part of the narrative.

An exception to this reading of the exorcisms is provided by the story of the exorcism of the Gerasene demoniac (Horsley 2001a:140–41). Of all the exorcisms in Mark's narrative, this one is distinguished by uncommonly violent proportions (Mark 5:1–20). A man possessed by demons has caused such raucousness that "no man could restrain him any more, even with a chain" (5:3). In answer to Jesus' question, he identifies himself as Legion, and upon the man's request the evil spirits enter a herd of two thousand swine, who rush into the sea to be drowned. In this case, it would be difficult not to acknowledge the anti-Roman sentiments. Both the intensity and the oppressiveness of violence, the naming of the demonic forces as Legion (a Roman military designation), their identification with swine (symbol of Gentile uncleanliness from a Jewish perspective), the large and precise number of swine, and, finally, their drowning in the sea add up to an unmistakably political, anti-Roman scenario. "The double meaning (of Legion) is not lost on the audience" (Horsley 2001a:18). On the narrative level the Gerasene demoniac represents Jesus' most massive excorcism; it takes place on Gentile territory and in repudiation of Gentile uncleanliness. Within the geographical coordinates of the Gospel the incident signifies Jesus' opening of new frontiers and a breakthrough toward a Gentile identity (Kelber 1979:30–33). However, the story clearly resonates with the experiences or reminiscences of a society haunted by demonic Roman violence and indulges wishful thinking of seeing the hated Roman "pigs" driven into the sea. The informed hearer may even discern an analogy between the drowning of the demonic oppressors and the paradigmatic drowning of the Egyptian pursuers of the fleeing Israelites in the red sea (Exod 14:26-28), although direct verbal links between the two stories are not discernible. The anti-Roman resentments, however, that are encoded in the exorcism story are recognizable as such only to the informed hearers who have ears to hear. Any overt confrontation with the Roman imperial authorities is carefully avoided.

Prior to his passion proper Jesus' emplotted activity is increasingly focused on the temple (Mark 11–13) and in fact in growing opposition to the central place. Having entered the temple to look at everything only to depart (11:11), Jesus enters a second time to judge and disqualify the temple by word and by deed (11:12–25). To all appearances, his act of condemnation (11:15–17) is motivated by his zeal for the religious identity of the temple. Exposed as a place of merchants who abuse the sacred place and rob people of their livelihood, the temple is ideally defined as a place of prayer open to members of all nations. The hearers of this story are never informed of the fact that Jesus' temple activities were fraught with political risks, since the temple precinct was the epicenter of power. Any interference at the center of religious and political power was bound to provoke fateful intervention on the part of Sadducean and Roman powers. As long as the Romans were in control over Israel, they kept a watchful eye on the temple, making sure that law and order prevailed according to Roman imperial interests. Mark's Jesus, however, not only departs from the scene of disturbance unchallenged but returns unharmed a third time to the temple—this time for the purpose of teaching, defining and defending his own authority against that of the temple (Mark 11:27–12:40). Following extensive teaching in the temple, he exits for the last time (13:1) and promptly predicts the physical destruction of the holy place (13:2). As far as Mark is concerned, Jesus' active demonstration in the temple and his verbal condemnation are religiously motivated and carry no overt political consequences.

When in his final speech, delivered to four select disciples on the Mount of Olives and in full view of the temple, Jesus informs them of wars, rumors of wars, and national uprisings (13:5–37), he pointedly apprises them of a time of unprecedented suffering (13:19). Regardless whether the speech addresses a situation prior to or after the conflagration of the temple, hearers are bound to associate "the worst time of suffering since God created the world" (13:19) with Israel's historical experience as a colonized people. However, nowhere is Roman aggression directly identified, let alone challenged, and never is God's judgment, or that of the Son of Man, called upon to punish the oppressive rulers. Indeed, the speech stays remarkably clear of judgmental language. Mark's strategy in dealing with the politically explosive issue of war and the unparalleled violence associated with it is to place it into a larger, a cosmic scheme of events. This larger framework entails the rise of fraudulent redeemer figures (13:5–6, 21–22), the proclamation of the gospel to all the nations (13:10), a shortening of the time of tribulation (13:20), cosmic darkness and a heavenly revolution (13:24–25), followed by the epiphany of the Son of Man (13:26) and the redemption of the elect (13:27). By thus integrating the time of tribulation into a providentially devised scheme of cosmic events, a context of meaning is generated that deactivates anti-Roman resentments and refocuses attention from violence to epiphany.

In the passion narrative, the high priests along with the scribes initiate and advance the plot on Jesus' life (14:1, 10–11, 43) and arouse the Jerusalem crowd against him (15:11). The politically explosive issue of the temple incident does come up in the hearing before the high priest, but it is dismissed as false and conflicting testimony (14:57–59). The accusation that brings about the death sentence is blasphemy (14:64), a religious rather than political charge. As far as Jesus' transfer from Jewish to Roman authorities is concerned, the narrator has Pilate surmise that it was motivated by the jealousy of the Jewish establishment (15:10). Pilate, the highest Roman official in charge of the case, remains unconvinced of Jesus' guilt (15:14), proposes to release him in place of a man of violence (15:6–9), and "wonders" (15:5: *thaumazein*) when Jesus is alive and still "wonders" (15:44: *ethaumazen*) after he is dead. Contrary to his well-founded historical reputation, the Pilate introduced by Mark into the Christian tradition is a man who tragically failed in his attempt to save the life of Jesus.

There is one scene in the passion narrative that seems to bespeak unbridled anti-Roman sentiments: Jesus' cruel mocking and torture by a battalion of soldiers (15:16–20). Clearly, the soldiers do not carry the blessing of the narrator, and Rome is placed in a blatantly negative light. Yet the scene of mocking is fraught with irony intimating that the direct sense is not entirely to be trusted. The soldiers, determined to make a brutal caricature of Jesus, clothe him with a purple cloak, place a crown of thorns on his head, and salute him as "King of the Jews." The rhetoric of their gestures suggests that a royal investiture, or more precisely the reversal of such an accession to power, has been enacted: Jesus is caricatured as king in an act of utter infamy. But the themes of coronation through humiliation and of induction into kingship by way of a crown made of thorns are entirely in keeping with the Markan narration of Jesus' death. For it is the Markan conception that Jesus acceded to royal power by surrendering all earthly power and by submitting himself to the most brutal of executions. Viewed in this light, the mocking scene does not, on a subliminal level, bespeak anti-Roman sentiments after all, for the soldiers who carry out the royal mocking enact the truth in ignorance and infamy.

There is, lastly, the centurion's affirmation made in full view of Jesus' death: "Truly, this man was Son of God" (15:39). Sanctioned by the heavenly voice both at baptism (1:11) and at the transfiguration (9:7), "Son of God" is the confessional designation fully befitting the Markan Jesus. It is the kind of confession the disciples should have made but never did make. As a matter of narrative fact, the Roman official in charge of the execution turns out to be the only human being in the narrative who ever makes the Son-of-God confession. Rome, not Jesus' own disciples, delivers the most appropriate response to Jesus' death.

Mark's representation of Jesus and God's kingdom is such that it studiously evades any direct confrontational engagement with Rome. While Jesus is a revolutionary who turned against the temple, or rather against those in charge of it, his temple activity is thoroughly depoliticized and the political charge dismissed in the trial. Projected as a figure of power, he turns traditional concepts of political power inside out: a successful exorciser, he dies engulfed in cosmic darkness (15:33); a popular performer of miracles, he suffers a nonmiraculous death; appointed in power, he dies abandoned by God in powerlessness (15:34). This inversion of power has the effect of disarming any perceived threat to Roman power. Far from exposing the brutality of the Roman punishment of crucifixion, the reversal of power constellations renders the crucifixion a source of strength and turns the Romans into unwitting executors of redemption. As for the politically imposed violence, past and present, it is reframed in a larger, a cosmic context. By transposing the source of violence into a transhistorical domain, the perspective on colonial violence is vastly broadened. The unprecedented tribulation and the demise of the temple need to be viewed in the larger context of the history of the kingdom of God and its struggle with the demonic forces of evil.

THE GOSPEL OF LUKE: AN ACCOMMODATION TO ROMAN POWER

Whether Theophilus was a Jew or a Gentile, a Jewish Christian or a Gentile Christian, Luke's formal address to him as *kratiste Theophilo* (Luke 1:3), and the reiteration of the personal address at the outset of Acts (1:1), expresses an authorial interest in introducing "the Way" (Acts 9:2; 19:9, 23; 24:14) to a person of high social ranking. To hold Theophilus's attention and to meet his likely political inclinations, Luke will be disposed to make a case for the compatibility of the new faith with the pro-Roman cultural elite in the Hellenistic world. This does not mean that Luke's often-observed cultural, political apologetic sells out the gospel to the Greco-Roman ruling class. As is well known, no other canonical Gospel shows greater contempt for the rich and more compassion for the poor than Luke (Degenhardt; Johnson). In this Gospel, human nature reveals itself—in part at least—by a person's relation to money and possessions. Assisting the poor has become an article of faith, and enslavement to possessions versus faith in Jesus, which manifests itself in giving alms to the poor, is an elementary conflict experienced by the followers of the "Way." Nor is the theme of the Roman apology the dominant one in Gospel and Acts, but it is a frequent subtext that ever so often surfaces and in the passion narrative and in parts of Acts clearly comes to the fore.

While the infancy Gospel (Luke 1–2) introduces John and Jesus the protagonist in Septuagintal language and with imagery derived from the Hebrew Bible, thus implanting them in a thoroughly Jewish context, it further links them with political figures who loom large on the stage of ancient Mediterranean history. The emperors Augustus and Tiberius, Quirinius the governor of Syria, king Herod and his brother Philip, and Lysanias the ruler of Abilene—to mention only the more important personages—represent the political coordinates of a history in the midst of which John and Jesus are shown to have been operative. The program implied in this impressive stage setting is that the Jesus movement, far from being an insignificant Jewish, messianic sect tucked away in a forgotten corner of the world (Acts 26:26), was from the beginning linked with eminent profiles in power. A revelation to the Gentiles and a glory to Israel (Luke 2:32), the movement had both a claim on the world and a responsibility for it.

In this spirit, John's preaching is expanded by a series of responses to questions addressed to him by the multitudes, tax collectors, and soldiers (Luke 3:10–14). His counsel amounts to a social and professional ethics of compassion and honesty "in which loyalty to the State is implicit" (Conzelmann: 138). John, who in Mark is presented as an apocalyptic figure, is thereby partially changed into a social reformer and advocate of civic responsibilities. In the case of Jesus, his parents' journey to Bethlehem (Luke 2:1–5) serves a threefold purpose. It has Augustus, the most powerful man in the ancient Mediterranean world, issue a decree that sets in motion "a train of events so far reaching as to excel all human might" (Flender: 57). Second, it has the parents abide by a census that was instituted for the purpose of administering Roman taxation. Any Zealotic implication as far as Jesus' birth, upbringing, and mission is concerned is thereby discounted. Finally, the journey to Bethlehem locates his birth "in the city of David a Savior, who is the Messiah, the Lord" (Luke 2:11), thus stipulating Jesus' Davidic messiahship. In sum, Jesus the Messiah in no way poses a threat to the imperial Roman system.

Luke enunciates peace as a recurring motif more than any other canonical Gospel. Mark uses *eirene* once, Matthew four times, John six times, and Luke (Gospel and Acts) twenty times (Morgenthaler: 92). In Luke, both John and Jesus are introduced as messengers of peace (Luke 1:79; 2:14). The angels heralding the messianic birth announce peace on earth (2:14), whereas the disciples accompanying Jesus on his entry into Jerusalem proclaim peace in heaven (19:38). The reality of peace is, therefore, not restricted to the immanent dimension of history. Rather, peace partakes of a dialectical mode of thought and action whereby events in heaven relate to corresponding events on earth, and vice versa (Flender: 37–56). In Jesus' own words, the trouble with Jerusalem is that it failed to recognize the things that make for peace (19:42). The first greeting extended by the Risen One to the disciples in Jerusalem is "Peace be to you" (24:36). Ideally, the early church lives in a state of peace and under the guidance of the Holy Spirit (Acts 9:31). In one of his speeches Peter summarizes the gospel in terms of "peace through Jesus Christ" (Acts 10:36). This Lukan motif of peace will resonate differently with hearers of the Gospel and Acts. For the most part it appears in contexts that have little to do with the cessation of war and strife; it may imply, but does not directly connotate, absence of violence. However, it shows greater affinity with the Jewish notion of *shalom,* which defines peace as a gift from God that restores harmony in the relationship between God and humans. However, an audience versed in Hellenistic culture may sense undercurrents that are reminiscent of the imperial propagation of the *pax Romana.*

Peace (*eirene*), savior (*soter*), good news (*euangelion*), and benefactor (*euergetes*) are part of the vocabulary of the imperial cult and liturgy. Imperial births and enthronements are tidings of joy that celebrate the emperor as savior and benefactor under whose governance land and sea will enjoy peace and well-being. But whether the Lukan Jesus, messianic herald of peace, is perceived in fulfilment of the *pax Romana* or in competition with it, he is in either case politically innocent of and immune to the Zealotic gospel of violence.

Yet appeasement of the Roman will to law and order does not fully characterize Lukan strategy. Already in the infancy Gospel, Mary's Magnificat (Luke 1:46–55) challenges positions of power and introduces the revolutionary theme of social reversal. In appealing to God as the one who "has scattered the proud in the imagination of their hearts" (1:51), the Gospel avails itself of decidedly provocative language, and in asserting that God "has put down the mighty [*dynastas*] from their thrones, and exalted those of low degree" (1:52), it is decidedly taking political risks. Statements of this kind carry positively social, even political implications that do not lend themselves easily to a spiritualized interpretation. Only slightly less precarious are Jesus' own words to the effect that among his disciples Gentile power relations ought to be reversed: whereas Gentile kings, who call themselves benefactors, rule over their subjects, among his followers the leader is destined to serve (22:25–26). This does suggest that the social structure enacted by the "benefactors" can only serve as a negative example for those who wish to follow in the "Way." At an earlier point in the Gospel the Lukan Jesus had emphatically denied that his mission was to deliver peace on earth. Instead, he intended to light a fire that would divide households and turn family members against one another (12:51–53). In this instance, peace as cultivation of family structures and values is subverted. As a general rule, imperial powers will not look favorably upon the dissolution of family ties, even though sayings of this kind are meant for internal, Christian consumption. There is, finally, the tantalizing Lukan episode regarding the two swords (22:35–38). Concluding his farewell speech, Jesus counsels the purchase of a sword and is promptly presented with two. There clearly is an air of violence hovering over the scene. However, the suspension that is building up in this scene is taken up and resolved in the following episode of the arrest (22:47–51). When violence erupts at the arrest and one of Jesus' followers (disciples?) puts the sword to action and cuts off the right ear of the high priest's slave, Jesus interferes and reverses the violence by performing his last healing. An overzealous follower is thereby repudiated, and Zealotism at a pivotal juncture in Jesus' life repudiated. For the most part, language that affronts Roman sensibilities is the exception rather than the rule.

More than the other canonical Gospels Luke has foregrounded Jerusalem and its demise. His narrative relates the military siege and destruction of the city in historically graphic terms: Jerusalem is "surrounded by armies" (Luke 21:20); the "enemies will set up ramparts [around it] and surround [it], and hem [it] in on every side, and crush [it] to the ground" (19:34-35); it will be "trodden down by the Gentiles" (21:24); and people "will fall by the edge of the sword" (21:24). But in spite of a historical awareness of both the military logistics and the human tragedy surrounding the event, the Gospel will issue neither complaint nor criticism concerning Roman brutalities and refrain from holding Roman military and/or political authorities responsible for the indescribable suffering of the people. What is lamented is Jerusalem, not the Romans. The fault, Luke argues, lies with the city and its citizens who habitually killed the prophets (13:34) and missed the appropriate time (*kairos*) of God's visitation (19:44). Additionally, Luke firmly draws a connection between the fate of the city and that of Jesus, a link already affirmed less emphatically by Mark. Notably, Luke abides by the Markan pattern in treating the destruction of city and temple in the context of Jesus' story, not, as required by historical chronology, in the context of his (Luke's) second volume, Acts. Over and above the Q lament (Luke 13:34–35) and Mark's apocalyptic anticipation (Mark 13:14–20 = Luke 21:20–24), Luke introduced two more lament scenes: Jesus' weeping over Jerusalem (Luke 19:41–44) and his grieving over the daughters of Jerusalem (23:27–31). Both scenes are placed in the passion narrative, one at the entry into Jerusalem and one on the way to crucifixion. In his last word prior to his execution Jesus wonders what will happen when the wood is dry if this was being done while it was still green (23:31), thereby linking his own demise with that of the city. Undoubtedly, Luke is in possession of detailed knowledge about Jerusalem's destruction, but his mode of argumentation is of a conventionally religious kind. He will not allow himself to express overt animosity toward the destructiveness of Roman political and military power.

In the passion narrative Luke further develops the *apologia Romana*, already in existence since Mark, into a programmatic theme. He has Jesus' opponents resort to the intensely political issue of Roman taxation in order to bring him to trial (Luke 20:20). When they deliver him to Pilate it is precisely on this charge of having committed a crime against the imperial government: "We found this man perverting our nation, forbidding us to pay taxes to the emperor, and saying that he himself is the Messiah, a king" (23:2). Kingship, messianism, revolution and Roman taxation constitute the core of the indictment, a potent political charge that is designed to bring about the death sentence. Luke, although not unaware of Pilate's insensitivity toward ethnic people and religious issues (13:1), nevertheless takes a major step toward promoting the Roman governor into a model Christian. Pilate responds not once, but three times: there was no basis for the charges (23:4), Jesus was not guilty (23:14), and there is, therefore, no judicial ground for granting the requested death sentence (23:22). This is the first time in the Christian tradition that a formal charge of political culpability has been brought against Jesus and that it has been formally dismissed, and dismissed by the principal Roman authority. Henceforth, the *apologia Romana* is firmly entrenched in Christian consciousness.

After Pilate has pronounced Jesus innocent, Luke will not have the latter tortured by Roman soldiers. In Mark, Pilate has Jesus scourged (Mark 15:15) before he turns him over to the soldiers, who in turn subject him to torture. Hence prior to his execution the Markan Jesus twice undergoes physical suffering on the instruction of Roman authorities and by Roman hands. Mark, Matthew, and John all report the so-called mocking by the Roman soldiers. In Luke, however, Roman soldiers verbally abuse and mock Jesus while he suffers on the cross (Luke 23:36), but neither they nor Pilate will subject him to physical torture prior to his execution. Instead, the Gospel projects Jesus' physical abuse by the soldiers backward into the courtyard of the high priest, where "the men who were holding" him subject him to mocking torture (22:63-65). This is a harbinger of things to come in the Christian tradition: the culpability for Jesus' death is increasingly transferred from Roman to Jewish authorities, and eventually to the Jewish people at large. The Gospel's Roman apology reaches its peak with the centurion, the Roman official in charge of the execution, pronouncing Jesus innocent in full view of his death (23:47). In short, as far as Luke is concerned, Jesus' death was a judicial error forced upon the Romans by the Jewish people and authorities of Jerusalem.

As far as Luke's concept of history is concerned, a major rationale for Jesus' birth, mission, and death was the inauguration of an ecumenical movement. However, with one exception Jesus himself refrained from pursuing the Gentile mission. He initiated it in his inaugural sermon at Nazareth (Luke 4:16–30, esp. 25–27), by way of a single, programmatic journey unto Gentile territory (8:26–39), and by his commissioning of the seventy (10:1-12), but the execution of the Gentile mission itself was the work of the early church and for this reason had to be relegated to the second volume, Acts.

Luke's so-called "great omission," the deletion of Mark 6:45–8:26, is a deliberate procedure undertaken in the interest of the theme of the Gentile mission. In Mark this segment corresponds exactly to Jesus' sanctioning of the Gentile mission. Luke deletes this narrative segment not because of lack of interest in the theme but because it is the theme to be treated in Acts.

In view of Luke's sympathy toward Gentile culture and Roman power, the goal and ending of his two-volume work is of particular interest. After Paul, who identifies himself as a Roman citizen by birth (Acts 22:25–29; 23:27) and appeals to the Roman emperor (25:10–12), arrives in Rome, he spends two years in the capital proclaiming the gospel that was meant for the Gentiles without any interference on the part of the authorities (28:16–30). Luke's work, as the construction of all narrative, entails to some extent a plotting backwards from its anticipated ending. This interior retrospectivity (Ong 1977b) implies that both Gospel and Acts are narrated with a view toward, and from the perspective of, the city of Rome that Paul was to reach at the end of Acts. In different words, Luke constructs both Gospel and Acts from the perspective of a Christianity that had safely arrived and settled in the capital of Rome.

Given the preeminence of the Gentile theme, Luke had to face up to the realities of the Roman Empire. His Roman apologetic arose out of a perceived necessity to devise a modus operandi with the imperial state and is not necessarily an ad hominem construction tailor-made for a particular social setting, conventionally called the Lukan community. Hence in effect, and probably in intention, Luke makes a case for the compatibility of Christianity with Rome. He is keenly aware that his case will be ineffective unless it addresses the controversial issue of Jesus' political culpability. Crucifixion by the Romans made Zealotic criminality, or rather the charge of Zealotic criminality, to be eminently plausible. In the course of his argumentation, Luke, therefore, had to concede that the charge of political criminality was indeed an issue in the case of Jesus and the principal reason for his judicial hearing before Pilate. The Roman declaration of Jesus' innocence constituted the linchpin of Luke's Roman apology. In following Mark, he reinforced his case by introducing a paradoxical twist: it was the Jews who entertained seditious sympathies because they requested the release of Barabbas, a known Zealotic insurrectionist. In the last analysis, therefore, no other than Pilate himself lent support to Zealotism by giving in to Jewish pressure and ordering the release of Barabbas. Admittedly, Jesus was a social and religious reformer, a revolutionary even, but he explicitly rejected the political gospel of violence.

The Apocalypse of John: A Subversion of Roman Power

John's Apocalypse dramatizes a global conflict between the forces of evil plotting destruction and death and those of redemption visualizing order and life. To stage the drama, the narrator operates with a collage of symbols creating a largely imaginative universe of compelling rhetorical persuasiveness. The fierce conflict is principally enacted by the Lamb, one like the Son of Man and the Bride, representing the forces of life, and at the opposite side the city of Babylon, the great Whore and the Beast impersonating the powers of destructiveness. While precise historical references are, we shall see, infrequent in the narrative, poetic language and images predominate. Symbols are used flexibly and at times interchangeably. Only with difficulty can they be reduced to steno-symbols that would require a one-to-one relation of symbol and meaning. For the most part John's Apocalypse employs symbols as tensive figures evoking a wide range of meanings that cannot be exhausted in any one apprehension of meaning (Wheelright; Perrin: 29–30; Schüssler Fiorenza: 183–86).

The rich legacy of connotations that the symbols carry derives in part from the Jewish tradition, especially the book of Ezekiel, and from the apocalyptic strands of it, and within the apocalyptic tradition above all from the Apocalypse of Daniel. In part, however, the Apocalypse summons symbolic representations that draw on deeper archaic sources. This applies especially to the combat theme that pits the forces of chaos, sterility, and death against those of order, fertility, and life. That theme derived from and resonates with an archaic Near Eastern myth of combat and creation (Gunkel 1895; A. Y. Collins). However, the Apocalypse's collage of symbols does not arise exclusively from primordial and apocalyptic memorial wellsprings nor exist exclusively in the harmonious configuration of its own interior world. It relates in complex ways to history. Symbols are being invoked in the historical context of readers/ hearers, and the symbolic dramatization is to a degree at least shaped from the perspective of and with a view toward the Apocalypse's recipients and their experiences in the present. This is why the collage of symbols can take on life in and for the historical audience/readership. Tapping a deep register and configuring it with a view toward the present, the vastly imaginative narrative reaches out to hearers/readers, inviting them to make sense of their historical experiences in the context of the apocalyptic narration. On this view, John's Apocalypse is neither an aesthetic world closed unto itself and without any social, historical, political parameters nor a poetic world that is limited to a one-to-one translation of its symbols into history. It rather appeals to hearers/ readers both as participants in, and victims of, history and as sharers in the memories of ancient myths. In short, the Apocalypse is a poetic narration that mobilizes hearers to explore their historical conflicts in an archetypal, symbolic dramatization of a primal conflict. The latter constitutes a combat of worldwide, indeed cosmic dimensions, parts of which have been set into motion "from the foundation of the world" (Rev 13:8). Insofar as the Apocalypse has globalizing implications, it functions as an explanatory mechanism that projects hearers into the cosmic drama and encourages them to comprehend their present crisis in global dimensions.

When the Apocalypse singles out Babylon as the quintessential rogue city, it taps into resentments that run deep in Jewish, Jewish-Christian consciousness. Ever since the ancient Babylonian Empire had humiliated Judah and destroyed Jerusalem's temple in 587 B.C.E. (2 Kgs 24–25), Babylon had become a proverbial expression of anguish and enragement in the face of foreign, imperial oppression. One of the pivotal features of John's Apocalypse is the fierceness and relentlessness of judgment that it pronounces on Babylon. The six direct references to Babylon are all placed in negative, judgmental contexts (Rev 14:8; 16:19; 17:5; 18:2, 10, 21). Employing the formulaic diction of a dirge or lament modeled on Isaiah (21:9), the Apocalypse announces mournfully the downfall of Babylon, the great city: "Fallen, fallen is Babylon the great!" (Rev 14:8; 18:2). Plagues in the form of "torment and grief," "pestilence and mourning and famine" (18:7-8) will be inflicted upon her. An unprecedented earthquake will split the city of all cities into three (16:18–19), fire will consume her (18:8), and she will become "a dwelling place of demons" (18:2). "Babylon the great" is beyond redemption and doomed to destruction.

The city-destruction rhetoric (Rossing: 62) comprises indictments of prostitution, murder, as well as of arrogant claims to universal power— all directed against the great city of Babylon. The charge of prostitution (*porneia:* Rev 14:8; 17:5; 18:3) is polyvalent and open to interpretations in terms of illicit relations with foreign cities (including sexual promiscuity), participation in imperial cult practices, and/or, we shall see, the advancement of commercial ties that compromised the integrity of the merchants and fed the great city's voracious appetite. There are, moreover, frequent expressions of anguish over the shedding of the blood of saints, prophets, and witnesses of Jesus, and in one instance at the very least these atrocities are attributed to Babylon (18:24). Ruling "as a queen" (18:7), "Babylon, the mighty city" (18:10) indulged herself in the narcissistic illusions and arrogance that is endemic to world powers (18:7). She has seduced and deceived the nations of the earth and contributed to their downfall (14:8; 18:23). However, her own imminent fall will bring about the collapse of the nations and "the cities of the nations" (16:19; cf. Isa 14:12). Hence, her day of doom will be cause for universal lament on the part of "the kings of the earth" (Rev 18:9–10), who had entertained relations with the glamorous queen, the "mother of whores" (17:5).

A conspicuous feature in the Apocalypse's narration concerns references to economics and commerce, with a special emphasis on issues pertaining to seafaring, navigation, and maritime trade. This is atypical in the rhetorical repertoire of apocalyptic language and for this reason deserves to be viewed as in some sense case-specific (Kraybill). "Clothed in fine linen, in purple and scarlet, adorned with gold, with jewels and with pearls" (Rev 18:16), enchanting Babylon is a city of unprecedented wealth. She is said to entertain a flourishing shipping trade, exporting numerous items and vast quantities of luxury items ranging from gold to the human cargo of slaves (18:11–13). Shipmasters, seafarers and sailors, kings and merchants, "the magnates of the earth" (18:23), such as those who traded and traveled on sea and who gained wealth from Babylon and benefited from her in numerous ways—all of them will be devastated by her demise (18:9, 14–15, 17–19, 23). In focusing on the shipping trade, the Apocalypse targets what tended to be a nerve center in ancient power politics: commerce, shipping, and imperial interests blended together and fed one another. Standing within a Jewish tradition of resistance to oppressive imperialism, the Apocalypse counsels a strategy of commercial noncooperation with corrupt and vainglorious Babylon.

With rare exceptions, the rogue city of Babylon is conventionally interpreted as a figure for imperial Rome. However, that interpretation entails complex hermeneutical configurations. As far as the Apocalypse's dramatized imagery is concerned, we are dealing first and foremost with an intricate symbolic interaction of Babylon, the evil Woman, and the evil Beast. The Woman clothed in luxurious garments and adorned with expensive jewelry is marked as the embodiment of all the impurities on earth. Representing both the wealth and the abominations of Babylon, she carries on her forehead an inscription that reads: "Babylon the great, mother of whores and of earth's abominations" (Rev 17:5). This identification is fully confirmed in nonsymbolic, propositional language: "The woman you saw is Babylon the great city that rules over the kings of the earth" (17:18). There is, moreover, the Beast arising out of the abyss of the sea (13:1) carrying blasphemous names on its head (13:1; 17:3) and uttering "haughty and blasphemous words" (13:5). It will receive homage from the tribes, nations, and peoples of the earth (13: 7–8) although its reign of terror is of limited duration. For forty-two months (13:5) it will exercise its military authority, make war on the saints (13:7), and assault the Lamb (17:14), but its end is destruction as it is conquered by the Lamb (17: 14). The scarlet Beast is linked to the evil Woman insofar as she takes her seat on it and, clothed in purple and scarlet, rides on it (17:3–4). Thus, Babylon, the great Whore, and the scarlet Beast are the three principal embodiments of evil. While the symbolic representations alternate between a city, a person, and an animal, their functions and attributes closely interact to the point of blending into one another. All three function as manifestations and agents of inordinate wealth, corruption, idolatry, blasphemy, and universal domination.

To the extent that Rome plays a role in the apocalyptic scenario, she is, therefore, represented not merely by Babylon but by all three principalities of Evil. There are a number of links connecting the symbolic world embodied by Babylon, the great Whore, and the scarlet Beast with imperial Rome. We have already seen that the extensive maritime language falls outside the symbolic world and appears to connect with historical realities current in the world of the author and audience. No city in the ancient Mediterranean fits the Apocalypse's diatribe against seafaring and maritime commerce better than Rome. Ostia, the city's principal port, was the center of a vast commercial network and the destination of countless trade routes. Merchants not only realized a hefty profit from Rome's boundless appetite for ordinary and extraordinary goods but also became dependent on Rome—its economic status, its currency, its cultural needs and tastes, and its political powers. Moreover, the Apocalypse expresses abhorrence of emperor worship (Rev 13:4, 12–17; 16:2; 19:20), raising the specter of links between seamanship and imperial cult practices (Kraybill: 123–32). Numismatic evidence displays the very alliance between commerce, Roman military, pagan gods, and imperial cults that the Apocalypse found deeply objectionable. Indeed, no mercy is held out for those who worship the Beast and its image (14:9–12). From the perspectives of the Apocalypse, all these practices and beliefs centered on the unholy alliance with Babylon/Rome.

This is evident as well from the Beast's deadly focus on the destruction of Jerusalem. It is said that the Beast conquers "the holy" or "the great city," which is the very city "were also the Lord was crucified" (Rev 11:2, 8). The streets of Jerusalem will be soaked in the blood and strewn with the bodies of her victims as a result of the conquest that will last forty-two months (11:2, 7–8; 13:5). The Beast is thereby unmistakably associated with the brutalities of the Roman military might, and the principal conquest with the fall of Jerusalem, the holy city. Clearly alluding to the tragic event of 70 C.E., which looms large in the background, the Apocalypse enjoins its hearers/readers to comprehend the struggle with Rome as the reactivation in the present of an old, archaic conflict. The Woman, finally, who rides on the Beast, is also seated on seven mountains (17:9), which is sometimes taken to refer to Rome as the city of the seven hills. In sum, the rogue city, the seductive Woman, and the abominable Beast are symbols with floating and interactive connotations whose core identity, however, is Rome, the paradigmatic city of imperial corruption and idolatry. Once we recognize that the Apocalypse's objection to Rome found expression through the principal trinity of evil representations, not by reference simply to the ancient city of Babylon, the profundity of its anti-Roman sentiments is difficult to overstate.

Given the depth of the Apocalypse's antagonism toward Rome, it may be tempting to view its symbolic language and imagery as a strategy borne out of political considerations. Yet the objective of the apocalyptic scenario, which draws on a rich source of established diction, imagery, and configurations, is ultimately not intelligible as, let alone reducible to, a rhetoric of political prudence. To be sure, Rome is invoked in a complex narrative web of symbols and images and never directly mentioned by name. More than that, it is doubtful whether the Apocalypse intends to invite hearers to decode its world, symbol after symbol and image after image. Indeed, many commentaries are still unduly preoccupied with determining links between the coded symbolic world and historical data, events, and personages, thereby treating the imagery as steno-symbols rather than as tensive figurations. But rather than translating each item into current history, the Apocalypse invites audiences to project themselves into its world. As hearers involve themselves in the dramatization of the conflict between Babylon, the great Whore, and the abominable Beast versus the heavenly Jerusalem, the Bride, and the Lamb (or one like the Son of Man), they locate their own roles and identities in the scenario. There is a sense, therefore, in which hearers are invited to reorient, to relive even, their present conflict with the world power of Rome. However, the symbols are often plurisignificant, evoking multiple floating and interactive representations. As the heavenly Jerusalem functions as an archetypal ideal, so also does Babylon function as its satanic parody. It does represent Rome, but also more than the human, imperial city. The scarlet Woman is also seated on the waters, which pass for "peoples and multitudes and nations and languages" (Rev 17:15). She does represent Rome, but also more than the human, imperial city of Rome. The Beast is a sea monster, which conjures up archaic, mythological anxieties (11:7; 13:1–10, 18; 15:2; 16:13; 17:7–14). It does represent Rome, but also more than the human, imperial city of Rome. Hence, the symbols not only assist hearers in identifying current events but also open up to a world that encompasses and transcends the present crisis, assisting hearers in recognizing themselves and their conflict as part of an archaic, global confrontation between chaos and order.

Conclusion

We have observed the early Christian appropriation of the scribal medium as an instrument of identity formation. As a marginalized group, the early Christians scribalized their traditions for the purpose of solidifying cultural memory and constructing a sense of history. In the case of Mark, scribality unified the selected memories of the recent past in the interest of identity formation at a decisive juncture in early Christian mnemonic history. Luke created a sense of Jesus' past history from the perspective of the subsequent history of the expansion of the new faith into the Gentile world. The Apocalypse designed a largely imaginary world, vastly expanding the universe of experiences and identifications and summoning its hearers/readers to find identity in it. In all three instances, scribality, cultural memory, and identity formation cooperated in the interest of constructing early Christian self-legitimation. In different ways this self-legitimation was affected by the relations one negotiated with the Roman world power. As a rule, the public medium of scribality had to process this explosive aspect of early Christian identity with utmost discretion. Mark's text of the life and death of Jesus articulated a cautiously couched program of an alternative to Roman power. Luke, while retaining vigorous, social ethics, nonetheless wrote what amounted to a program of acculturation to the new political realities of Roman supremacy. The Apocalypse, finally, articulated an uncompromising condemnation of the world power, but its anti-Roman scenario was judiciously camouflaged in the coded diction and imagery of an apocalyptic dramatization. In this way early Christians prepared the way into the Roman Empire for the message of and about the one who was crucified as criminal by Roman law and authority.

Practicing the Presence of God in John: Ritual Use of Scripture and the *Eidos Theou* in John 5:37

Jonathan A. Draper
University of Natal

1. Introduction

My interest in this essay is the ambivalent role of a sacred text in a situation of colonial domination, such as first-century Palestine after the fall of Jerusalem in 70 C.E. On the one hand, it is utilized consciously or unconsciously as an agent of control by the colonial authorities and their surrogates. The colonized elite uphold an ideological control of the sacred text, determining what constitutes legitimate interpretation and what constitutes "heresy." On the other hand, resistance to colonial domination in the early Christian movement seems increasingly to have taken the form of resistance, not so much to the Hebrew Scriptures as to ideological control of the Scriptures by the elite. Early Christian interpreters can be seen as *bricoleurs* exploring counterstrategies of appropriation. It often takes the form of a hunt for a hermeneutical key to unlock the dynamic potential of the controlled text as living word. Always the assumption is that the Word mediates power and that discovering the key unleashes divine power. The power of the liberated, orally mediated Word then provides a counterpoint to colonial control through the textual word. The work of Bryan Wilson in *Magic and the Millennium* has proved a helpful starting point. He attempts to differentiate indigenous responses to colonialism and provide some pointers to the relationship between historical context and the particular responses of specific indigenous movements. The particular "sectarian" response to colonialism relevant to the present study is the "introversionist" response, which is marked by experimentation with new cultural combinations. Here the model of the *bricoleur*, as this is developed by John and Jean Comaroff, is helpful. Where ideology fails to legitimate hegemony, gaps appear at the edges, which provide space for play ("liminal space," utilizing the terminology of Victor Turner!) and innovation, and these in turn allow for the emergence of resistance and reconstruction.

The material for the new construct does not come *ex nihilo* but from elements of the collapsing indigenous worldview and the dominating worldview of the conquerors. Always the quest is for power perceived to lie in these elements, whether fully understood or not. The attempt is made to turn the culture of the conquerors against them and to preserve the indigenous culture from further collapse (see Ranger: 211–62). This essay starts from the premise that John's Gospel is the product of a marginalized and alienated section of the elite of a subjugated indigenous people in a colonial situation after the destruction of the old hegemonic order, emphasizing the continuity of revelation, of living Word revealed by the sacred text but continuing to be revealed to the community of believers, as representatives of a heavenly order that, against all appearances, is in control of events: "My kingdom is not of this world" (John 18:36).

The starting point is, to be sure, the absence of God: "no one has ever seen God" (1:18; 6:46), but the affirmation of the text is, in the end, that the absent has been made present through the Logos. "He who sees me sees the One who sent me" (12:45); "He who has seen me has seen the Father" (14:9); "the glory which you have given me I have given to them, that they may be one even as we are one, I in them and you in me, that they may become perfectly one" (17:22). Certainly, Jesus goes to the Father, and where he goes they cannot come now, but "you shall follow afterwards" (13:36). They cannot worship the Father seeing his face directly, but Jesus goes to prepare the *hekhaloth* within the heavenly temple for them (14:2). Jesus is absent from the *kosmos*, yet the Paraclete is present and makes Jesus present, and Jesus is, after all, the Logos of God, the knowable, communicable presence of God who was with the Father from the beginning, before creation. It is a question of emphasis. What is it that John's community is promised in the Gospel: presence or absence? the possibility of experiencing the presence and glory of God in his Word now or the impossibility of direct mystical experience?

It seems to me that the primary possibility opened up by John is not absence but presence, not silence but Word, not a closed heaven but an open heaven: "where I am, there shall my servant be also" (12:26). It is, of course, paradoxical and hedged around with qualifications, for obvious reasons, but the possibility of experiencing the divine presence is affirmed in the Word. In what follows, I will sketch the outlines of my understanding, which has been substantiated already in more depth in other papers (Draper 1993; 1997; 2000; 2003b). The identification of Jesus with the divine *logos* of Greek philosophy is an act of *bricolage* that serves as a hermeneutical key to counter the emphasis on text and only text, legitimating control, and to some extent also empire, which was represented by the newly dominant scribal elite after the destruction of the temple. The *logos* is not only a device for opening the Scripture to new interpretation but also the device for continuing revelation. While it is true that the sayings of Jesus abound in John's Gospel, they are not, on the whole, the sayings of the primitive Jesus tradition. These form the nucleus of the wealth of the words of Jesus in the text, to be sure, but only the nucleus. The Gospel abounds with Jesus speaking directly to the community in long discourses. This is well known. The author(s) of the Gospel can continue to hear the voice of the living Jesus and report it to his community.

The particular focus of this essay is provided by John 5:37–39, where the text asserts that the "Jews," by which I understand the authorities in Judea rather than an ethnic designation, have never heard the voice of God nor seen his form and do not have his word remaining in them, because they do not believe. The rhetorical force of this is that those who do believe do hear the voice of God and see his *eidos*—a radical claim indeed, but one already implicit in 1:18. It is no accident that the vision of God is linked with the presence of the word within the believer and the desire of the Judeans to "search the Scriptures" mentioned in 5:39. This essay explores the link between heavenly vision and ritual meditation on the "Scriptures" in John. Elsewhere I have argued for a link between the destruction of the temple, the presentation of Jesus as the wilderness tabernacle presence of God, and aspects of what comes to be called "merkabah" mysticism (Draper 1997; 2000; 2002; 2003). Here this theme is taken up again with a specific focus on the use of Scripture meditation to induce heavenly visions. The link between the word and heavenly vision established in John 5 is taken up in the presentation of Jesus as the "bread which comes down from heaven," which must be eaten to participate now in "eternal life." This, again, is linked with heavenly vision in the climactic, if enigmatic "What if then you should see the son of man ascending where he was before" in 6:62. Clearly the discussion in John 6 is central to the self-understanding of the Johannine community, since it provides the substance of its dispute with others who "stopped following him and no longer went about with him" in 6:66. Perhaps it was the claim of the Johannine community to direct access to the heavenly vision of God that was central to that dispute.

2. Two Powers in Heaven?

In his groundbreaking study of the "two powers in heaven" heresy[1] attacked by the rabbis, Alan Segal (1977) has concluded that the earliest

---

1 This term is used without prejudice as to their own perspective here, to denote their status in the eyes of the rabbis.

debate centered on interpretations of Scripture, and Exodus in particular, with respect to angelic mediator figures.

> It seems clear, then, that the synagogue and academies in Palestine were the locus of the debate and defense against "two powers." Exegesis was the earliest battleground of the conflict. Although the answers to the heretics were worked out by the academies, the question must have been raised in relation to Bible-reading and by groups who were interested in hearing the Jewish bible expounded. (Segal 1977:154)

In other words, this was largely an "inner-Jewish" dispute in origin, rather than a late external threat. Furthermore, Segal argues that the debate about the intermediary angel was very early, since the standard defense against the heresy, to emphasise the "two faces of God," namely, "justice" and "mercy" to explain his two appearances, was already current in the time of Rabbi Akiba and Rabbi Ishmael. Yet they use an argument that contradicts this principle.

> Whenever they developed, the basic traditions concerning the angelic figure are older than the time of R. Akiba and R. Ishmael because the rabbinic defense against the heresy contradicts the rabbinic doctrine of divine mercy and justice which was known to both of them. (151)

The conflict also shows that the rabbis lived in close contact with the "two powers" heretics in Palestine, since the debate slackened when the center of gravity for the rabbis moved to Bablylon (154).

While Segal points to several texts that were utilized in the struggle over this doctrine, the key ones seem to me to relate to the description of the mediation of the law, particularly Exod 20:20–22; 24:9-11; and 33:7-23. The profoundest contradiction is suggested by the flat denial of the possibility of theophany in 33:20: "But," he said, "you cannot see my face; for no one shall see me and live," when it is stated in 24:9–10, "Then Moses and Aaron, Nadab and Abihu, and seventy of the elders of Israel went up, and they saw the God of Israel." It seems from the research of Segal that some heretics solved the problem with the aid of Exod 23:20–21.

> I am going to send an angel in front of you, to guard you on the way and to bring you to the place that I have prepared. Be attentive to him and listen to his voice; do not rebel against him, for he will not pardon your transgression; for my name is in him.

The angel bearing the name of God mediates the presence of the Lord. The passage that follows assists in the ambiguity, since there is a fluctuation between the use of the first and third person for God, even within the same sentence (23:25): "You shall serve YHWH your God, and I will/he will bless your bread and water, and I will take sickness away from the midst of you." The Masoretic Text has וברך, while the Septuagint and Vulgate have εὐλογήσω and *benedicam* respectively. The latter allow the possibility that it is the name-bearing angel YHWH who shall be served, while it is God who blesses. The former also allows the possibility that the "he" and the "I" are two different figures. Since it is then said of the elders of Israel that "they saw the God of Israel" (ויראו את אלהי ישראל) and that, moreover, "they saw God and sat down and ate and drank" (ויחזו את־האלהים ויאכלו וישתו), the conundrum of the vision of the invisible God can be solved with recourse to the name-bearing angel. The "two powers" heresy is then able to generalize on this basis to explain all theophanies as mediated by the angel.

The rabbis oppose this on the basis of a rigid monotheism, while later also allowing that the Shekinah or Memrah of God is the subject of difficult passages. However, there is no doubt that this group of passages, so central to the covenantal faith of Israel, presents openings for speculation. There is no doubt, either, that an overly rigid transcendant monotheism presents problems for any understanding of the immanence of God. Segal and others (e.g., Borgen 1968; Rowland 1981; Fossum 1995a; 1995b; Hurtado; Gieschen) have shown the extent to which this problem and the angel-mediation solution played a role in Jewish thinking prior to John's Gospel and after it in the apostolic fathers.

3. The "Two Powers" and John's Gospel

John's Gospel enters into this controversy in the Prologue itself in the bold assertion of both halves of the conundrum: θεὸν οὐδεὶς ἑώρακεν πώποτε· μονογενὴς θεὸς ὁ ὢν εἰς τὸν κόλπον τοῦ πατρὸς ἐκεῖνος ἐξηγήσατο (1:18). No one can look on God and live, as Exod 33:20 declares, yet the vision of God is mediated by a second "God." A few late texts have μονογενὴς υἱός, but these are outweighed by the witness of P[66,75], ℵ, B, C*, and others, and μονογενὴς θεός is certainly the *lectio difficilior*. The invisible God is made known by the "only begotten" or "only coming into being" God.[2] This "only coming into being" God is identified by John as the Logos who was with God from the beginning and was God. While there is no doubt that John understood himself as a monotheist (since Jesus says, "I and my Father are one" [10:30]; see also 17:11, 22), his formulation seems to match fairly closely the profile of the "two powers" heretics

---

2 For a discussion of this word, see Büchsel; the meaning could be "unique," but "what John means by ὁ μονογενὴς υἱός in detail can be known in its full import only in the light of the whole of John's proclamation" (741).

attacked by the rabbis. It is interesting to note here that this statement is made in the context of a contrast between Moses and Jesus, in which the derived nature of the gift of the Torah (ὅτι ὁ νόμος διὰ Μωϋσέως ἐδόθη) is contrasted with the immediacy of the "grace and truth" that comes through Jesus Christ (ἐγένετο; 1:17). It seems as if the thinking of John's Gospel concerning the mediatorial role of Jesus is linked in the mind of the author with speculation on the exodus and the giving of the law. We know that there was a tradition concerning the intermediary role of an angel(s) in the giving of the law (e.g., Acts 7:34).

While John (the author, with no assumptions as to historical entity) uses the Greek word and concept of the Logos to explore the nature of the relationship between the unmediated and the mediated God, the concept of the name of God is already present in the Prologue also: ὅσοι δὲ ἔλαβον αὐτόν, ἔδωκεν αὐτοῖς ἐξουσίαν τέκνα θεοῦ γενέσθαι, τοῖς πιστεύουσιν εἰς τὸ ὄνομα αὐτοῦ (1:12). That this is not accidental, but contains many of the features of the name-bearing angel as mediator, is shown in the use of "name" in 12:28 (πάτερ, δόξασόν σου τὸ ὄνομα. ἦλθεν οὖν φωνὴ ἐκ τοῦ οὐρανοῦ, Καὶ ἐδόξασα καὶ πάλιν δοξάσω) and 17:6 (Ἐφανέρωσά σου τὸ ὄνομα τοῖς ἀνθρώποις οὓς ἔδωκάς μοι ἐκ τοῦ κόσμου. σοὶ ἦσαν κἀμοὶ αὐτοὺς ἔδωκας καὶ τὸν λόγον σου τετήρηκαν; see also 2:23; 3:18; 5:43; 10:25; 14:13–14, 26; 15:16, 21; 16:23–26; 17:11–12, 26; 20:31). This has been explored in more detail by Jarl Fossum (1995a). Charles Gieschen (70–78, 271–80) points to the close relationship between *name* and *glory* in the angelomorphic mediator tradition of Judaism and argues that the concept Word may have its roots in the same kind of hypostatic tradition that lies behind the rabbinic use of *memra YHWH*. However, it seems to me that John's development of this tradition is aware of, and draws extensively on, the hermeneutical possibilities of the Greek philosophical tradition of the Logos, in a way similar to, but independent of, Philo of Alexandria (see Borgen 1968). This enables John to link creation, theophany in the history of Israel and in Jesus, without relaxing his insistence on the unity of God, since the idea of mind and its expression in thought/word permit an ontological unity that the angelomorphic tradition by itself does not.

I have argued elsewhere (1993; 1997; 2000; 2003b) that John's Gospel interprets the Hebrew Scriptures in a targumic way. By this I do not mean that *Targum Jonathan* was extant at the time of John or that he himself knew it. Rather, I mean that John works with the Hebrew text and exploits the problems of translation and the semantic potential of words no longer properly understood in terms of Aramaic concepts and cognates. He may also be in touch with traditions of interpretation and with textual variants that allow him to reread the "dead text" in a creative fashion. Although John does quote the Hebrew Scriptures directly from time to time, his text is not that of the Septuagint. Moreover, his indirect use of the Scriptures shows even more that he is using the Hebrew text (e.g., 1:51, on which see Odeberg: 33–40; Rowland 1984:498–507; Fossum 1995b). John may write in Greek, but he thinks in Aramaic.

4. JOHN 5:37–47

In the context of the dispute with Judean authorities over the healing of the paralyzed man on the Sabbath at the pool of Bethzatha, Jesus asserts that his work is the work of the Father (5:17), a charge that they understand to be blasphemous (ἴσον ἑαυτὸν ποιῶν τῷ θεῷ) and therefore punishable by death. Jesus' response is that he does only what he is shown by the Father (5:20) and, indeed, that the works he does are the testimony of the Father to his identity. He does not need human testimony, not even that of John the Baptist, important as it was from a human point of view (5:33–34), since the works he does shows that the Father has sent him (αὐτὰ τὰ ἔργα ἃ ποιῶ μαρτυρεῖ περὶ ἐμοῦ ὅτι ὁ πατήρ με ἀπέσταλκεν; 5:36). All of this is somewhat puzzling, since John speaks as if he is referring to a proof text, "and the Father who sent me has himself borne witness to me" (5:37), even though there is no obvious reference. It is also not immediately clear what the connection is between this and the assertion that it is Moses who will accuse them of unbelief since he wrote about him (5:45–47). However, it is clearly linked to the Johannine version of the feeding of the five thousand that follows in John 6, since there, too, the story turns on Moses and the exegesis of accounts of the wilderness period. I would like to argue that there is a very specific tradition lying behind this argument and that it is precisely the kind of "two powers" speculation on Exodus identified by Segal that lies behind this passage in John.

The passage in John 5:36–47 is tightly structured into three units, each in turn structured into three sections.

1.
1α ἐγὼ δὲ ἔχω τὴν μαρτυρίαν μείζω τοῦ Ἰωάννου·
    τὰ γὰρ ἔργα ἃ δέδωκέν μοι ὁ πατὴρ
      ἵνα τελειώσω αὐτά,
    αὐτὰ τὰ ἔργα ἃ ποιῶ μαρτυρεῖ περὶ ἐμοῦ
      ὅτι ὁ πατήρ με ἀπέσταλκεν·
1β καὶ ὁ πέμψας με πατὴρ
    ἐκεῖνος μεμαρτύρηκεν περὶ ἐμοῦ.
    οὔτε φωνὴν αὐτοῦ πώποτε ἀκηκόατε
    οὔτε εἶδος αὐτοῦ ἑωράκατε,
      καὶ <u>τὸν λόγον αὐτοῦ</u> οὐκ ἔχετε ἐν ὑμῖν μένοντα,

ὅτι ὃν ἀπέστειλεν ἐκεῖνος,
   τούτῳ ὑμεῖς οὐ πιστεύετε.
1γ ἐραυνᾶτε τὰς γραφάς,
   ὅτι ὑμεῖς δοκεῖτε
     ἐν αὐταῖς ζωὴν αἰώνιον ἔχειν·
   καὶ ἐκεῖναί εἰσιν αἱ μαρτυροῦσαι περὶ ἐμοῦ·
   καὶ οὐ θέλετε ἐλθεῖν πρός με
     ἵνα ζωὴν ἔχητε.
2.
2α Δόξαν παρὰ ἀνθρώπων οὐ λαμβάνω,
   ἀλλὰ ἔγνωκα ὑμᾶς
     ὅτι τὴν ἀγάπην τοῦ θεοῦ οὐκ ἔχετε ἐν ἑαυτοῖς.
2β ἐγὼ ἐλήλυθα ἐν τῷ ὀνόματι τοῦ πατρός μου,
   καὶ οὐ λαμβάνετέ με·
   ἐὰν ἄλλος ἔλθῃ ἐν τῷ ὀνόματι τῷ ἰδίῳ,
     ἐκεῖνον λήμψεσθε.
2γ πῶς δύνασθε ὑμεῖς πιστεῦσαι
   δόξαν παρὰ ἀλλήλων λαμβάνοντες,
     καὶ τὴν δόξαν τὴν παρὰ τοῦ μόνου θεοῦ οὐ ζητεῖτε;
3.
3α μὴ δοκεῖτε
   ὅτι ἐγὼ κατηγορήσω ὑμῶν πρὸς τὸν πατέρα·
     ἔστιν ὁ κατηγορῶν ὑμῶν Μωϋσῆς,
     εἰς ὃν ὑμεῖς ἠλπίκατε.
3β εἰ γὰρ ἐπιστεύετε Μωϋσεῖ,
   ἐπιστεύετε ἂν ἐμοί·
     περὶ γὰρ ἐμοῦ ἐκεῖνος ἔγραψεν.
3γ εἰ δὲ τοῖς ἐκείνου γράμμασιν οὐ πιστεύετε,
   πῶς τοῖς ἐμοῖς ῥήμασιν πιστεύσετε;

From a rhetorical point of view, the text sets up a set of oppositions between text and word in (1) and (2), which is connected also with Jesus' identity and the possibility of knowing God. The refusal of the Judean authorities (Ἰουδαῖοι; see Draper 2000) to receive Jesus, the one sent by the Father, means that they do not have "his [the Father's] word" (τὸν λόγον αὐτοῦ), also linked with the "love of God," abiding in them. Instead, they "search the Scriptures thinking to have eternal life in them." Moses wrote about Jesus, so that failure to believe in Jesus means that they do not believe the Scriptures and so do not believe Jesus' "words" (τοῖς ἐμοῖς ῥήμασιν). In other words, the Scripture as text to be searched is ambiguous, in that it speaks of Jesus but does not in itself mediate "life" (ζωή αἰώνιον). Life can be obtained only by "coming to Jesus" or "believing in him." Therefore "text" also brings condemnation (κατηγορήσω) to those who read it and do not see that it points to Jesus, while "word" abiding in the one who makes an act of faith in Jesus (πιστεύετε) gives life (ζωή).

This set of oppositions between text and word is matched by another set of oppositions in the central section (2) between receiving glory from humans by coming with one's own name and seeking the glory that is from the only one of God (τὴν δόξαν τὴν παρὰ τοῦ μόνου θεοῦ) who comes with the name of the Father (ἐν τῷ ὀνόματι τοῦ πατρός).[3] An implicit link between the two sets of oppositions would imply that "searching the Scriptures" to seek life is linked with coming in one's own name and receiving glory from one another, while "having the word abiding in one-self" is linked with believing the only one of God who comes with the name of the Father and reveals the glory that is from the only one of God. This set of oppositions underscores the conflict between Jesus and the Judean authorities, but it is not an absolute opposition, since the Scriptures do point to Jesus: Moses does write about Jesus. If they were to search the Scriptures with faith they would find life! There is no opposition between Jesus and Moses, but the relationship is that of witness to that of the thing witnessed to. Again, this is a theme from the Prologue already, where there is no adversative construction and no negative relating to Moses: "Because the law was given through Moses: grace and truth came into being through Jesus Christ" (1:17).[4]

I suggest that the opposition between text and word, which we have noted, relates to a different way of using the Hebrew Scriptures. The opposition is between "searching the Scriptures" as a means of settling disputes in the manner of halakah and internalizing the Scriptures through meditation until they become "Word abiding in you," a mystical way of practicing the presence of the Word, of knowing the Unknowable God through the one he has sent. In this process, Jesus as the one bearing the name of God in himself is recognized as the one behind the revelatory words of Scripture. From the creation of the world through the Word spoken by the Father (יְהִי אוֹר), the Word has been shining in the darkness and the darkness has never prevailed against it (καὶ τὸ φῶς ἐν τῇ σκοτίᾳ φαίνει, καὶ ἡ σκοτία αὐτὸ οὐ κατέλαβεν). It is this continuing presence of the Word in the world from creation that makes all theophany in the Scriptures (and elsewhere potentially) christophany.

---

3 Here the Greek word ἐν is taken in the instrumental sense "with" to signal that he is bearing the divine Name within him, rather than "in," signaling that he is a representative.

4 A few manuscripts (P[66] (W[s]) it sy[h**] bo) do insert δέ, but these must be regarded as attempts to smooth the text and introduce the usual opposition between law and grace found in Paul.

The reference to Jesus as the one who comes "with the name of the Father," taking the instrumental sense of ἐν, seems to be clearly linked to concepts of Jesus as the name-bearing angel, as several scholars have already seen (Rowland; Gieschen; Ashton). Most significant is the possibility opened up by its negation in 5:36, as many have observed:

> You have neither heard his voice ever,
> Nor have you ever seen his appearance,
> And you do not have his word abiding in you
> Because you have not believed in the one whom he [God] sent.

The Judean authorities do not hear and see, but the possibility of hearing the voice and seeing the form of God is affirmed, provided that one believes in the one whom God sends. In other words, Jesus is portrayed as the intermediary between God and human beings. The premise is set out in the Prologue to the Gospel in 1:18:

> No one has ever seen God ever:
> The only coming-into-being God
> Who was in the bosom of the Father,
> He has made him known.

The background to this conception lies in Exod 33:20, where God refuses to allow Moses to see him directly: "No human being shall see me and live." Yet God's "face" or "presence" (פנים) will go with Moses and give him rest (33:14); God's glory and goodness passes before Moses, and God pronounces his name (33:18–19). Moses is allowed to see the back but not the full glory of God directly (33:23). The text seems to demand an intermediary figure. This theme is, as we have seen, already present in the Prologue, where the Logos made flesh in Jesus mediates the glory of the only coming-into-being God in 1:14 (καὶ ἐθεασάμεθα τὴν δόξαν αὐτοῦ, δόξαν ὡς μονογενοῦς παρὰ πατρός, πλήρης χάριτος καὶ ἀληθείας).

So Jesus as the intermediary angel makes God known to Moses and also makes it possible to see the glory and presence of God for the believer now. Gieschen takes the primary reference here to be to Exod 3, the appearance of the Angel of YHWH in the burning bush. However, it seems that this section of John needs to be taken as a more specific reference to Exod 23:21, one of the central passages in the development of angel christology, which the rabbis came to call the "two powers" heresy. John Ashton concludes his study of the angelic mediator figure in the Hebrew Scriptures:

> The ambiguity and oscillation between Yahweh and his angel that is found elsewhere in Exodus, as in Genesis, Numbers, and Judges,

appears in Exod. 23:20 in an especially direct and dangerous form. When adapting or commenting upon this passage, however, later Jewish authors, starting with LXX, do their best to conceal the indiscretion, not wishing to leave room for an angel figure who, credited with an independent existence, might be thought to be related to Yahweh not as an ally or amanuensis but as a rival. (Ashton 1994a:80).

5. Exodus 23:20–22

(20) הנה אנכי שלח מלאך לפניך לשמרך בדרך ולהביאך אל המקום
אשר הכנתי (21) השמר מפניו ושמע בקלו אל תמר בו כי בקלו אל תמר
בו כי לא ישא לפשעכם כי שמי בקרבו (22) כי אם שמע תשמע בקלו
ועשית כל אשר אדבר ואיבתי את איביך וצרתי את צרריך

Several features of this passage are very suggestive as the background to John 5:37. In the first place, here the one writing may be assumed to be Moses (from the perspective of a first-century Judean), but the speaker is God. God testifies that he is sending his angel before the people of Israel. Hence Jesus can say that he has a μαρτυρία greater than John, namely, the works the Father has given him to do, and, indeed, the Father himself testifies on his behalf (καὶ ὁ πέμψας με πατὴρ ἐκεῖνος μεμαρτύρηκεν περὶ ἐμοῦ). Second, the Exodus passage instructs the people of Israel to "observe his face" and "hear his voice" and not to rebel against him. Jesus argues that the Judean authorities have never heard God's voice or seen his appearance because they do not believe the one whom he has sent. So the element of judgment is implied here, and this taken up also in the warning of Exodus: If the people of Israel do not heed the Angel of the Lord, he will not forgive their trespass (לא ישא לפשעכם). This is why the theme of judgment emerges in the Johannine text in section 3. It is not Jesus who accuses before the Father, but Moses. The warning stands there in what he has written concerning the Angel of the Lord. If they believed in these words of Moses, then they would also believe in the one of whom Moses writes.

Key to the whole picture is the description of the angel as bearing the name of God not just "upon himself" but within himself (בקרבו). John describes Jesus as having come "with/in (ἐν) the name of my Father." He represents the Father, he is one with the Father, through the agency of the name. Therefore he also bears the glory of the Father, and yet the authorities are not willing to seek the glory of God in the face of his angel. Bearing the name is synonymous with being the glory of the Father. "He who has seen me has seen the Father." Instead, the authorities are accused of coming in their own name and seeking glory from one another. I wonder to what extent the rabbinic formula, which is common later on, in which the rabbis give their judgments on the Torah in their own name or in the name of another rabbi, lies behind this idea. Then the picture is one where the formula "Rabbi so and so said in the name of rabbi so and so" is contrasted with I am come in "the name of the Father." You accept one another's names and glorify each other but refuse to seek the name and glory of the Father.

6. The Link between John 5 and 6

It is surely more than coincidence, if this background of the Angel of the Lord in Exod 23 lies behind John 5, that John 6 takes up the theme of the bread from heaven and the manna of Moses. There is another one of the cruces for "two powers" speculation in 23:25, since the subject switches between third and first person:

ועבדתם את יהוה אלהיכם וברך את לחמך ואת מימיך והסרתי מחלה מקרבך

"You shall serve the Lord your God and he will bless your bread and your water, and I will take the sickness away from the midst of you." The Septuagint and Vulgate have "I will bless," but either way the text is open to the kind of interpretation favored by the advocates of angel mediation between God and humankind. The person blessing is different from the "I" representing the voice of God. The person blessing is the Angel of the Lord. "Who gave the bread from heaven?" asks John in 6:32, "It was not Moses who has given you the bread from heaven, but my Father gives you the true bread from heaven." Of course, there are other themes running through this complex and rich discussion of Jesus as the bread of life, but speculation on the Angel of the Lord in Exod 23 would already have suggested the theme.

7. John 14:1-4

Another suggestive parallel to the text of Exod 23:20 is offered by the promise of Jesus that he will go to prepare a place. The language is particularly close. In John 14:1 God and Jesus are set side by side as "two powers" who are really one: "Believe in God and believe also in me." Then the task of the Angel of the Lord matches that of Jesus, "I go to prepare a place for you." The use of the Greek word τόπος, which is otherwise puzzling, is explained on this reading by the underlying reference to the Hebrew המקום. The Angel of the Lord will "bring you to the place that I have prepared" (ולהביאך אל המקום אשר הכנתי). Jesus suggests that they know the way he is going (καὶ ὅπου [ἐγὼ] ὑπάγω οἴδατε τὴν ὁδόν), something that Thomas doubts. Of course, the major task of Jesus as Angel of the Lord is to keep the people of Israel "on the way" (לשמרך בדרך), so that this theme is present in the Exodus account also. John develops it characteristically, so that Jesus is the way, the truth, and the life, the only way to the Father. Since Jesus is the Angel of the Name, he also reflects the image and glory of the Father who sent him. The person who knows and sees Jesus has known and seen the Father (14:7). So Philip is out of order in asking Jesus to show them the Father, since "The one who has seen me has seen the Father." There is no difference between the one sending and the one sent (the identity of agency).

8. CONCLUSION

John seldom quotes Scriptures as γραφή, either as citation or proof text. I make the tally eleven direct references, and several of these are problematic. When he does quote Scripture, the text is not that of the Septuagint; indeed, Günter Reim (188–89) has characterized his use as "astonishingly inaccurate." Yet the Gospel is everywhere saturated with Scripture in an indirect form, such as, for instance, the notorious promise of Jesus to Nathaniel that "you will see the heavens opened and the angels of God going up and coming down upon the Son of Man" in 1:51. Interpretation of the passages concerned really depends on the metanymic referencing of the underlying scriptural passages, using the terminology of John Miles Foley (1991). It depends on long traditions of debate over the interpretation of the Hebrew Scripture, which can still be traced in the rabbinic writings (in this case see Borgen 1968:145–46; Rowland 1984:498–502; Fossum 1995b). The seed falling in the ground as a sign for the return of the diaspora of the "Greeks," for instance, depends on an interpretation of Isa 6:13 that can be found also in the Targum of Isaiah (Draper 2000). The reference to the angels at the head and feet of Jesus in the tomb depends on an interpretation of the theophany in Isa 6:1 (Draper 2003b). Reim suggests that this way of referring to the Hebrew Scriptures is the result of "lack of acquaintance with the written text of the Old Testament in the composition of the Gospel," but this seems unlikely, given the skilled nature of the appropriation of the texts, which utilizes known interpretive trajectories.

Rather, the "inaccurate references" are the result of a particular use of the Scriptures, in which the Word is believed to underlie the words at every point. If the Scriptures are the revelation of the presence of God in the history of Israel, then they are the revelation of the Word coming from the Father creating, sustaining, and revealing itself. God is at every point only known or seen through the one who bears his name and mediates his presence and glory. Ritual meditation on Scripture and its internalization is the means by which God's glory and presence are realized. The appropriation of the Word in the words is the way to the Father, the way the Father is known, the means of experiencing the mystical ascent to the throne of glory.

RESPONSES

Rabbinic Oral Tradition in Late Byzantine Galilee: Christian Empire and Rabbinic Ideological Resistance

Martin S. Jaffee
University of Washington

Professor Draper, in his introduction to this collection, has already spelled out ways in which each essay contributes its own distinctive angle of entry into the cluster of issues regarding oral tradition, writing, and the promulgation of or resistance to colonialist political structures. So there is no need here of an "afterword" that situates the various contributions. Accordingly, the present essay, commissioned specifically as a "response from the perspective of rabbinic oral-traditional studies," is somewhat selective in its focus. I shall not attempt to respond even broadly to each author. Rather, my plan is to isolate parts of several essays that, in my view, do demand a specific and immediate response "from the perspective of rabbinic oral-traditional studies." Response is called for in the present context either because a particular essay in this collection appears to me to have an immediate potential to advance work in rabbinic oral-traditional studies or because, at least from where I situate myself as an onlooker, work in rabbinic oral-traditional studies might suggest other approaches to the material discussed by several essays. So, in recognition that the study of oral-traditional literature in the political context of colonialism is a paradigm in the process of construction,[1] I note those areas that appear most immediately relevant to problems in my own field or those in which contributions from my own area of inquiry might be most immediately useful in grasping some broader issues currently under exploration. Thus, first of all, I take up John Miles Foley's definitions of the spectrum of oral-traditional literature in order to test their application to classical rabbinic sources. Second, I engage the essays of Richard Horsley and Werner Kelber in an effort to clarify ways in

---

1 See, for example, *Journal of the American Academy of Religion* 71:1 (2003), which devotes a number of essays to the theme of "Religion and Empire."

which we might think about the relation of rabbinic ideas of oral tradition and the writings associated with them to the larger political context of Judaism in Second Temple through Byzantine times.

The Rabbinic Text as a "Voice from the Past"

It was largely through the early work of John Miles Foley on oral literature that I began to see new ways of approaching the question of the orality of rabbinic literary tradition. So it gives me enormous pleasure to report that I have found his contribution to the present collection most stimulating for my own thinking. One of the puzzles that attracted me to an "oralist" hermeneutic of rabbinic literature was the paradoxical fact that the surviving literature of rabbinic antiquity—numbering into many thousands of manuscript pages—is identified in rabbinic culture as oral tradition and is classified in rabbinic legal and hermeneutic thought as "Oral Torah" (Jaffee 1999). The ideological issues surrounding the representation of rabbinic writing as an orally transmitted tradition and Oral Torah—in contrast to the biblical canon of "Written Torah"—shall be taken up later in relation to other contributors to this volume. But for now what interests me is the way in which Foley's construct of a "spectrum of oral poetry" helps to situate the particulars of rabbinic literary productivity within a cross-cultural comparative setting.

Prior to Foley's work, many scholars of rabbinic literature had recognized that the formulaic style of much rabbinic literature indicates a mnemonic system designed to facilitate memorization of the texts for oral performance (e.g., Gerhardsson; Neusner 1987; Zlotnick). But most have assumed that such mnemonic systems were responsible for the composition of the precise texts before us, which could then be read as written "recordings," so to speak, of the original "oral performances" or "oral publications" of the texts. In this view, the texts we have were composed for oral-performative transmission, and the texts we have are the substance of the oral performance. What is now written down is what was once memorized without reference to writing. There is, so to speak, a kind of one-to-one correlation of the surviving text with the oral tradition it reflects.

Foley's construction of a "spectrum of oral poetry" should help students of rabbinic oral-traditional literature to refine this view and to explore concrete strategies for "reading orality" in the various compilations of rabbinic legal, exegetical, and narrative tradition. Similar to such staples of oral-traditional studies as the *Odyssey, Beowulf,* or the *Song of Roland,* rabbinic literature betrays broad hints of origins in oral-performative settings yet survives in a written form that deeply transforms the oral remnants and reframes them. Once the manuscript copies are received as "authentic" embodiments of the tradition—especially within the "native" communities who received and transmitted the texts as part of their own cultural heritage, but even to a significant degree within the "scientific" communities of textual and literary scholarship—these texts became themselves the subject of memorization and oral performance. But the reoralized manuscript text is a rather different oral-performative event than the scribal representation of the oral-performative tradition[2] that yields the earliest manuscripts in the first place. This, I take it, is one of the principle hermeneutical challenges and opportunities presented to scholars by those texts that Foley has designated as "voices from the past." As cultural icons that "monumentalize" the tradition, they obscure as much of the oral culture behind them as they disclose. The hermeneutical task for the contemporary scholar is to develop programs of "reading" these texts that keep open the wide range of compositional/performative possibilities that may have yielded these versions before us, to somehow train the reading eye to see behind the frozen texts' patterns of motion that were at one point perceptible also to the ears of living audiences.

Rabbinic Judaism is, from a textual point of view, a culture that specializes in the production of textual "voices from the past." Certainly its Scripture—the Hebrew Bible—is a classic example of living tradition received as a "voice from the past" that still speaks. But this the rabbinic sages of the early centuries of the Common Era had already received from earlier Judaic civilization in Second Temple period Palestine. In the vast body of rabbinic oral traditions, however, which cohered over the first millennium C.E. into a remarkable collection of textual compilations, the rabbinic sages produced their own body of texts that came to be received by the inheritors of rabbinic tradition as "voices from the past" as well. What follows is an illustration of how recognition of the oral-performative dimension of written rabbinic "voices from the past" can help to identify both the oral-traditional substrate of written texts as well as the likely contributions of scribal formulations and editorial interventions in their creation.

The first two selections are from separate tractates of the Mishnah, usually regarded as the earliest compilation of rabbinic tradition, stemming from the first half of the third century C.E. (Stemberger 1995a: 133–40).[3] Mishnah Tractate *Avot* as a whole is best characterized as a collection

---

2 For my usage of the term "oral-performative tradition," see Jaffee 2001:8: "the sum of performative strategies through which the oral-literary tradition is summoned from memory and delivered in diverse public settings."

3 Mishnaic texts are cited from the edition of Albeck.

of rabbinic wisdom sayings,[4] and 5:1 in particular introduces a subcollection of material (5:1–15) organized around the mnemonic principle of number ("With ten Divine Utterances...," "With ten trials was Abraham tested...," "There are seven traits of the clod and seven of the Sage...," "There are four types of human character," etc.) The second selection, from Mishnah Tractate *Sanhedrin* 4:5, is extracted from a tractate on judicial procedure. It represents the charge given by a judge to witnesses in a capital case, reminding them of the consequences for posterity of their testimony. These passages have nothing in particular to do with each other. However, as shall become clear, the third passage before us preserves the record of how at least one rabbinic composer of traditions heard them as deeply intermeshed. This third passage is extracted from *Avot d'Rabbi Natan* (hereafter *ARN*), a postmishnaic compilation of rabbinic traditions, edited perhaps as late as the sixth century, that broadly follows the plan of Mishnah *Avot* and now serves as a sort of companion to it (Lerner 1987b). Two recensions of *ARN* survive: Version A and Version B. The selection below is from Version A, chapter 31.[5]

Readers will notice rather quickly the very obvious fact that the composition of *ARN* appears to coordinate materials known already from the mishnaic passages. This fact is highlighted in the translation by distinct typefaces. Italicized type indicates material shared almost verbatim in Mishnah *Avot* and *ARN*. Bold type indicates material shared almost verbatim in Mishnah *Sanhedrin* and *ARN*. Passages in plain type are unique to the compositions in which the larger passages are found. Here, then, are the texts.

MISHNAH *AVOT* 5:1
With ten Divine Utterances was the world created.
And what does the Scriptural Teaching [of Gen 1:1ff.] propose? Could it not have been created by a single Utterance?
Rather, this is to punish the wicked *who destroy a world that was created by 10 Divine Utterances,* and to grant a good reward to the righteous *who sustain a world that was created by 10 Divine Utterances.*

According to the earliest rabbinic exegetical traditions, the "ten utterances" are the various formulations of "and God said" that can be found

---

[4] Mishnah *Avot* is generally described as having been redacted somewhat later than the rest of the Mishnah and to have been included in the mishnaic "canon" rather informally (Lerner 1987a).

[5] Text cited from edition of Schechter. I have discussed this passage at greater length in "What Difference Does the Orality of Rabbinic Writing Make for the Interpretation of Rabbinic Writings." That essay will appear in Krauss.

in the Genesis creation account (see *ARN* B:36, paralleled in *Midrash Genesis Rabbah* 17:1). The opening line of the Mishnah thematizes this textual fact into a proposition about the intentions of the Creator, while the response turns it into a puzzle: Why couldn't God have created the world with one utterance? The answer to the question makes the point: the fact that no fewer than ten acts of divine speech were invested in creation increases the preciousness of the world—enabling God to enhance the reward of those whose acts sustain creation and to increase the punishment of those whose acts diminish creation.

MISHNAH *SANHEDRIN* 4:5
Civil suits are not comparable to capital crimes, for in civil suits a person renders his money and he is absolved, while in capital crimes, his blood and the blood of his offspring hang in the balance until the end of the world.
For so do we find regarding Cain who killed his brother, since it is said: "your brother's bloods cry out." (Gen 4:10) It does not say "your brother's blood," but rather "bloods"—that is, his blood and the blood of his offspring....
For this reason Adam was created as a single individual, in order to teach you that **anyone who destroys a single[6] life is acknowledged by Scripture as one who destroyed an entire world; and anyone who saves a single life is acknowledged by Scripture as one who saved an entire world.**
And, furthermore, for the sake of peace among people, so that no one will say to his neighbor, "My father is greater than yours."
And also to testify to the greatness of the Blessed Holy One, for a person can stamp many coins with a single mold, and each is identical to the next, but the King of Kings of Kings, the Blessed Holy One, stamps each person with the mold of the original Adam, but none of them is identical.
For this reason, each and every person must say: "for me was the world created!"

The Mishnah's judges are reminding the witnesses that when an innocent person is executed, the result is to cut off not only that life but all lives that the victim might have spawned. The thought is demonstrated exegetically by recalling the odd locution of Gen 4:10, which, indeed, does refer to the "bloods" (Hebrew *damim*) of Abel. The point yields a second regarding the larger purpose behind the biblical depiction of the creation of humanity through a single prototype: a single human life is

---

6 I follow here the text of the Kaufman manuscript of the Mishnah, for reasons that I discuss momentarily.

equivalent to an entire cosmos, just as the entirety of the human race was contained in its single forebear. This explanation of the singularity of the human creature, appropriate to the theme of the value of even the accused murderer's life, is now extended to a new topic: from the singularity of Adam we learn also about the equality of nations and the uniqueness of every human individual. In all, this is as elegant a piece of theology as one finds anywhere in the Mishnah. It is, indeed worthy of being included in Mishnah *Avot*, the most theologically oriented of all mishnaic compilations.

And that is precisely what the scribal tradent behind *ARN* A:31 seems to have concluded as well.

AVOT D'RABBI NATAN A:31
With ten Divine Utterances was the world created.
Now, why do the world's inhabitants need to know this? Rather, this is to teach you that one who performs a single commandment, or one who observes a single Sabbath, or one **who saves a single [Jewish][7] life is acknowledged by Scripture as if one who saved the entire world** *that had been created with ten Divine Utterances.*
And one who commits a single transgression, or one who desecrates a single Sabbath,
Or one **who destroys a single [Jewish] life is acknowledged by Scripture as one who destroyed the entire world** *that had been created with ten Divine Utterances.*
For thus have we found regarding Cain who murdered Abel his brother, as it is said: "The voice of your brother's bloods cries out to me!" (Gen 4:10)
He spilled one blood, but many bloods are spoken of here.
Rather, this teaches that the blood of his children, his grandchildren, his great grandchildren, and all his descendants until the end of all generations that would have proceeded from him, all of them arose and cried out to the Blessed Holy One.
Thus you learn that a single person is as valuable as the entirety of Creation!

---

[7] The word "Jewish" (*miyisrael*) does not appear in the first edition of *ARN*. Shechter includes it in his edition in brackets on the basis of manuscript readings. As I explain momentarily, and as Schechter argues, this reading seems correct for the tradition reflected in *ARN*. A comprehensive study of the textual history of this passage was offered in 1961 by Ephraim E. Urbach in a Hebrew article entitled, "Whoever Sustains a Single Life…: Textual Vicissitudes, the Impact of Censors, and the Matter of Printing." The article first appeared in the journal *Tarbiz* and has been reprinted in Urbach. On page 178 of the present essay I explore some of the implications of Urbach's discussion.

Before us is a remarkably clear example of how the rabbinic scribe/ composer behind *ARN* works with and transforms the elements of the inherited oral-performative literary tradition to create a new, yet utterly tradition-bound, articulation of its meaning. Mishnah *Avot*'s assertion about the "ten utterances," mobilized there as part of a discourse on reward and punishment, is now thoroughly rethought in light of Mishnah *Sanhedrin*'s charge to the witnesses about the uniqueness of human individuals. As in Mishnah *Avot*, the origin of the world in ten "divine utterances" is the ground for defining the preciousness of the world, but now, in *ARN*, those who sustain or destroy God's precious world are particularized. They are no longer simply the "righteous" or the "wicked." Rather, they are Jews, whose engagement with Scripture's covenantal commandments determine the fate of the world. The core of the creative synthesis of oral-traditional elements lies in the balanced pair: **one who saves/destroys a single [Jewish] life as acknowledged by Scripture as one who saved/destroyed the entire world** *that had been created with ten Divine Utterances.* From that point, the transmitter/composer moves backward to Mishnah *Avot*'s assertion that the world was created through ten divine utterances and forward to the celebration of the uniqueness of human life.

Let me reframe this observation in terms opened up by the suggestions of John Miles Foley regarding the ways in which we must explore the possible interplay of various registers of orality and inscription in that specific category of text that falls under the rubric "voices from the past." It is likely that the textual snippets represented in the above passages by italicized and boldface texts circulated as core oral-compositional elements analogous to the epithets so often noticed by students of oral-epic composition or *topoi* employed by rhetoricians and public speakers in Greco-Roman antiquity. They were the phrases and clichés that made up the thesaurus of "words" that could be deployed in the transmission of orally managed tradition. In the present settings in Mishnah *Avot* and Mishnah *Sanhedrin*, however, they have been set down in written texts. Each rendering of the *topoi* exemplifies one of many possible ways of deploying the orally managed material in the purpose of creating new discourses upon the received themes.

The text of *ARN* displays one such way. Few scholars doubt that by the late Byzantine period, during which *ARN* was probably edited, written texts of the Mishnah were in circulation. Yet, as we shall see later on in this discussion, the training of disciples required them to memorize the texts from orally transmitted versions. So the scribe/composer of *ARN* would have surely known these written versions, but his own appropriation of those versions reveals the aural and oral mastery of the text distinctive to the oral-performative tradition, mixing and matching diverse traditional elements of ten divine utterances and the uniqueness of Adam for new theological work.

As it happens, the innovative character of this work has had an important affect upon the representation of the very text that ARN receives as a "voice from the past." Attentive readers will have noticed that Mishnah *Sanhedrin*'s reference to a "single life" has been changed, in the manuscript versions of the *ARN*, to "a single Jewish life." This in itself makes sense in terms of the context of *ARN*, which equates sustaining of the world with the performance of commandments and the Sabbath, which are the particular responsibility of the Jews. It also signals an ethnocentric move in rabbinic thought away from the rather broad universalism of Mishnah *Sanhedrin* or even Mishnah *Avot*, with its generic reference to the righteous and the wicked.

At this point we are in a position to take account of a perplexing fact of the text produced in most printed texts of Mishnah *Sanhedrin*. Most versions *also* read: "one who saves/destroys a single Jewish life!" The classic ninteenth-century edition of the Mishnah and its major commentaries, produced by the Romm family of Vilna, preserves this reading. Yet it notes in its list of *variae lecciones* that this reading is attested neither in the Munich manuscript of the Babylonian Talmud, the Kaufman manuscript of the Mishnah, nor in Maimonides' twelfth-century quote from the text in his code of Jewish law (*Laws of the Sanhedrin* 12:3). The reading of the printed editions, moreover, is most infelicitous in the context of Mishnah *Sanhedrin* itself, which stresses the Adamic (that is pre-Judaic) origins of humanity. Obviously, the transmission of the text of Mishnah *Sanhedrin* as reflected in the printed editions has been inflected by the parallel in *ARN*, where the reference to "a Jewish life" is contextually almost a necessity.

It is not clear to me that *ARN*'s "particularist" appropriation of Mishnah Sanhedrin's "universalist" reference to the value of a single life is motivated by much other than the new context provided by *ARN*'s composer, in which the subject matter of observance of commandments clearly highlights the Jewishness of the life in question. Requiring explanation, however, is how *ARN*'s revision of Mishnah *Sanhedrin*'s oral-traditional text is then exported into manuscript and printed editions of that very Mishnah to yield the reading "single Jewish life." Recall that manuscript traditions up until the twelfth and thirteenth centuries preserve the "a single life" reading for Mishnah *Sanhedrin*, while the altered reading is attested thereafter in the manuscript traditions and into the age of print. These were centuries of desperation for much of European Jewry, marked by mass violence against Jews centered around a series of blood libels (extending from England in 1144 to Trent in 1475) and a string of communal expulsions: from England in 1290; from France in

1306, 1322, and 1394; and from Iberia in 1492–97. It is very likely in this historical-social setting that the "particularist" reading of *ARN* might have served as the inspiration for "correcting" the text of Mishnah *Sanhedrin* 4:5 in light of a reading well attested in *ARN*. The price of some subtle violence to the text of Mishnah *Sanhedrin* was worth bearing in an age in which many "single Jewish lives" were lost to the predations of hegemonic Christendom.

Surprisingly, our reflection upon some rabbinic "voices from the past" has highlighted the possibility that a situation of Christian political domination of the Jews in the High Middle Ages may be have occasioned at least one act of "textual resistance" in which a Jewish copyist, exploiting the malleability of scribal texts of Oral Torah, "corrected" his version of Mishnah *Sanhedrin* in light of a text known from *ARN*. This may, then, be a good moment for us to recall the obvious—that virtually the entire history of the textual tradition identified by the rabbinic sages as Oral Torah, from third-century Galilee to tenth-century Baghdad, was worked out under conditions of colonialist domination by a succession of imperial administrations. In the following we explore a second dimension of the impact of the colonial context upon rabbinic oral tradition. We shall focus, however, not on the issue of the transmission and composition of traditions but on the very way in which rabbinic communities constructed and inflected the concept of Oral Torah as an ideological model for oral-traditional texts that were also handed on in written copies.

PHARISEES, RABBINIC SAGES, AND THE POLITICS OF ORALITY

The essays of Richard Horsley and Werner Kelber demonstrate the extraordinary promise that a focus on various models of anticolonial resistance holds for a deeper grasp of what might be called the "political economy" of orality and writing. Horsley performs a great service in linking the Galilean origins of Christian tradition to the half-millenium of political jockeying in the Judean temple-state—among hegemonic empires, imperially sanctioned priestly establishments, and various (compliant and/or dissident) scribal communities—that enabled the production and circulation of what would become the "great tradition" of Israel's canon of Scripture. Horsley's depiction of the Galilean Jesus movement, as an assertion of the oral "little tradition" of Galilean peasants over against the literate scribal experts (including, but not exclusively, the Pharisees) who jockeyed for the political power to exert exegetical control over the "great tradition," is particularly helpful. It offers a vivid illustration of the way in which the cultivation of "oral tradition" can serve marginalized communities as a focus of resistance to political and social elites who control, as it were, the "means (and terms) of communication."

While Horsley's essay highlights the strategic role of the Galilean Jesus community's oral tradition against the background of the imperial politics of canonical scripturalization in Second Temple Palestine, Kelber's construction of the dynamics of scripturalization and oral tradition in Second Temple Judaism has a rather different focus. His concern is not so much to explain the function of early Christian oral tradition in the context of inner-Judaic responses to Roman imperialism; rather, he explores ways in which the background of power politics and literacy shaped ways in which Christian scribes chose to draw upon the early Christian oral tradition in order to "entrust their message to the scribal medium in view of Roman imperialism."

Both Horsley and Kelber, to a greater or lesser extent, mount their studies of early Christian oral tradition on the backs of rich depictions of the social and political contexts of orality and literacy in Second Temple Judaism. In my own studies of the background of rabbinic oral tradition, I have also had to make my own sense of this matter (Jaffee 2001:15–61). In doing so, I have reached conclusions that cohere rather more neatly with Horsley's picture of the role of oral tradition among the Pharisees in particular than with that offered by Kelber. That is to say, I suppose that virtually all Second Temple scribal communities must have had a variety of what I term orally mediated text-interpretive traditions[8] that accompanied written records of prophetic pronouncement (i.e., scriptural works and those competing for such authoritative status). Some of these, as Horsley proposes, would have surely stemmed from those aspects of "a wider range of Judahite/Israelite law and tradition" that, having been excluded from the imperially backed Persian-era version of the Torah of Moses, "continued to be cultivated orally, certainly among the peasantry and apparently even among (rival) priestly and scribal circles" (133). Others would have emerged in reflection upon the official Torah (in whatever textual state it might have embodied in any given era) that grounded the authority of various temple regimes under Persian, Seleucid, Hasmonean, and Roman hegemony. However, in the entire literature of Second Temple Judaism (if, as I believe we must, we read Josephus through the lens of Steve Mason's brilliant exegeses in Mason:230–43) I find no claim that the authority of these orally mediated traditions of interpretation is superior to or even in competition with that of the written prophetic book. That is to say, while orally mediated text-interpretive traditions surely governed what scribal readers understood their written prophetic works to mean, it did not occur to them to establish the authority

---

8 I define the meaning of this term as "a body of interpretive understandings that arise from multiple performances of a text (written or oral)" (Jaffee 2001:8).

of oral tradition per se as a sovereign source of hermeneutical insight or an independent normative tradition. Thus, when Second Temple scribal groups compete about the meaning of Torah (however the textual boundaries of this term might be defined), they appeal to *other* written texts as authoritative interpretive sources.

Horsley is admirably circumspect in defining the media in which the conflict of scribal interpretations was disseminated. In describing the competing interests of scribal groups associated with "the Sadducees, the Pharisees and the dissident priestly-scribal community at Qumran/the Essenes" (122), he is careful to point out that each group would have developed "a sense of their own authority associated directly with the official Scripture or associated with alternative revered traditions..., authority independent of their aristocratic rulers-patrons" (122). Note that he does not take a specific stand upon the medium associated with the dissemination of such traditions. Werner Kelber is rather more definite about the *medium* of such "alternative revered traditions" than is Horsley. Thus, in my view, he courts a certain degree of anachronism in his depiction of the nature of Pharisaic text-interpretive tradition in particular. To be sure, the burden of Kelber's essay is to explore early Christian textuality in the late first and early second centuries rather than to reconstruct the Second Temple setting of Judean scribalism. Nevertheless, it seems to me that certain representations of Pharisaic tradition in particular are no longer tenable and should be used with rather more hesitation than Kelber employs here.

Kelber introduces the Pharisees as challengers to the Sadducean priestly establishment of Jerusalem. This is a point with which no one would argue. However, Kelber goes on to characterize the scribal character of the first-century Pharisees and the relationship of their scribalism to their conceptions of tradition. I reproduce the most crucial characterizations here:

> [T]he Pharisees were known for their interest in and cultivation of the written word..., for the Pharisees infused the scroll with a sense of sacrality that exalted it to a point where it was viewed as something like a portable temple or even the promised land. When, therefore, in 70 C.E. the center of the temple went up in flames and the Pharisees—along with the Jesus people—turned out to be the principal survivors among the dissenting groups, they were already conditioned to conduct their religious and civic life apart from the temple.... In retrospect, therefore, we can see how the Pharisaic cultivation of the written word unwittingly prepared the people for a diasporic existence in the absence of the physical center.
>
> In contrast, and indeed opposition, to the Sadducees, the Pharisees additionally cultivated the spoken word, or the Oral Torah, as they called it.... In contrast to the Sadducean concept of the chirographically

rooted will of Yahweh, the Pharisaic embrace of the Oral Torah implied that divinity was not to be limited to a narrowly confined body of manuscripts. Hence, not only what was written down, but memorable sayings, ethical instructions, and notable stories enjoyed authoritative validity as they were placed on the same footing with a select group of scrolls. From the perspective of the Pharisees, therefore, the Oral Torah signified an ongoing revelation apart from and in addition to the scribal medium. From the perspective of the Sadducees, on the other hand, the privileging of oral tradition violated the Written Torah and, significantly, placed revelation outside of their control. In thus viewing ancient history as media history, we see how the seemingly esoteric quibble over the Oral Torah among Pharisees and Sadducees in effect constituted a power struggle over the control of the media. (136–37)

In light of the past twenty years or so of scholarship on the relation of Second Temple Pharisaism to the rabbinic communities whose earliest texts derive from the early third century, very little of Kelber's picture remains intact.[9] Indeed, one of the scholarly references cited by Kelber is quite clear that the attempt of earlier scholars to bestow upon the Pharisees credit for development of the characteristic rabbinic distinction between Written Torah (Scripture) and Oral Torah (rabbinic oral tradition stemming from Sinai) "sounds plausible, [but] the path by which it is reached is a combination of total trust in a very late rabbinic text with an enthusiasm for hypotheses. The method is very questionable from a scholarly point of view" (Stemberger 1995b:95).

I criticize my colleague, Werner Kelber, here at length for two reasons. First, his deserved stature in the study of early Christian oral tradition lends a certain credibility to his discussions of materials over which he has only a secondary control. Thus I would point scholars interested in the question of orality in Second Temple Pharisaism and other Judean groups to more up-to-date sources. But, more importantly, Kelber ascribes to the Pharisees an economy of written and oral tradition—and a theory of their status as complementary revelations—that is most properly the creation of third-fifth century C.E. Galilean rabbinic Judaism. So my complaint is not simply that Kelber offers a rather anachronistic account of Pharisaism, confusing later rabbinic ideologies of oral tradition with reports of Pharisaic cultivations of "ancestral traditions." More importantly, his account of Pharisaism obscures one of the key issues that

---

9 Compare, for example, the following cautious judgment of Hezser 2001:201, who is more sympathetic than I to Kelber's conception: "The notion of the Oral Torah was a relatively late rabbinic concept not used by the Essenes or the Pharisees before.... While the *concept* of the 'Oral Torah' was specifically rabbinic, its *function* seems to have been similar to the Pharisees' presentation of their own views as 'ancestral traditions.'"

animates the essays in this volume: the role of oral tradition and its inscription in the life of marginal communities responding to colonialist pressures. What I wish to point out is that the emergence of the ideas of Written Torah and Oral Torah in Judaism must, as Kelber supposes, be understood in the context of resistance to colonialism. However, the colonialism is not that of Second Temple Judea, in which scribal and priestly communities squabbled over scriptural verses in order to retain political authority that could only be legitimated by Rome. Rather, the colonialism at issue is that facing Galilean sages and their disciples during the century of transition of Rome to a formally Christian empire. So the route into understanding rabbinic oral tradition in the context of colonialism requires us to recall that, as much as Christianity emerges in resistance to colonialism, it later becomes an imperial power itself—with important consequences for the Judaism that would be shaped in part under Christian hegemony.

My thinking about the relationship of rabbinic ideas about oral tradition to the imperial contexts of Jewish existence has recently been stimulated by Seth Schwartz's provocative study of the transformations of Judean society and religion from roughly the late Second Temple period to the fall of Byzantium to Islam. Schwartz notes a remarkable, and previously under-appreciated, pattern of correlations between Roman imperial systems and expressions of collective Jewish identity within such systems:

> [A]ttempts to make sense of the remains of ancient Judaism must consider the effects of shifting types of imperial domination. The complex, loosely centralized but still basically unitary Jewish society that may be inferred from the artifacts of the last two hundred years of the Second Temple period was in part produced by a long history of imperial empowerment of Jewish leaders. The fragmentation characteristic of the Jewish remains of the high imperial period imply a profound but partial accommodation to direct Roman rule, hastened by the disastrous failures of the revolts of 66 and 132. The Jewish cultural explosion of late antiquity, which can be read from a revival of literary production and the emergence and diffusion of a distinctively Jewish art and archaeology, is in complex ways a response to the gradual christianization of the Roman Empire. (Schwartz: 291)

This is not the setting for an extended analysis of Schwartz's argument, based largely as it is upon readings of archeological evidence in particular. His point, however, is very important: in the centuries between the final destruction of the Judean temple-state and the Christian transformation of Roman Palestine, what had once been a vigorous national-religious Judean identity fell into precipitous decline. This decline was caused not by persecution per se but rather by the relative disinterest of the Roman imperium in the Jews themselves as a collectivity. With its formal political leadership and the center of its cultural traditions in total disarray, Jewish culture in the Greco-Roman world from the second through the early fourth centuries began to fragment into incoherence.

The post-Constantinian transformation of the empire into a formally Christian state, however, and especially the construction throughout Palestine of Christian pilgrimage sites that transformed the Palestinian landscape into a material mnemonic of Christian historical memory, served paradoxically as a spur to Jewish cultural memory and self-assertion as well. For now, in contrast to the situation under pagan Rome, Jews and Judaism became an official and crucial element in the cultural memory of the empire. Theologians designed theological strategies for interpreting the meaning of Judaism in the midst of a Christian empire, and emperors presided over legal codifications that would simultaneously protect and constrain the social and economic lives of Jews. Whereas Jews under pagan Rome had experienced large degrees of social and cultural integration into the communal, polyglot landscape, the emerging cultural and legal ethos of the empire was devoted to their isolation and marginalization.

In Schwartz's view, the Jewish response to this marginalization manifested itself primarily in an efflorescence of cultural activity surrounding the synagogue as a center of Jewish communal life, exemplified most importantly in the emergence of a consistent iconographic language in synagogue art, a liturgical poetic tradition, and a focus on the local community as a center of religious identity (Schwartz: 240–74). Jewish responses to Christian Rome's renewed focus upon Judaism, and to Rome's desire to limit the ability of Judaism to appeal to Christian subjects of the empire, was to retrieve and transform elements of Jewish social and cultural cohesion that had, in fact, been on the wane for over a century and more. In an intentionally provocative turn of phrase, Schwartz depicts the resurgence of a coherent Jewish religious-cultural identity under Christian hegemony. The political and cultural Christianization of the empire "had a direct impact on the Jewish culture of late antiquity because the Jewish communities *appropriated* much from the Christian society around them. That is, quite a lot of the distinctive Jewish culture was, to be vulgar about it, repackaged Christianity" (179).

That is to say, the impact upon the Jews of Christian Rome's obsession with controlling Judaism was, ironically, the resurgence of Judaism. But the cost of that resurgence was the creation of a Judaism that would incorporate within itself not a little of the structure of the dominant culture. This, it seems to me, is a classic "colonial scenario" familiar from countless studies of European colonialist enterprises in Africa, Asia, and the Americas. It is within this setting that I believe we can learn some important things about the emerging rabbinic culture of the Galilee in particular.

I share Schwartz's skepticism that the nascent rabbinic communities of the Byzantine period were key players in the resurgence of Palestinian Judaism (Schwartz: 238; compare Levine; Goodman; and Hezser 1998–2002). The substantial archeological record yields few examples of the dominance of rabbinic religious or cultural ideas within the reawakening sense of Jewish national and cultural identity, but the fact remains that the early Byzantine period witnesses the consolidation of postmishnaic rabbinic oral-traditional learning into manageable textual recensions (Hezser 1997) and the consolidation as well of an emerging ideological commitment to the idea of oral tradition as a form of theological and cultural resistance to the "nations of the world." Although the rabbinic "conquest" of Judaism would await the coming of an Islamic imperial order in the seventh through the tenth centuries, many of the cultural and ideological tools that would facilitate the rabbinic rise under Islam were forged under Christian domination in the fourth to sixth centuries.

Central among these ideological tools is the development of the idea that the orally mediated legal traditions of the rabbinic sages constituted a corpus of principles that were mediated to Moses on Sinai, along with the scriptural Torah. These constituted an Oral Torah that served as both the hermeneutical context for interpreting the text of the Written Torah and the legislative framework for determining the application of the divine commandments. This distinctively rabbinic conception of Oral Torah emerged within a century and a half of the origins of the primitive Christian communities, but it would be too much to claim that the rabbinic idea of Oral Torah was in some sense, at its origins, a response to the emergence of primitive Christianity as a distinct "counter-Judaism." It is more likely that the rabbinic claim to possess an authoritative record of orally transmitted traditions stemming from the originary moment of the Sinaitic covenant is bound up with inner-Judaic ideological discourse in the post-70 era. But the early outlines of such discourse are lost. No Jewish literature composed prior to 70 addresses the conception of Oral Torah, pro or con, and virtually the only post-70 Jewish literature to survive into the third century is in the orbit of the rabbinic sages and so treats the concept of Oral Torah as more or less a settled matter, offering only the most obscure references to the earliest contexts in which the concept was employed.[10]

---

10 The earliest references to the concept of Oral Torah appear in compilations of biblical exegesis compiled in the late third–early fourth centuries. One of these (*Sifre Deuteronomy*

The earliest significant rabbinic dispute about Oral Torah at the ideological level concerns neither its origins nor its authority but rather the role of written texts containing the legal traditions of Oral Torah in the training of rabbinic disciples (Babylonian Talmud, tractate *Temurah* 14b; paralleled at *Gittin* 60b):[11]

> And thus said Rabbi Abba, the son of Rabbi Hiyya b. Abba, said Rabbi Yohanan: Those who write down legal traditions might as well burn the Torah. And one who studies [the oral tradition] from them [in written form] receives no reward.

> Rabbi Yehudah b. Nahmani, Resh Laqish's Expounder, offered an exegesis: One verse says: "Write for yourself these words" (Ex.34:27). And one verse says: "But these things are transmitted orally"[12] (*al pee hadevarim ha-eleh*: Ex.34:27).This tells you that teachings given orally you may not recite from writing; and teachings given in writing you may not recite orally.

All parties assume that there are "those who write down legal traditions," that is, who make written copies of the orally transmitted material at the heart of rabbinic learning. The Palestinian Talmud itself mentions early fourth-century figures who were said to write traditions in notebooks or on walls (Jaffee 2001:141–42; cf. the contrasting position of Hezser 2001: 203–4), and a late Byzantine synagogue in the Bet Shean valley preserves a substantial rabbinic text on its mosaic floor (Zussman 1982). The real issue before us here is the role played by written recensions in the performance of the oral tradition. In the formal oral-performative setting in which disciples displayed their mastery of the traditional Oral Torah, it is

---

351 [to Deut 32:2]), describes an early second-century sage (Rabban Gamaliel II) as explaining the concept of Oral Torah to "Agnitos the Hegemon," a Roman official. Thus, in rabbinic memory, there is a suggestion that the concept of Oral Torah is bound up with an attempt to explain the authority of rabbinic teaching to early second-century imperial authorities, an explanation perhaps associated with some bid for power. The much later *ARN* locates the idea in the Second Temple period, in the efforts of the sage Hillel to teach Torah to "a man," or "a certain person," who was an apparently illiterate Jew (*ARN* A:15/B:29). The student is described in the talmudic parallel in Babylonian Talmud *Shabbat* 31a as a "Gentile." So the most one can say is that the concept of Oral Torah emerges in some sense after the Jesus communities have made an impact upon Palestinian Judaism but well before the authority of the church was formally linked to the power of Rome. There is no suggestion in the sources, however, that polemics with Christians gave rise to the idea of Oral Torah.

11 I follow the standard printed editions unless otherwise noted.

12 The literal rendering, followed in most translations, is "in accordance with these things." I translate the sense assumed in the rabbinic text, which depends upon the wordplay of *al peh* (orally) and *al pee* (according to).

here deemed impermissible to declaim rabbinic oral traditions by reading them from a written copy.

In order to clarify what is at stake here, we should recall that Jews everywhere had for at least two centuries read their scrolls of the Mosaic Torah directly from the written text in the setting of the emerging Torah cult of the synagogue. Should, now, the traditions of the sages, regarded as Torah, also be read from a document in the public learning of the rabbinic house of study? By insisting that public recitations of Oral Torah in the rabbinic study circle should avoid written texts, the Galilean sages were erecting around the Oral Torah a ritual demonstration of its conceptual distinction from the Written Torah. Let the synagogue do what it will, but, when rabbinic disciples would learn the Torah distinctive to the oral tradition, they would master it in the "traditional" way—as a discipline of memory in which written texts had no substantial role.

If the talmudic attributions of these ideas to third-century Galilean sages are accurate, and there is little reason to call them into serious question (Kraemer), then it appears that the rabbinic privileging of Oral Torah surely precedes the political rise of Christian fortunes in the Roman Empire. As I have tried to suggest, the target audience of the idea of Oral Torah is neither emergent Christianity nor imperial Rome. In the third century, the target audience of the rabbinic idea of Oral Torah was the scattered and demoralized Jewry of the Galilee and, increasingly, the masses of Mesopotamian Jewry in the Sasanian Empire, which had for roughly a millennium practiced its Judaism without the guidance of rabbinic tradition at all.

By insisting upon the essentially oral methods of instruction pioneered by the sages, the rabbinic groups sought to ensure the direct control of sages over the Torah imparted to disciples. Torah was not found in books; it was found in sages. Only the sages had received the Oral Torah in an unbroken tradition going back to Moses; only they could transmit it; and only those who undertook their orally grounded discipline of memory and performance could hope to embody it. Accordingly, we now read in the Palestinian Talmud the following discussion peppered with the names of third-century sages (y. Peah 2:6, 17a and parallels):[13]

> Said Rabbi Zeira in the name of Rabbi Yohanan: if a legal tradition comes to your attention and you can't comprehend it, don't set it aside for another matter. For, indeed, many legal traditions were spoken to Moses on Sinai, and all of them are embedded in the oral-performative tradition (*mishnah*)....

---

13 I cite from the Leiden manuscript in accordance with the edition of Zussman 2001.

Rabbi Haggai in the name of Rabbi Shmuel b. Nahman: some things were spoken by mouth and others in writing—but we would not know which is more precious but for this which is written: "I have established a covenant with you and with Israel through these things taught orally (*al pee hadevarim ha-eleh:* Ex.34:27). This proves that things spoken orally are more precious.

Rabbi Yohanan and Rabbi Yudan b. Rabbi Shimon:
    one said—if you preserve [the laws transmitted in] oral tradition and you preserve [the commandments of] Scripture, I will establish my Covenant with you. But if not, I will not establish my covenant with you.
    The other said—if you preserve oral tradition and you fulfill what is [commanded] in Scripture, you will be rewarded. But if not, you will not be rewarded.

It is written: "And on them was written according to all the words which the Lord spoke to you on Sinai" (Dt.9:10)
    Rabbi Yehoshua b. Levi said: instead of "on them" we read "AND on them." Instead of "all" we read "ACCORDING TO all." Instead of "words" we read "THE words." [These stylistic superfluities indicate that] Scripture, the oral-performative tradition (*mishnah*), dialectics (*talmud*), and homiletics (*aggadah*)—and even what a trained disciple will in the future expound before his master—all were already spoken to Moses on Sinai.

The exegetical exertions of this passage wring every hint from the recalcitrant texts of the Written Torah concerning the worldly authority of the sages of the oral tradition and the transcendental covenant-bearing import of their orally transmitted tradition. All of Sinaitic oral tradition is preserved in the rabbinic oral-performative curriculum, and even the discoveries of disciples in the distant future has its roots in that oral-traditional corpus of revelation.

Now this conception is profoundly sectarian in its impulses, for it restricts the rabbinic community to rather intimate face-to-face conventicles of experts trained in arcane lore. If the oral-performative tradition is not in written form, its covenantal implications cannot be enacted except through discipleship to the sages of the Oral Torah. And this sectarian impulse makes a good deal of sense in the context of third-century Galilee as described by Schwartz—one in which Judaism as a whole is fragmenting into diverse constintuencies and losing a sense of a coherent center. The sages, with their ideology of oral tradition, are "closing the wagons" around their own traditions of learning, restricting their transmission to carefully chosen circles of adherents.

When we move to the fifth century and later, however, it becomes clear that the emergence of Christianity to political and cultural dominance has a subtle impact upon the rabbinic conception of Oral Torah as well. We can find traces of the impact of Christianity on rabbinic thinking about Oral Torah in collections of Galilean midrashic traditions stemming from the fourth to the sixth centuries, and perhaps even later. The earliest pre-Constantine traditions about the origins of Oral Torah, which we have just reviewed, are more concerned to demonstrate its unbroken continuity with Sinai and to restrict its covenantal implications to a self-selecting elite. In texts edited in the late Byzantine or early Islamic settings, by contrast, we note an explicit innovation in the ideological commitment to the primacy of preserving the Oral Torah and its orally managed system of performance.

The first passage, from the *Midrash Tanhuma* (*Ki Tissa* 17),[14] begins with a minor reworking of the Palestinian Talmud *Peah*'s claim that the Sinaitic Oral Torah included all innovations that later disciples would discover in it. The text continues:

> When Moses had mastered all [the oral tradition disclosed on Sinai], the Blessed Holy One said to him: Go and teach it to my children! Said Moses: Lord of the World! Write it down for your children! He replied: I would give it to them in writing, but I know that one day the Nations of the World will subdue them and seek to take it from them, so that my sons will become like the other Nations. Rather: let them have the Scriptures in writing. But the oral-performative tradition, homiletics, and dialectics shall remain in oral form.

> "And the Lord said to Moses: write for yourself" (Ex.34:27)—this refers to Scripture.
> "But these things are taught orally" (Ex.34:27)—this refers to the oral-performative tradition and dialectics, for these distinguish between Israel and the Nations of the World.

The shift in emphasis, from the early Byzantine Palestinian Talmud to the late-Byzantine *Tanhuma,* is important: while the Talmud is concerned with the orality of tradition as a means to safeguard its interpretation in the closed world of discipleship, the Tanhuma is concerned with orality as a means of preserving the Torah for Israel *as a whole* in the context of attempts by the nations of the world to appropriate it. That is, where the oral transmission of Oral Torah preserves for the Talmud the boundaries of a Jewish sect from competing Jewish sects, *Tanhuma*'s Oral Torah protects all Israel from imperial attempts to subvert Israel's collective covenantal possession.

---

14 I cite from the edition of Buber.

The Christian context of this thematization of Oral Torah is even more explicitly evident in a somewhat later midrashic compilation, *Pesiqta Rabbati* 14b[15] (paralleled in *Midrash Tanhuma*, ed. Buber, *Vayera* 6, 44b):

> The Blessed Holy One foresaw that the Nations would translate the [Written] Torah and read it in Greek. And they would say: "They [the Jews] are not Israel!"
>
> Said the Blessed Holy One to Moses: "O, Moses! The Nations will say, 'We are Israel! We are the children of the Omnipresent!' And Israel, too, will say: 'We are the children of the Omnipresent!'"

And the scales are in balance!

> Said the Blessed Holy One to the Nations: "What do you mean that you are my children? But I recognize only the one who holds my mystery (*mistoryn*) in his hands. He alone is my son!"
> They said to Him: "What is this mystery?"
> He replied: "The oral-performative tradition" (*mishnah*).

Here the thematization of Oral Torah as a defense against Byzantium's colonialist appropriation of Israel's covenantal identity and its sacred literature is as explicit as one might wish. Byzantium has already, so to speak, stolen from Israel its sacred Scripture and turned it into a polemical weapon against Judaism's own covenantal self-understanding. Accordingly, the preservation of the oral-performative tradition in its nonwritten form is constructed here as an act of national resistance. Most importantly, the community of resistance is not merely the rabbinic disciple community among other Jewish groups. Rather, the sages resist Rome as the nation of Israel as a whole.

In this connection we observe the loaded terminology with which the oral-tradition's theological status is described. It is a "mystery." Elsewhere in Byzantine rabbinic literature this same term can apply to the covenantal rite of circumcision (e.g., *Midrash Tanhuma* [Buber] *Lekh Lekhah* 23) as well, which distinguishes Jewish "insiders" from non-Jewish "outsiders" to the covenantal promise of Israel. The ascription of this term to the oral tradition, however, particularly in conjuction with the metaphor of Israel as God's "son," seems explicitly to invoke and deny the parallel claims of Christian theology to possess, in Christ, a covenantal mystery that secures the church's identity as the covenantal treasure of God. Indeed, as Marc Bregman has noted, in a long-delayed essay on the meaning of the oral tradition as a "mystery," a distinctly parallel usage of

---

15 I cite from the edition of Friedmann.

the Latin cognate, *mysterium*, appears in the work of the fourth-century Latin theologian, Hilary of Poitiers (Bregman). In his commentary on the Psalter (Ps 2:2–3), Hilary describes as *mysteria* an oral tradition of scriptural interpretation, delivered to Moses and transmitted to the seventy elders, that ultimately guided the work of the translators of the Septuagint. As Bregman observes,

> What does seem clear is that the passage cited from the works of Hilary and the tradition attributed to R. Yehudah bar Shalom belong to the same realm of polemical discourse in which we find both Christians and Jews claiming to possess a 'mystery' ... that had been communicated orally in a chain of transmission going back to Moses. (manuscript: 5)

It seems, then, that the rabbinic construction of oral tradition as a "mystery" that cannot be set down entirely in books mirrors at the level of ideology what Schwartz has observed in the resurgence of coherent Judaic iconic and liturgical vocabularies in late Byzantine synagogues.

Innovations in synagogue iconography and liturgical poetry, that is, testify to Jewish appropriations of circumambient and politically ascendant Christian tropes that function, after Judaic resignification, as discourses of resistance to the Christian colonization of the Palestinian landscape and appropriation of Jewish historical memory in supercessionist theologies. This embrace of Christian iconic and liturgical traditions, characteristic of Jews as yet relatively unconcerned with rabbinic oral tradition, is modeled no less clearly within the circles of rabbinic tradition, in the distinctively Byzantine modulations of the rabbinic ideology of the meaning of Oral Torah. Moreover, in a later imperial system, underwritten by an Islamic civilization for whom Christianity posed a far greater problem than Judaism, the rabbinic ideology of Oral Torah framed in Byzantine terms would support the eventual "rabbinization" of Judaism and the transformation of rabbinic Judaism itself from a sectarian formation into the "Judaism" that would greet the colonialist threats to Judaism posed by early European modernity.

ORALITIES, LITERACIES, AND COLONIALISMS IN ANTIQUITY AND CONTEMPORARY SCHOLARSHIP

Claudia V. Camp
Texas Christian University

This volume's overt (entitled) aim is to connect two large and impor-tant scholarly conversations—on orality and literacy, on the one hand, and colonialism, on the other—with the study of (mostly Mediterranean) antiquity. It could be said, however, that the volume's aims are both nar-rower and (mostly much) wider than its title. The narrowness has to do with the limitation on the kind of literacy addressed. Professional village letter-writers, inscribers of marriage contracts, teachers of abecedaries for future keepers of mercantile records—such persons and their documents are rarely mentioned here, though they could be. All play a role in the mediation of orality and literacy, the maintenance and alteration of class status, and, ultimately, the political and economic functioning of empire that these authors discuss. As I shall suggest, their absence in the present discussion occasionally makes its presence known. The emphasis here, however, is on oral and written traditions that bear, at least, the cultural weight of identity, artistry, or profound thought and, at most, the author-itative burden of sacrality. It is this emphasis that, to a significant degree, also produces the unentitled overflow of this collection of essays, the (too) many issues that need to be addressed to gain some purchase on both the title and the specters that lurk in its margins.

I perceive three large dynamics running through the volume. One is the question of the interrelationship of (culturally weighty) written litera-ture with a largely oral culture. But here the overflow begins, for to answer this question requires consideration of several others, all complex and sometimes contentious. Given that the textual products of an oral-dominant culture are infused with varying degrees of orality, how do we identify and interpret the oral in the written (Foley)? How different (the question is both quantitative and substantive) are oral-dominant cultures from those anchored by writing, and what are appropriate (that is, nonethnocentric) methodologies for dealing with this question (Botha, Loubser)? Given the fact that students of history have no choice but to rely on texts (and occasional images), how do we "hear" the now-absent oral majority (Decharneux, Horsley)? Why do people in largely oral cultures write (Solère, Horsley, Kelber)? What political force does writing have in an oral culture, and how does it get its clout among both the literate and the nonliterate (Horsley, Kelber, Draper)? How does orality continue to affect writing not simply in terms of art and form but in terms of its connection to social power (Decharneux, Horsley, Draper)? One of the lurking issues for biblical scholars in all this has to do with the emergence of a religiously authoritative written canon as a specific aspect of the oral-written interface. We have here a particular form of the relationship both of literacy to orality and of literacy to power—in the case of the Bible, precisely to colonial power. I shall call attention to some ways this particularity of the issue might have been usefully more underscored.

The second major dynamic in the volume has to do with the notion of colonialism itself and how the scholar stands in relationship to it. Let me be blunt: no one these days wants to think of themselves as representative of a colonizing project, whether political or intellectual. And all members of the world's white elite stand in danger of this accusation. Let me assume, the table of contents notwithstanding, that all due effort was made to include in the enterprise that produced this volume, which originated in the university elite of South Africa, persons representing the colonized as well as the colonizers. (And let me be clear that I do not regard my own lone female voice, white elite that it still is, as remedy to this absence: I am making allowances; it is not my place to absolve.) All this said, there are still challenging ambiguities of identity surrounding the notion of colonialism as it appears in these essays.

The use of the term in the theoretical essays of Foley, Botha, and Loubser has to do with the potential for orality/literacy theory itself to undergird a colonial ideology, as well as its potential to resist precisely that. Is there an implicit hierarchy of written over oral in the theory, or does the theory's appreciation of the oral help overcome ethnocentrism on the part of the literate, especially scholars? Is the theory, in other words, an expression of colonialism or of postcolonialism? Surprisingly little reference to orality/literacy theory shows up at all in the essays devoted to ancient society. This is disappointing in itself; one would have liked to get a clearer sense of how these theories might be usefully applied. Susan Niditch's *Oral World and Written Word* (1996), to which I shall refer, has made a significant advance in applying the work of Foley and other folklorists to the Hebrew Bible, but there is much more to be said on this. Further, what difference to our understanding of the ancients would Botha's discussion of differences in cognition have made? And what would be the gains of applying Loubser's media-studies approach to this social-historical context? Beyond this general gap between theory and practice, however, is the particular one regarding colonialism, for the relationship of colonialism to communication modes appears in this second section less as a theoretical issue than as a historical one; that is, the role of orality and literacy in the power dynamics of groups within the Persian, Greek, and (mostly) Roman Empires, while highlighted, goes relatively untheorized. Nonetheless, the role of the Bible in more contemporary contexts of colonialism runs sometimes close to the surface of these historical discussions.

The third major dynamic concerns the kinds of interdisciplinary conversations in which biblical scholars might fruitfully engage. Importantly, the fascinating essays of Solère on Plato and Decharneux on Mithraism join those on orality/literacy theory itself to offer a cross-cultural dimension to the collection as well as a methodological one. So one must finally ask: What has biblical scholarship to do with the writing Greeks and the nonwriting Romans?

The number and complexity of issues at stake in this volume force choices on a respondent! Although I shall try to integrate all its essays into my comments in one form or another, the reader will find that a considerable portion of my attention is spent on two, Botha's and Horsley's. The reason has largely to do with the considerable scope of each one, Botha's on theory and Horsley's on historical reconstruction; each thus brings a variety of the issues into play.

Pieter J. J. Botha's "Cognition, Orality-Literacy, and Approaches to First-Century Writings" makes overt the curious paradox that marks the conversation about orality and literacy when conducted with sensitivity to ideological issues. Botha cites Malina's concern (drawn from Tuman) that approaches to the issue are "burdened with ethnocentric presuppositions" (39). Botha, to the contrary, contends that failure to consider the differences between oral and literate cultures is itself ethnocentric. A recent article by Emevwo Biakolo attacks as culturally imperialistic some of the sources Botha claims support his position, compelling some further consideration of the question of ethnocentrism. Biakolo's reference to a remark by Derrida is emblematic of the dilemma: Derrida suggests that orality/literacy theory is ethnocentrism masquerading as antiethnocentrism (1976). Still, it appears obvious that there are differences between cultures depending on whether they are or are not marked by pervasive literacy. The question then becomes how to sort this difference out, how much of it to assign to literacy as such, and how to ascertain its relevance for understanding ancient culture, without falling into the trap of cultural imperialism.

There are, I think, several different issues that get wrapped together in these discussions. One is the issue of how to overcome the "Great Divide," as in Foley's "Indigenous Poems, Colonialist Texts," that is, how to describe a complex continuity between "oral" cultures and "literate" ones based on the composition and reception of their texts. This effort is based on the demonstrable fact that there is in fact no Great Divide but that many cultures operate with both oral and literate components interacting in various ways. As far as the Bible is concerned—and, indeed, in any textually based effort to understand the ancient past—the written literary artifact is the prime "given." In this instance a typology such as that offered by Susan Niditch (1996) is useful, which traces a more specific continuum than Foley's. Operating in effect within his "voices from the past," she distinguishes texts that represent (1) oral performances recorded as dictation or later from notes; (2) repeated oral performances resulting in crystallization of the work, which is written down at a much later time; (3) literature produced in writing but with conscious appropriation of oral forms; and (4) literature that makes use of earlier texts in its production.

The problem of "colonialism" at work here is that articulated by Foley: the bias toward literary texts, with a "set of sacrosanct, unexamined assumptions about verbal art" (10). The great value of enterprises such as Foley's and Niditch's lies in overcoming this bias by demonstrating that orality and literacy—and, more particularly, oral traditions and written texts—are not mutually exclusive. In Niditch's work, moreover, a further issue important to ancient world studies is addressed, that of distinguishing different levels and kinds of orality involved in the production of an ancient text, thus allowing her to theorize certain aspects of the production of the Bible itself.

Such typologies do not solve all the problems, of course. At the most basic level is the question of what defines "orality" and distinguishes it from "literacy." It is easy enough when one observes a performance in person to label it as oral, but are there features of such a performance that are definitive of its orality as such that can be applied to traditions whose oral performances are inaccessible to us? Students of oral literature believe so. Thus Niditch (drawing on but not wedded to Parry and Lord) can list and give biblical examples of such features of the "oral register" as repetition, formulas, epithets, longer formulas, quotations of a specific text or traditional referentiality, and patterns of content (1996:13–21). Yet in her effort to respect the particularity of the biblical material, she alters to some degree the Parry/Lord model to suit the data provided by a written text. The text, then, is an inescapable presence for the student of ancient culture.

We do know, of course, that the biblical writings were produced in a culture where the vast majority of people were nonliterate and artistic production was traditionally oral. But while most students of oral culture agree that repetition, for example, is a hallmark of oral art, Biakolo, citing Ruth Finnegan, argues that

[a]nyone who goes on "to take the occurrence, or a specific proportion, of repetition as a touchstone for differentiating between 'oral' and 'written' styles is ... bound to be disappointed" [Finnegan 1977:130]. The concept of repetition is so wide and its application so various that to delimit it in more precise definition is to lose its universality.

We might further note Goody's argument that certain aspects of repetition, such as rhyming and use of formulas, are "more characteristic of oral performance *in literate cultures*" (2000:27; emphasis added). Biakolo urges, then, the study of particular oral pieces in terms of their own individual style rather than as the source for "grandiose pronouncements" about the oral style.

Scholars have, however, varying motivations for wanting to make such generalizations. Biakolo's concern is not, finally, the technical difficulties in discerning an oral register in written works but rather ethnocentrism, insofar as the labels "orality" and "literacy" implicitly, even if unintentionally, presuppose "primitive" and "advanced." If Niditch's work raises a question about where one draws the line between oral and written in an ancient text, as does Foley's model for a broader sweep of literature, these two authors do not, I would argue, fall under the ideological critique. Both are concerned with exactly the sort of variations and interpenetrations of oralities and literacies that Biakolo calls for.

More problematic is an argument such as Botha's, where easily (or at least potentially) verifiable observations about the degree of literacy and nonliteracy in a society and theorization about how a predominant orality might manifest itself in written texts are extended to claims about differences in cognitive capabilities, cultural characteristics, and worldview between "oral cultures" and "literate cultures." His impulse as a historian cannot be gainsaid: it is clear that modern scholars from a highly text-dominant culture must find ways of understanding one in which texts played an important (how else would we have ended up with a Bible?) but much narrower role. Orality-literacy issues are, as he claims, "*one of the factors* making up the first-century Mediterranean world" (39; emphasis original). The question is, as Loubser well puts it: "How can one approach the issue of cultural difference without reverting to a colonialist discourse?" (65).

Botha's concerns center not so much on features of literature but on the distinction between speech and writing in a far more comprehensive sense; he takes his cue particularly from studies in cognitive and especially cultural psychology. The reader should be warned, however, that both the results and the implications of the research he cites are the subject of contentious debate not only by a biblical scholar such as Malina but also among anthropologists, folklorists, and philosophers. Malina is reliant upon Tuman, and I have also noted Biakolo's recent citation of

Finnegan's work from 1977. One might also mention the objections of
Jacques Derrida and Brian Street, with whom Goody, one of Botha's main
theoretical supports, is still arguing in 2000. The latter work is to be recommended for Goody's nuancing of the issues as he refutes some of the
objections raised to his work. (On the other hand, one might still worry
about the passing reference to "magic" as opposed to "religion"
[2000:24].) The overarching problem I have with Botha's essay is the failure to distinguish easily challenged results of the research from those
with more critical promise.

Botha's main agenda here is to critique the work of Scribner and Cole
on which Malina relies for his dismissal of orality/literacy issues. This
critique is in many respects well taken, but its results are pressed too far
in the other direction. If Scribner and Cole's study "contains evidence for,
against, and irrelevant to orality-literacy theories" (56), then we are, in a
sense, starting at square one, for theories with too much "against" them
may need radical modification, with the evidence "for" incorporated into
some more adequate formulation. Where then from here?

The answer, I think, lies not back in the direction of Luria and Vygotskiĭ, whose work is presented too uncritically here. Repeating without
qualification old notions—that illiterate people do not tend to think in
"'abstract,' 'logical' ways" because their thought is "context-dependent," that they "experienced difficulties with self-evaluation and
analysis," that they were "found unable to formulate abstract superordinate categories," and that they "refused to solve verbal problems
when the proposed premises contradicted their actual experience"
(42–43)—is an invitation to being at best misunderstood. Goody (2000:
esp. 1-25), claiming himself to be misunderstood, has recently reiterated
the important qualifications in response to criticisms such as Biakolo's
(more directly, to the earlier work of Street): it is crucial to recognize
that (1) demonstrable cognitive differences, especially that between so-
called abstract and concrete or context-dependent modes of thought,
are relative, not absolute (that is, while writing encourages and possibly
transforms certain cognitive tendencies, it does not transform consciousness wholesale); (2) there are different kinds of logics and
rationalities: a "low score" on the Western philosophical and scientific
version does not mean a culture or individual is "illogical" or "irra-
tional"; (3) writing is not the sole cause of what differences may exist
but works in combination with many cultural factors; (4) there is a complex interface between the oral and the written; (5) there is no such
thing as "instant literacy" leading to immediate changes in thought patterns or ways of life, and "cognitive techniques and practices that one
might attribute to writing ... are themselves subject to long-term developments" (2000:12).

Monocausation, technological determinism, and oral/written binarism are ethnocentric pitfalls of orality/literacy theories that can distort the user's intended antiethnocentrism. Botha clearly seeks to avoid these traps, as is evident, for example, in his stress that orality/literacy issues are *"one of the factors* making up the first-century Mediterranean world" (39; emphasis original). Yet problems remain. Let me take a brief excerpt as an example. Botha states that

> Luria follows Vygotskiĭ in stating that writing is context-independent, is addressed to an unknown interlocutor, and uses longer sentences, more relative clauses, and fewer direct quotes; it also makes us conscious of language (Luria 1981:164–68). (43)

There are three different kinds of claims made here. "Longer sentences, more relative clauses, and fewer direct quotes" are empirically observable features of literature; if found in enough literature from enough different cultures, they may well be said to mark the "written" end of the oral/written continuum. But this says nothing in itself about difference in cognition. The second sort of claim has to do with the significance of context in orality and literacy. But whether or not writing is context-independent and addressed to an unknown interlocutor is itself highly dependent on the kind and context of the writing involved, as Foley's and Niditch's work makes clear. Luria/Vygotskiĭ's assertion typifies modern writing but applies sometimes more and sometimes less in more traditional cultures. Not all speech is equally "evanescent" (witness Niditch's category 2 regarding "crystallization" of oral works through repeated performances), and not all writing is context-independent (witness her category 1 and Foley's category 2, both of which deal with texts produced from oral dictation). Again, no cognitive difference is inherent in these (complexly related rather than polar) attributes. Decharneux's work in this volume on the Mithras cult, moreover, shows the capacity of an oral tradition to extend itself over vast geographical areas, which also calls for qualification on the question of "context" and orality, at least as it appears in an empire that is otherwise informed by literacy.

Caution is needed, moreover, in arguing from context (in)dependence to further claims regarding cognitive distinctions. For example, the finding that "there is an enforcing relation between context-dependent communication and egocentrism (absolutizing one point of view)" (43–44) surely needs a more complex explanatory framework than that provided by a monocausal approach to literacy/orality. Writing certainly involves "practice in the use of linguistic contexts as independent of immediate reference" (Greenfield: 174), in contrast to the face-to-face interaction required of oral discourse. But how much practical effect does this skill have independent of other factors? And how much of the skill does one need to have to make a difference? Completely nonliterate societies are typically isolated from the influence of other points of view and are small enough that most communication need only be face to face. Nonliterate individuals, by the same token, are unlikely to have encountered others much different from themselves. Learning to write may well provide a Wolof schoolchild of Greenfield's study with a range of imagined experience she is unlikely to have in real life, but this broadened "experience" may not be a function of writing alone. (It is perhaps worth noting that my experience of teaching college in Texas confronts me with any number of bright, well-educated young people who seem extraordinarily incapable of seeing things from multiple points of view, a fact I attribute substantially to cultural isolation.) Botha reports Denny's important critique of Greenfield's "overinterpretation" of her evidence as indicating the cognitive trait of abstraction, rather than relating it to the tendency to decontextualize as societies grow larger. But this perspective comes late and appendix-like in the essay rather than being prominently placed as a corrective to ideologically slippery claims about the role of literacy in cognition.

The final assertion in the passage quoted above is that writing "makes us conscious of language." Here, finally, is a cognitive matter as such, but it may also be one of those overinterpretations or overgeneralizations of the evidence. What defines such "consciousness," and how is its presence or lack thereof tested? If I may invoke the foibles of my dear students once more, highly literate people may produce both thinking and writing that show no evidence of the "deliberate analytical action and 'deliberate structuring of the web of meaning'" (41) that presumably accompany awareness of the structure of language. But this fact, as Goody reminds us, is not decisive for two reasons: literacy does not replace orality, and it is variously prominent even within a so-called "literate" culture. The more important issue is the implication that people in oral cultures are not conscious of language. Surely, though, one would not imagine one of Lord's singers of tales to be unconscious of language, nor indeed the singer's listeners, who comment easily on the greater or lesser mastery of one performer relative to another. Do people in mainly oral cultures have, then, instead simply *different* consciousnesses of language, and are these the same from one culture to the next, whether written or oral? To get an answer to this, the specific kinds of tests involved—for example a person's willingness to consider that the sun might equally well, and equally arbitrarily, be called the moon—would have to be run in many different cultures and the specific kinds of responses analyzed. Botha cites Denny's caution about "how precariously small the actual 'empirical' and comparative data base of anthropological and cross-cultural research actually is" (59).

"Consciousness of language" can be related in Botha's argument to his appropriation of the proposals of Goody and Olson that "reading objectifies language and encourages abstract thought" (44). He cites research that suggests that

> the more literate subjects tend to classify in terms of nominal (superordi-nate) categories by constructing abstract taxonomies such as "tools" or "vehicles." The less literate or illiterate participants have a greater tendency to use perceptual categories ("red things," "small things") or functional categories (classifying an ax with a tree rather than with other tools). (44)

This is, I think, a very interesting insight when it comes to the Bible. One must first, of course, acknowledge that the difference here is not between logic and illogic but between different kinds of logic that mark different kinds of discourse. To frame this distinction within somewhat different theoretical terms:

> The development of a discourse may take place along two different semantic lines: one topic may lead to another either through their similarity or their contiguity. The metaphoric way would be the most appropriate term for the first case and the metonymic way for the second, since they find their most condensed expression in metaphor and metonymy respectively.... In normal verbal behavior both processes are continually operative, but careful observation will reveal that under the influence of a cultural pattern, personality, and verbal style, preference is given to one of the two processes over the other. (Jakobson: 90)

To refer to Jakobson's metaphoric and metonymic ways (compare de Saussure's associative and syntagmatic planes of language and, more recently, Lakoff's study of metaphor and metonymy as cognitive modes) as respectively logical and illogical is patently ethnocentric. To refer to them in the more contemporary social-scientific parlance as more and less "abstract" is perhaps technically accurate but not, I think, most helpful when it comes to thinking about the Bible. It may be that literacy encourages the development of metaphoric discourse. Jakobson, who was studying aphasia, presumably assumed the literacy of his subjects. But he also alludes to traditions of verbal art, both written and oral (the parallelism of biblical poetry and Finnic and Russian oral traditions), where he finds that "the interaction of these two elements is especially pronounced." Further, he suggests that "poetry is focused upon the sign" and driven by the principle of similarity, while the focus of "pragmatical prose [is] primarily upon the referent" and is thus "forwarded essentially by contiguity." Thus, "for poetry, metaphor, and for prose, metonymy, is

202 ORALITY, LITERACY, AND COLONIALISM IN ANTIQUITY

the line of least resistance." Jakobson is, however, describing tendencies, not absolute distinctions, as can be seen in his interest in the interaction of the two in the study of verbal art and also in his observation of different styles of poetry, where he notes that "romanticism is closely linked with metaphor," while realism is tied to metonymy; likewise, "in Russian lyrical songs ... metaphoric constructions predominate, while in the heroic epics the metonymic way is preponderant" (Jakobson: 91, 95, 96).

Consideration of metaphor and metonymy as modes of discourse may be useful in interpreting both the test results of cultural psychologists and anthropologists as well as biblical literature. If metonymy is tied to prose, to narrative, and to "realism" (broadly construed), then it is no wonder that a nonliterate person, whose life is typically constrained by the circumstances of "real" life, more immediately associates "ax" with "tree" than with "tool" (note, again, Denny's emphasis on decontextualization as an important way of understanding what has been called "abstraction"). One interesting question then becomes, however, What happens in the various forms of this person's verbal art? Jakobson notes the mix of metaphor and metonymy in biblical poetry, with its required parallelism. But is this an example of the influence of writing? Some have argued that parallelism is an oral device; for example, form criticism of the Psalms often assumes an oral background. On the other hand, the popular proverbs that appear in biblical narrative do not use the parallelism that marks those in the book of Proverbs, suggesting perhaps a development in style under the influence of literacy (Fontaine). Again, literacy may be a factor in promoting "the metaphoric way," but a deeper cultural understanding depends on getting beyond the labels "abstract versus nonabstract" and considering, among other things, the genre and context of language use within the given culture.

One way or another, however much metaphor may appear in biblical literature, it is safe to say that the level of abstraction there, despite the fact that it is of course all now written, is substantially less than in modern languages coming from literate cultures. There are few if any Hebrew words, for example, that translate into nouns ending in "–ion"! Thus, again, with Goody, if orality/literacy is indeed the best way to understand degrees of abstraction, we must still account for a continuum and an interface of modes, with literate tendencies emerging slowly over time. One wonders whether appeal to an ongoing metonymic (oral?) style of thinking would explain the willingness of biblical editors to maintain multiple versions of similar stories, often in close literary proximity to each other. The metaphoric mode tends toward substitution, while the metonymic prefers contiguity. From this perspective, for example, the linkage of the creation of the humans at the end of Gen 1 to the further discussion of their relationship to each other in Gen 2 would be a perfectly "natural" train of thought, without a worry about the "conflict" between two stories of creation, which turns out to be the product of a preference for superordinate nominalization perhaps fostered but clearly not produced by literacy alone.

Before leaving this topic, let me introduce one further observation from Biakolo, who is critical of work on African oral culture that "equates all traditional thought with traditional religious thought."

> The assumption ... is indeed a common one, perhaps the commonest in all anthropological-philosophical discourses of this sort. This is the notion that the magical, with its connotation of, and connection with, ritual and religion, is the dominant characteristic of all primitive thought and behavior.

One question Biakolo raises about this assumption is that of why, in comparing "oral" to "literate" societies, "the comparison is not made within the same experiential domain, say, between traditional religious thought and modern Western religious thought. Or, alternatively, between an instance of traditional nonreligious thought and science?" The evidence from my own anthropological research base, college students in Texas, suggests that there is not a great deal of difference in the underlying structures of their religiosity from what is often called "magic" (though their use of a written canon will deserve further comment in a moment). Indeed, they are typically (orally?) quite happy with the metonymic approach to Gen 1 and 2 proposed above and highly resistant to the superordinate nominalization that would require them to compare two variations of the category "creation story."

The conflation of traditional culture with "orality" and "magic" leads to some questionable results. Drawing on Goody, Botha argues that

> [t]he religious systems of societies without writing lack the concept of a religion, "partly because magico-religious activities form part of most social action, not being the attribute of a separate organization, partly because of the identification with a people, as in 'Asante religion'" (Goody 1986:173). It follows that a society with a heavy oral residue will lack the experience of "religious conversion." Whereas a written tradition articulates beliefs and interests in a semipermanent form that can extend their influence independently of any particular political and cultural system, oral traditions are inextricably linked to their contexts, where one can only experience incorporation. "Conversion is a function of the boundaries the written word creates, or rather defines" (1986:10, 172). (47)

While it is arguably true that traditional societies lack the concept of "religion," it is open to question whether and how this lack is related to lack of writing rather than to other factors. Biakolo would have us question the assertion that "magico-religious activities form part of most social action" (what counts as "social"—trading in the local market? food preparation? sex?). Nor is it obvious that the development of separate organizations of "religious" specialists is necessarily connected to having the concept "religion" (which a number of scholars today associate with the development of the academic discipline). Traditional societies often lack the ways and means of distant travel. Might lack of contact with peoples who "religion" in significantly different ways correlate with having no notion of "conversion" (to what?)? The identification of a religion with the people who practice it is partially related to this lack of contact with difference but can be further theorized in terms of Peter Berger's "sacred canopy," an ideological form that has functioned powerfully until the modern period even in societies where writing had taken significant hold.

There is a further problem, I believe, in Botha's appropriation of Goody's argument about written traditions and conversion, if I understand the latter correctly. (I do not have the 1986 source available, but the essence of the discussion appears in the 2000 book.) Botha states that "a society with a heavy oral residue will lack the experience of 'religious conversion'" (47). Goody's argument, however, concerns the necessary role of authoritative, written religious texts in the spread of religion beyond local boundaries. In the ancient world, however, the development of an authoritative text—whether Jewish, Christian, or Muslim—did nothing to change the dominantly (hardly "residual") oral mode of the societies involved. It was precisely under such conditions of orality that most conversion did take place. It is the role of canon in all of this, as much as of literacy in general, that the student of these ancient societies needs to understand. How do authoritative texts "work" in a largely oral culture, both when they are used to produce conversions, as with Christianity and Islam, and when they are not, as with Judaism?

In sum, then, largely because of its focus on problematizing scholarly dependence on the conclusions drawn by Scribner and Cole against the effects of literacy, Botha's essay seems to minimize the complications of orality/literacy theories, not least of which is some residue of ethnocentrism. Goody has, to be sure, dealt with many of the criticisms, but there remain considerations that cannot be dismissed simply as "(unwarranted) political suspicions" (47). The irony, of course, is that a research agenda that began by trying to overcome the myth of the "savage mind" by reference to sociocultural experience risks being snared by the net of, as it were, savage culture. Caution, not repudiation, is urged.

For surely it is true, as Botha asserts, that "what the mind can do relates to the devices provided by one's culture," that representational systems mediate our interaction with the world (45). What is needed is a more developed account of how "mind" in an individual sense and "culture" come together in the matter of orality and literacy. Research in cognitive development and cultural psychology shows the association of gaining (certain sorts of?) literacy and the acquisition of certain mental skills, and the theory that the written word liberates language from concrete situations, thus clearing the way for symbolic manipulation, is attractive. However, as Goody emphasizes, the emergence and effects of literacy in a given culture is not an autonomous process. The historical understanding that Botha seeks by means of theories of orality and literacy requires far more precisely *historical* specification. Both his concluding remarks and, interestingly, some of his footnotes point clearly in this direction. Here we find stressed the importance of bearing in mind the fact that "even the 'literates' were literate in a preprint culture" (63). Further, he encourages the recognition of "*particular* literacy—and its specific circumstances of acquisition and use" (62) and thus of conceptualizing both written and oral traditions in terms of their specific functions. Such considerations return us to the question of the interface of, rather than the difference between, orality and literacy.

The pursuit of these ends is helpfully advanced by means such as the media-studies approach of Loubser's "Moving Beyond Colonialist Discourse: Understanding Oral Theory and Cultural Difference in the Context of Media Analysis." As noted, Loubser poses the crucial question: How can one approach the issue of cultural difference without reverting to a colonialist discourse? Essential to an answer, he argues, and lacking in most studies of how orality and literacy shape societies and texts, is a general theory of culture and, in particular, "an adequate theory for dealing with cultural difference" (65). To this conversation he offers an exploration of the relationship of media and culture.

Loubser's overview of communication media typical of different types of social formations (from hunter-gatherer societies through the nation-state) shows how "media usage corresponds with and depends on the other elements of a cultural system and cannot be isolated from those other elements" (75). He proposes a definition of culture as "*the symbolic representation of concepts by means of media*" (75). If, then, "the medium ... is an integral component in every process of symbolic representation, it follows that an analysis of media usage is profitable for the study of cultural differences." The focus is put, then, on "media texture," that is, "*the network of signs in a text* [including oral texts] *that relate to the management of the media used in the production of meaning*" (76).

There are, first of all, media properties that regulate the *production* of messages, including the manipulability of the medium, the volume of signs it can carry, the density of signs it can carry, and its physical mass.

Second, there are media properties that relate to the *format* of messages (form, style, and demarcation of units). The codes required for the management of sound in time (e.g., repetitive formulae) generate different genres than those required for the management of marks in space. Further, a medium's "multimedia capacity," the spectrum of other media it can incorporate, "has a direct b.;aring on the length and style of the message" (78). And its mode of intertextuality influences the form in which references to other texts in the same medium appear. Third, media properties influence the *distribution* of messages. "How far and wide messages are distributed depends on the durability, affordability, range of reception, copying, and storage capacity allowed for by the medium, as well as the type of censorship that is possible" (78). Fourth, there is a series of media properties with bearing on the *reception* of messages, namely, accessibility, aesthetic impact (including aspects of the message that *cannot* be included in the medium, e.g., intonation in writing), opportunities for reflection and feedback, and the level of distortion.

A media-focused study such as Loubser's allows for, as he suggests, "more sophisticated typologies" (82) of culture when it comes to matters of orality and literacy. It also creates the possibility, I would suggest, for a more culturally specific, and thus more culturally sensitive, understanding of the how orality and literacy might variously affect cognition.

The understanding of "colonialism" takes a different turn in the essays dealing with ancient texts and traditions. Whereas Foley, Botha, and Loubser were concerned with colonialist bias in theories of (or assumptions regarding) orality and literacy, most of the other authors in this volume focus on how orality and literacy function within a colonized or colonizing environment. (Naturally, the theories are also being produced in such an environment, but only a rarefied version of intellectual politics comes into play in the essays themselves.) The generalizations about "oral culture" that haunt the theories tend to be mitigated by focus on particulars, for the given historical circumstances force attention to the *interaction* of orality and literacy rather than to their theoretical opposition. The assumption in all cases is that students of ancient texts need to attend to the predominant orality of the ancient culture. The colonialist bias toward written texts is thus apparently staked through the heart. At points, however, the idealization of orality becomes as worrisome as its opposite.

This is not the case in Werner Kelber's essay, however, "Roman Imperialism and Early Christian Scribality," which, more than the others, focuses almost entirely on the production of written texts. The essay opens up some promising categories of analysis and at the same time raises questions. Citing J. Assmann, Kelber proposes that "scribality, literacy, identity formation, and cultural memory constituted a syndrome that could well serve the self-legitimating interests of religious-political powers" and, by the same token, be used by dissident groups "to construct their identity vis-à-vis dominant power structures" (135). Like Loubser, he proposes we view "ancient history as media history" (137).

Kelber has, of course, done groundbreaking and ongoing work on orality and literacy; however, the promise of these opening conceptualizations is not realized in this essay. This is true in part because the dynamics of the relationship of power to media is not worked out, and in part because the subsequent discussion of how three of the New Testament writers "entrust[ed] their message to the scribal medium in view of Roman imperialism" (137) is enacted mainly by an ideological reading of those texts that, for all its own merits, owes little to any theory of orality/literacy as such. We learn how (in Kelber's interpretation) these three authors dealt with the politically fraught memories of Jesus' life and death, but we learn nothing about how the fact of writing made a difference in this process, other than making it risky because of distribution issues.

What more would I ask? Kelber makes an initial observation that "those in positions of power shared a vested interest in advancing the cause of scribality because control over the medium allowed them to govern the public discourse," and, further, that "most frequently and influentially, scribality was applied for the purpose of recording people's stories and history," thus determining how people would remember the past and think of their identity (135). But these assertions need some unpacking. Was scribality most often employed for recording stories and history? What about its regular use for letter writing, contracts, economic transactions, and the like? Some clearer indication of the forms, agents, and circumstances of literacy implied here would be useful.

Even more important in the present context, though, is the question of the relationship of power and scribality, especially alongside dominant cultural nonliteracy. How is it, exactly, in a nonliterate culture that control over scribality allowed control of public discourse? How in this framework are written texts understood to influence the nonliterate? Is the assumption that texts are produced in order to be read aloud? If so, to whom and in what settings? Or are the nonliterate regarded as too powerless to need influencing, with texts thus directed only to the small percentage of people who could read them? One way or the other, *how do texts come to determine identity when few can read?* Kelber's excellent question—how did early Christian writers compete with Greco-Roman powers on the marketplace of scribal communication?—is answered here only in terms of the content of those writings. No theory of orality and literacy provides advantage over the many content analyses available in the marketplace of contemporary scholarship. Missing is the media-historical approach that Kelber so provocatively enjoins. One wishes for a Loubserian analysis of how the production and distribution of these documents took place and, especially, how constitution of these documents as written rather than oral effected and affected their reception. Writing can reinforce power. It can also be consigned to dust. Who read, and what did reading do for them?

Both Richard Horsley and Jonathan Draper run into some of the same sands when it comes to accounting for the written-and-readness of the New Testament literature, but both offer much of value along the way. Horsley's "The Origins of the Hebrew Scriptures in Imperial Relations" is a highly ambitious attempt to locate these texts in a broad sweep of social and political history, from the mid-fifth century B.C.E. to the first century C.E. There is a concerted and important effort here to show how considerations of orality and literacy interconnect in varied ways with the circumstances of colonialism and also to show how written texts gain authority in a largely oral culture. I want to respond in two ways to his argument. First, while recognizing the important contribution he makes to our understanding of the roles of scribes, in particular, in the pre-Roman period, I take some exception to his historical reconstruction. This leads me, in turn, to offer an alternative scenario to make sense of the evidence for a developing authoritative written tradition among the scribal and priestly groups. Second, I shall be more directly critical of what I see as unwarranted idealization in his proposal regarding the "little" tradition that informed the Jesus movement and the early Christian writings.

First, Horsley takes up the recent scholarly view of the postexilic period as one in which ostensibly indigenous manifestations of religion— temple and Torah—are in fact instruments of imperial rule. This reconstruction needs more nuancing than it receives here, as the essays in James Watts's recent edited volume, *Persia and Torah* (2001), make clear. It seems likely that imperial involvement with the temple, with all the social-political apparatus it involved, was more direct and meaningful than with the text. Temples house people in power; scrolls house ideas. The latter are very important for social control in the long run, but not in so immediate a way. It is, I think, not surprising that the historicity of Ezra and the "book of the law" is more open to question than that of Nehemiah and the temple. In several publications Lester Grabbe makes a strong case for doubting, if not the existence of a "historical Ezra," then most of what is said about him (see, e.g., Grabbe 1998 and 2001). Certainly we cannot, as Horsley seems to do, take the so-called commission of Ezra by Artaxerxes (which one?) as a historical record clearly related to the establishment of an authoritative text. The notion of a foreign imperial force behind the origin of the biblical canon makes a neat irony for religious skeptics, but it may well prove a double-edged sword, giving undeserved historical credibility to a textually produced myth of origin.

Consideration of orality and literacy and their interrelationship proves valuable at this point, if we do not fall too quickly into sweeping political generalizations. For the question is, as Horsley correctly sees, that of *what kind of literacy* is involved with "Ezra's law book." I would suggest that the information the text provides us on this question says more in the first instance about literacy and authority in a largely oral culture than it does about imperial relations. And what it says is quite interesting, though more complicated than Horsley allows.

He suggests, first, that the ceremonial reading of the book as depicted in Neh 8 indicates its quality as "sacred-magical writing," that is, writing that is *received* not as content to be studied but as an "icon" (so Niditch 1996:43), powerful in itself because of the power it symbolizes and conveys. All writing regarded as sacred has such a quality (so even today, as when the Sunday scripture reader begins by intoning, "hear the word of the Lord"). Yet a simple view of the scroll as a "numinous sacred object" seems belied by the further indication that the writing was interpreted or translated by the Levites for the people. While not an object of general study, "Ezra's book" as presented in this narrative seems yet to be regarded as more than mere object, however sacred. Those who cannot read must nonetheless understand. Horsley's reference to the tradition of "found books" (with Speyer) is also interesting and reinforces the magical quality associated with authoritative texts. Yet here too there is complexity: one might well ask whether (like the book in Josiah's temple) this book was really "found" (or *mutatis mutandis*, suddenly "appeared" with Ezra) or whether this is *the story that was told about it*. If this scene is more fictional than not, then it is less easy to assert in a direct sense that "Ezra's 'book of the law of Moses' was written to authorize a new foundation of the temple-state under the Persians" (114). It was written to authorize something, to be sure—and under the conditions of colonialism, too—but what, exactly, and when, and by whose power? One prior question, of course, is, Which "it" are we talking about?

The story of the timely arrival of some text or another, accompanied by a transformative ceremonial reading, seems likely to be just that, a story. It was an important story in the long run, as we know, but one useful thing we might learn from this is precisely the role of such stories in the authorization of a text in an oral society: the text needed such authorization before it could do any authorizing itself! Those who promoted such a story were most likely representatives of, or at least responsible to, the empire, and it was in their interests to connect "the law of God" to "the law of the king," but I suspect this was as much a bottom-up enterprise (from colony to colonizer) as a top-down one. The priests, not the king, are running the textual show (cf. Grabbe's conclusion from the available inscriptional evidence that "the Persian bureaucracy would respond to particular petitions from its subjects, especially if granting the request did not inconvenience or contravene its own operations" [2001:110-11]). The fact that we do not know the content of "Ezra's" text should not be ascribed too quickly to its "sacred-magical" quality; most likely, we do not know because this content changed considerably over the long and complex process of mutual reinforcement of the authority of the literate and their products.

One aspect of Horsley's argument traces the supposed development in appropriation of the authoritative text from that of (1) a numinous object to (2) an object of study and interpretation to (3) a source of justification for the roles and prerogatives of its interpreters. Such a typology offers insight both into the question of how a written text gains authority in an oral culture and how it functions in relation to power (in the case of the Bible, in a situation of colonial as well as local power). Yet I am not sure the development through these stages is as neat as Horsley suggests. He himself notes, and I have emphasized, that the public reading recorded (or dramatized) in Neh 8 is accompanied—almost awkwardly so—by acts of interpretation. The fact that Ben Sira's (extant!) book contains little actual scriptural interpretation does not necessarily mean he was not doing it. One might wonder whether he represents one of those "elders" whose *oral* tradition so exercises Jesus. Orality may be functioning powerfully here, not only in ritual public performance in the cult but also in a relatively more private ritual performance, that is, in the act of teaching. Is it possible that the *written* interpretations in 4QMMT are an innovation not in the reception of the written law but in the written transmission of its interpretation? Has an alternative locus for doing textual interpretation, outside the normative grounds of the temple, led to the use of a new medium?

It is true, and important, that when Ben Sira wants to authorize his own work he does not call on the text but on direct personal inspiration. But the reason for this, I would suggest, is that he is still self-consciously in the process of text-making himself and seeking to authorize his own text as a worthy addition to those he studies. In this sense, he is a case study in that process of scribal development to which Horsley points in which the scribes develop a sense of their own authority and status alongside (and to some extent over against) that of the priests. For all Ben Sira's adulation (and concomitant ideological support) of the high priest, I find reason to doubt Horsley's claim that here "the law/Torah was surely not under the custody of the scribes/sages as its interpreters" (116).

If there is no obvious progression among the scribes from the law-as-numinous-object to the law-as-studied-and-interpreted, there may likewise be no neat movement from the studied text to the text used as the basis for roles and prerogatives. Horsley associates the latter shift with the resistance to the Jerusalem establishment beginning in the late third century and especially to the Hellenizing moves of the high priests under Antiochus IV.

> While the sacred scrolls of the Torah stored in the temple functioned as magical writing authorizing the temple-state, it may well be that the written text itself was first studied and claimed as an authority by dissident groups of scribes and priests attempting to justify their dissent from the imperial/colonial order. (134)

While it is possible that resistance motivated a shift in how the Torah was utilized by scribes and priests, it may rather be, as noted above, that the circumstances of resistance (removal from the power center) merely promoted a shift in how interpretation was transmitted. The larger point would be, however, that, if there was no Ezra, then there also may have been no authoritative written text with which to justify roles and prerogatives until much later than the fifth century. In other words, did resistance lead to interpretation of the authoritative text, or did a newly authoritative text lead to interpretation, both that committed to the status quo and that resisted it? Study of developing canons by Jonathan Z. Smith suggests that authoritative and increasingly fixed texts create just such a need for interpretation. What is interesting is that, as far as we know, the first *written* interpretation seems to have been done by the resisters. Such a perspective lends an additional meaning to Horsley's observation that certain scribes made alternative use of their literacy in resistance to imperial domination: they perhaps not so much *read* differently as they *wrote* newly.

Texts in a largely nonliterate culture likely have, to some degree, a magical quality to those select few who write them. But a writer can also not help but be aware of his or her ability to manipulate those texts. However reverential, the writer exercises some control over the text. Reverence must be learned and taught along with the teaching of those means of control over what is revered. Although he does not put the point quite this way, Horsley's emphasis on oral performance is, I think, crucial in understanding how a text comes to be experienced as authoritative for a man like Ben Sira. It is not simply that orality continues to be more important than textuality in general in the culture; rather, it is that texts are in some way deployed in ritual so that the sanctity of the occasion is conferred on the object. Some such connection of text and ritual seems to lie behind Ben Sira's hymn of praise to the ancestors that uses the biblical story to glorify (and authorize) the high priest in his ritual function. This does not mean that the scribe can only then relate to the text as a numinous object; rather, it means that all the scribe's work with the texts, that is to say, his interpretive endeavors, are also vested with this sacred quality. Ritual itself, then, may be one of the means by which scribes come to have a sense of their independent identity and authority, despite their economic dependence on others, as well as a means by which others accept this self-image.

The "origin of the Hebrew Scriptures in imperial relations" is, then, part and parcel of the question of how a text becomes authoritative in a largely oral culture. Up to this point, the analysis has considered this process among the literate. But what, then, about the nonliterate? Horsley appropriately turns our attention from the scribes to the peasants, who may be precisely *not* accepting this authority. Here the concepts of great tradition/little tradition and hidden transcript are useful to a point, but necessarily limited for the ancient context, as he notes, by the fact that the little and the hidden leave few records to the ages. We are left, as always, seeking the methodological means to discern the oral in the written. I would make two comments on Horsley's effort. The first, briefly, is a comparison with Kelber's essay. Notably, where Horsley sees Mark as an "oral-derived" work that with apparent transparency delivers to us an antiestablishment social-political reformer or even revolutionary, Kelber argues that Mark deploys literacy to "disguise any pronounced opposition to Roman imperial power" (138). It is beyond both my purpose and my capability to judge between these two views. It is worth noting, however, that while they both seem to understand the historical Jesus in about the same way, they differ precisely on the role of literacy in the early Christian movement vis-à-vis the colonizers. Methodological issues clearly remain.

There is, though, a subtler issue that I think runs through Horsley's essay and also informs that of Draper. Any effort by biblical scholars to connect consideration of orality and literacy with the issue of colonialism is to some extent driven by contemporary concerns. In the case of this volume, the role of the Bible, first in the colonization of nonliterate African peoples and then its subsequent role in African religious (and political) life as literacy spread, runs between many of the lines about both modern theory and the ancient world. The impulse toward critical self- and cultural reflection is a vital one. With both sympathy and respect for it, I want to raise a concern that justifiable ideological considerations not drive what should be a complex analysis into polarized categories. The arguments of both Horsley and Draper move at points into the discourse of liberationist hermeneutics. This can make for better theology than history.

This tendency is most obvious in Horsley's repeated and uncritical assumption that there was something that can be called "Israelite/Judean tradition," presumably identified with the "Mosaic covenant," that was maintained by "indigenous" priests and scribes but, most importantly, by the peasantry. The use of the term *Israelite* itself is anachronistic and sometimes tendentious. Judas the Galilean may well have represented a "more radical faction among the scribal retainers of the temple-state" (121). Josephus's brief description of this revolt, however, gives slim basis for asserting that these radicals, by taking "the content of their Torah most seriously[,] found revolutionary implications in the Mosaic covenant" (121). Moreover, such a reading of a "stricter popular tradition" acknowledging YHWH alone as Master, and thus opposed to paying tribute, flies in the face of some important data. Jeremiah, for example, the quintessential "Mosaic" prophet, advocated not resistance but acquiescence to imperial rule. Nor am I sure what the evidence is that by the time of Jesus "Mosaic covenantal law ... had apparently been cultivated among Israelite villagers for centuries" (123), such that the Mosaic covenant functioned as the "core" of the "Israelite popular tradition." To the contrary, both biblical and archeological evidence shows considerable lack of (latter-day?) orthodoxy outside Jerusalem (thus presumably involving "peasants") regarding worship of YHWH alone. Horsley engages in an unwarranted essentializing of a "Mosaic covenant," not to mention an apparent historicizing of its eponym, among a romanticized body of peasantry capable of carrying on an ideologically untainted version of it for "centuries." If any idea breaks all known rules of "orality," with its assumption of flexibility and change in traditions (as well as disinclination toward "abstraction"!), surely this one does.

It would be politically quite useful in the modern context to be able to imagine an ancient hidden transcript combining right worship and revolutionary freedom in the oral tradition of first-century peasants that stands against the corruption of the written text (and its concomitant oral interpretation) by the imperial power or its lackeys. But I fear that this is a form of wishful (theo? ideological) thinking (akin to Gottwald's premonarchic free peasantry) that can only impair our ability to apply orality/literacy theories in methodologically rigorous ways. I am neither a New Testament scholar nor the daughter of one, but what I know of the historical Jesus debates engenders only despair of certainty about the man's real intentions. Are there indications of a political agenda in the "render unto Caesar" episode? It would appear so, but no less are there eschatological indications elsewhere and teacher/sage indications elsewhere yet. Revolution—inevitably laced with religious rhetoric—was in the air in first-century Palestine, and Jesus was no doubt caught up, perhaps even directly involved, in it. But tax resistance and support for conventional norms such as supporting elderly parents do not a centuries-old (implication: pure and original?) Covenant (capital C) tradition make. This sort of idealization impedes Horsley's important effort to address the complex question of how orality and literacy mix and match in the ancient world and, in particular, in a situation where a written tradition was gaining increasing power within a largely oral culture.

Jonathan Draper's is the most theological of the biblical essays in this volume and also the one that comes closest to an overt articulation of its subtext. His interest "is the ambivalent role of a sacred text in a situation of colonial domination" (155). Though he makes no direct hermeneutical move in the direction of contemporary (South) Africa, it seems waiting in the wings in a context where the role of scripture as a means of both oppression and resistance still awaits full exploration. The question, then, is whether theories of orality and literacy can help further Draper's important inquiry regarding sacred texts and colonial power. While I learned much from this essay, theology seemed in the end to outweigh theory and, thus, to stop the political analysis prematurely.

Draper refers early on to Bryan Wilson's study of indigenous responses to colonialism—the relevant one being the "introversionist," "which is marked by experimentation with new cultural combinations"— and to the model of the *bricoleur*, which he takes from Comaroff and Comaroff (though note Biakolo's critique of this concept as used by Lévi-Strauss). Thus,

> [t]he identification of Jesus with the divine *logos* of Greek philosophy is an act of *bricolage* that serves as a hermeneutical key to counter the emphasis on text and only text, legitimating control, and to some extent also empire, which was represented by the newly dominant scribal elite after the destruction of the temple. The *logos* is not only a device for opening the Scripture to new interpretation, but also the device for continuing revelation. (156–57)

The essay then turns to a fascinating analysis of the intra-Jewish debate about the "two powers" heresy as it relates to John's portrayal of Jesus in connection with his mediatorial role in both the giving of the law and the conveying of the presence of God to the believer. Draper argues, convincingly to this non–New Testament scholar, that

> the opposition between text and word [in John] relates to a different way of using the Hebrew Scriptures. The opposition is between "searching the Scriptures" as a means of settling disputes in the manner of halakah and internalizing the Scriptures through meditation until they become "Word abiding in you," a mystical way of practicing the presence of the Word, of knowing the Unknowable God through the One He has sent. (163)

But what does this focus on differences in interpretive modes have to do, first, with orality and literacy and, second, with colonialism?

It is both obvious and at the same time noteworthy just how extraordinarily literary this whole scenario is. The rabbis and the "two powers heretics" are clearly debating about written scripture precisely *as written;* the kinds of details that engage them are only apparent to close readers of a text. John's Gospel likewise presents on one level a written response to a written problem. Where, then, does orality enter in? Does it lurk in Draper's passing (despite the featured position in the title) references to "ritual" as part of the process by which one achieves John's desired mystical effect? Does textuality itself produce a certain kind of (meditative?) ritual? I wish more were said on the topic, for, as Horsley points out, ritual is one context for important oral-written interface. Or is orality implied in the notion of Jesus as the Word that both opens and opposes written texts? If so, this is a heavily theologized, not to say literate, version of the orality/literacy framework! Have we not just ended up with a powerful valorization of the written text—of this particular written text—once more, by means of the rhetoric, rather than the actual practice, of orality?

One wishes here for more sociological grist for the theological mill, in particular more exploration of the "premise that John's Gospel is the product of a marginalized and alienated section of the elite of a subjugated indigenous people in a colonial situation after the destruction of the old hegemonic order" (156). Not just the presence of but also the high level of literacy in the Gospel does indeed suggest an elite, but who are they exactly? Draper's argument that they "think in Aramaic" presumes Jews, while their adaptation of Greek philosophy says well-educated, or at least cosmopolitan, Jews. Where did these people come from, and how exactly were they related to "the old hegemonic order" now destroyed? Whom are they writing to and for, and how do they imagine their writing will interface with a predominantly oral culture? One may take for granted that, in a situation of political and social devastation, new forms will arise if a tradition is not to die, but why in the case of John do these forms take the deeply literary character that they do? Is it John himself who wishes, with the rabbis, to be called "Rabboni"?

Theologizing language also gets in the way of the analysis of the Gospel's relationship to "colonialism."

> Always the assumption is that the Word mediates power, and that discovering the key unleashes divine power. The power of the liberated, orally mediated Word then provides a counterpoint to colonial control through the textual word. (155)

Such a statement confuses me. First, what does "power" mean here? Surely not power in a political sense vis-à-vis the Romans. In what way, then, does a liberated, orally mediated Word (if this is what the highly literate John represents) provide a counterpoint to colonial control? Indeed, what is the relationship between colonial control and the textual word after the destruction of the temple? What have Pharisees (or other Jewish scribes) to do with Romans at that point?

The liberationist theo-ideology short-circuits a historical analysis informed by orality/literacy theories. There are really two questions here, one historical and one contemporary. The second one (What role has sacred text played in situations of colonial domination in our own immediate history, and thus what role might it play in a postcolonial situation?) needs to be put on the table. The Bible has not always served well the cause of justice. But do we not simply reinscribe its magic when we read history through the newly rose-colored glasses of orality, seeking that ideal moment of liberation behind or within the text, if not captured by it?

I regret the lack of expertise that would let me comment as richly on the essays of Solère, on Plato, and Decharneux, on the Mithras cult, as they deserve. Let me conclude, nonetheless, with some questions they might raise for the study of the ancient Jewish and Christian worlds and their literature.

Solère's essay includes no consideration of colonialism in either theory or context. If there is any comparison to be made, however, between classical Athens and Hellenistic/Roman Palestine, it does raise some interesting questions. What, for example, might the suspicion of at least certain kinds of writing that appears in Plato and continues in the neo-Platonic tradition suggest about the development of written tradition in Judaism and Christianity? Does Ben Sira perhaps distinguish between things that are properly written and things that should remain oral? If so, his book is clear indication that the former would include instructions in living for scribes-to-be, hymns, prayers, and recitation of historical narrative. But there is a tradition of "riddles" (*ḥidoth*) among the sages going back at least to Proverbs. The ability to speak well was always a prime professional desideratum for at least a certain kind of scribe, but "riddles" suggest a more esoteric sort of oral knowledge. And what happens, then, when writing itself gains caché? Why, in the first place, given the Platonic tradition, does it do so? I do not suggest that Athens, or Plato in particular, is the only possible model for ancient views on writing. But some account must be given of why people in one context resist writing while those in another come to view it as the word of God. As Jaffee argues in his response essay in this volume, the later rabbinic tradition will take a version of the view that there are some things properly written and others not. Or, to be more precise, everything may be written, but some things must only be *performed* orally. Does this distinction begin already as early as Ben Sira, thus explaining Horsley's observation about the sage's (perhaps only) apparent lack of interest in interpreting the Torah? Is oral interpretation of scripture for him the current version of *ḥidoth*? And is scripture itself, like Plato's proper writing, understood as written for a select few? The same question might also be asked of the written Jesus and kingdom of God traditions analyzed by Kelber and Draper. Is our difficulty in discerning their audience because they are not intended to have much of one? Are they in this regard different from Paul, who seems to cast his rhetorical net widely? Are there, in other words, different understandings of writtenness (and thus orality) in early Christianity? Such is the implication of Draper's argument, but I think it requires a subtler scaling than the simple one of liberating orality versus colonializing text.

This subtle interrelationship of writing and orality is present in Decharneux's study of the Mithras cult as well. The historical evidence for the vast geographical spread of this cult is at first glance somewhat astonishing, given what seems like an anthropological truism, namely, that oral traditions are local traditions, with written texts required for geographical mobility. Two things have happened here. The obvious one is the Roman Empire, with its widespread armies and its trade routes. The other, less obvious, factor, noted by Decharneux only in passing, is that the *imposed* orality of the cult—its "overturn of writing in favor of orality"—takes place among otherwise often *literate* people. "Indeed, the circles in which the rites were developed and the members assisting the assemblies probably had access to written documents" (101–2). One can only guess at the degree to which written communication supported the diffusion of this determinedly oral tradition.

As with the biblical sages' "riddles," and the later rabbis' promotion of Oral Torah, the choice for orality in religious practice where writing is an option seems to be a choice for the secrecy, or at least special knowledge, needed to maintain the identity of an in-group over against outsiders. Few may be able to read and write, but the very fact of writtenness seems to have been acknowledged to include the potential danger of unauthorized access. The relationship of literacy and orality to power is, then, a complex business, and understanding John's written glorification of an oral Logos over against a written tradition may require several turnings of the screw.

WORKS CONSULTED

Akinnaso, F. Niyi. 1982. The Literate Writes and the Nonliterate Chants: Written and Ritual Communication in Sociolinguistic Perspective. Pages 7–36 in *Linguistics and Literacy*. Edited by William Frawley. New York: Plenum.

———. 1985. On the Similarities between Spoken and Written Language. *Language and Speech* 28:323–59.

———. 1991. Literacy and Individual Consciousness. Pages 73–94 in *Literate Systems and Individual Lives: Perspectives on Literacy and Schooling*. Edited by Edward M. Jennings and Alan C. Purves. Albany: State University of New York Press.

Albeck, Chanoch, ed., 1965. *The Six Orders of the Mishnah* [Hebrew]. Jerusalem: Bialik; Tel Aviv: Dvir.

American Heritage Dictionary of the English Language. 3rd ed. Cited 7 May 2001. Online: http://www.dictionary.com/cgi-bin/dict.pl?term=table.

Aronsson, Karin. 1988. Language Practices and the Visibility of Language: Reflections on the Great Divide in the Light of Ethiopian Oral Traditions. Pages 73–83 in *The Written World: Studies in Literate Thought and Action*. Edited by Roger Säljö. Berlin: Springer-Verlag.

Asante, Molefi K., and Abu S. Abarry, eds. 1996. *African Intellectual Heritage: A Book of Sources*. Philadelphia: Temple University Press.

Ashton, John. 1994a. Bridging Ambiguities. Pages 71–89 in idem, *Studying John: Approaches to the Fourth Gospel*. Oxford: Clarendon.

———. 1994b. *Understanding the Fourth Gospel*. Oxford: Oxford University Press.

Assmann, Jan. 1992. *Das kulturelle Gedächtnis: Schrift, Erinnerung und politische Identität in frühen Hochkulturen*. Munich: Beck.

Bain, B., and A. Yu. 1991. Qin, Han and Huang: Text Reproduction and Literacy in Rural China, a Case for Euclid and Homer. *Canadian Modern Language Review* 47:861–77.

Balogun, F. Odun. 1995. *Matigari*: An African Novel as Oral Performance. *Oral Tradition*, 10:129–64.

Barrett, C. K. 1955. *The Gospel according to John*. London: SPCK.

Bauman, Richard. 1977. *Verbal Art as Performance*. Prospect Heights, Ill.: Waveland.

———. 1986. *Story, Performance, and Event: Contextual Studies of Oral Narrative*. Cambridge: Cambridge University Press.

Bauman, Richard, and Donald Braid. 1998. The Ethnography of Performance in the Study of Oral Traditions. Pages 106–22 in Foley 1998b.

Bauman, Richard, and Pamela Ritch. 1994. Informing Performance: Producing the *Coloquio* in Tierra Blanca. *Oral Tradition* 9:255–80.

Baurain, Claude , Corinne Bonnet, and V. Krings, eds. 1991. *Phoinikeia grammata: Lire et écrire en Méditerranée*. Namur: Société des Études Classiques.

Beck, Roger. 1982. The Mithraic Torchbearers and "Absence of Opposition." *Classical Views* 26/1:126–40.

Bennett, Jo Anne, and John W. Berry. 1991. Cree Literacy in the Syllabic Script. Pages 90–104 in *Literacy and Orality*. Edited by D. R. Olson and N. Torrance. Cambridge: Cambridge University Press.

Benvéniste, Emile. 1966. *Titres et noms propres en iranien ancien*. Travaux de l'Institut d'études iraniennes de l'Université de Paris 1. Paris: Klincksieck.

Berger, Peter. 1967. *The Sacred Canopy: Elements of a Sociological Theory of Religion*. Garden City, N.Y.: Doubleday.

Berquist, Jon. *Judaism in Persia's Shadow*. Minneapolis: Fortress.

Berry, John W., and Jo Anne Bennett. 1989. Syllabic Literacy and Cognitive Performance among the Cree. *International Journal of Psychology* 24:429–50.

Bertrand, Jean-Marie. 1999. *De l'écriture à l'oralité: Lecture des Lois de Platon*. Paris: Publications de la Sorbonne.

Biakolo, Emevwo. 1999. On the Theoretical Foundations of Orality and Literacy. *Research in African Literature* 30/2: 42–65.

Bidez, Joseph, and Franz Cumont. 1938. *Les mages hellénisés: Zoroastre, Ostanès et Hystaspe d'après la tradition grecque*. 2 vols. Paris: Belles Lettres.

Blenkinsopp, Joseph. 1987. The Mission of Udjahorresnet and Those of Ezra and Nehemiah. *JBL* 106:409–21.

———. 1991. Temple and Society in Achaemenid Judah. Pages 22–53 in *Second Temple Studies 1: Persian Period*. Edited by P. R. Davies. Sheffield: Sheffield Academic Press.

———. 2001. Was the Pentateuch the Civic and Religious Constitution of the Jewish Ethnos in the Persian Period? Pages 41–62 in Watts.

Boethius. 1973. On the Hebdomads and De Trinitate. In idem, *The Theological Tractates*. Edited by H. F. Stewart, E. K. Rand, and S. J. Tester. 2nd ed. LCL. Cambridge: Harvard University Press.

Borgen, Peder. 1965. *Bread from Heaven: An Exegetical Study of the Concept of Manna in the Gospel of John and the Writings of Philo*. NovTSup10. Leiden: Brill.

———. 1968. God's Agent in the Fourth Gospel. Pages 137–48 in *Religions in Antiquity: Essays in Memory of Erwin Ramsdell Goodenough*. Edited by J. Neusner. Leiden: Brill.

Botha, Pieter J. J. 1991. Orality, Literacy and Worldview: Exploring the Interaction. *Communicatio* 17(2):2–15.

———. 1992. Greco-Roman Literacy as Setting for New Testament Writings. *Neot* 26:208.

———. 1993a. Living Voice and Lifeless Letters: Reserve towards Writing in the Greco-Roman World. *HvTSt* 49:742–59.

———. 1993b. The Social Dynamics of the Early Transmission of the Jesus Tradition. *Neot* 27:205–31.

———. 1993c. The Verbal Art of the Pauline Letters: Rhetoric, Performance and Presence. Pages 409–28 in *Rhetoric and the New Testament: Essays from the 1992 Heidelberg Conference*. Edited by Stanley E. Porter and Thomas H. Olbricht. Sheffield: Sheffield Academic Press.

———. 1999. Schools in the World of Jesus: Analysing the Evidence. *Neot* 33:225–60.

———. 2001. Towards an Ethnography of Communication in the First-Century Mediterranean World. Unpublished paper. Context Group. University of Pretoria.

Bradbury, Nancy Mason. 1998. Traditional Referentiality: The Aesthetic Power of Oral Traditional Structures. Pages 136–45 in Foley 1998b.

Brague, Rémi. 1978. *Le Restant: Supplément aux commentaires du Ménon de Platon.* Paris: Les Belles Lettres.

Bregman, Marc. Forthcoming. Mishnah and LXX as Mystery: An Example of Jewish-Christian Polemic in the Byzantine Period. In *Continuity and Renewal: Judaism in Eretz Israel during the Byzantine-Christian Era.* Edited by L. Levine.

Bright, William. 1982. Literature: Written and Oral. Pages 271–83 in *Analyzing Discourse: Text and Talk.* Edited by Deborah Tannen. Washington, D.C.: Georgetown University Press.

Brill de Ramírez, Susan Berry. 1999. *Contemporary American Indian Literatures and the Oral Tradition.* Tucson: University of Arizona Press.

Brown, Duncan. 1998. *Voicing the Text: South African Oral Poetry and Performance.* Cape Town: Oxford University Press.

Brown, Mary Ellen. 1996. The Mechanism of the Ancient Ballad: William Motherwell's Explanation. *Oral Tradition* 11:175–89.

Brown, Peter R. L. 1996. *The Rise of Western Christendom: Triumph and Diversity, AD 200–1000.* Cambridge: Blackwell.

Brown, Raymond. 1966–70. *The Gospel according to John.* 2 vols. AB 29–29A. New York: Doubleday.

Bruner, J. S., and D. R. Olson. 1978. Symbols and Texts as Tools of Intellect. *Interchange* 8(4):1–15.

Buber, Salomon, ed. 1963. *Midrash Tanhuma.* Israel: n.p. [Orig. 1912–13]

Büchsel, F. μονογενής. *TDNT* 4:737–41.

Bultmann, Rudolf. 1971. *The Gospel of John: A Commentary.* Translated by G. R. Beasley-Murray. Edited by R. W. N. Hoare and J. K. Riches. Philadelphia: Westminster.

Burkert, Walter. 1987. *Ancient Mystery Cults.* Cambridge: Harvard University Press.

Byrskog, Samuel. 2000. *Story as History—History as Story: The Gospel Tradition in the Context of Ancient Oral History.* WUNT 123. Tübingen: Mohr Siebeck.

Callahan, Allen Dwight, Richard A. Horsley, and Abraham Smith, eds. 1988. *Semeia* 83/84.

Cambiano, Giuseppe. 1988. La démonstration géométrique. Pages 251–72 in Detienne and Camassa.

Campbell, Leroy A. 1968. *Mithraic Iconography and Ideology.* Leiden: Brill.

Carter, Charles E. 1999. *The Emergence of Yehud in the Persian Period: A Social and Demographic Study.* JSOTSup 294. Sheffield: Sheffield Academic Press.

Cavallo, Guglielmo. and Roger Chartier. 1967. *Histoire de la lecture dans le monde occidental.* Paris: Éditions du Seuil.

Chandler, Daniel. 2001. Marxist Media Theory. Cited 3 May 2001. Online: http://www. aber.ac.uk/media/Documents/marxism/marxism13.html.

Chao Gejin. 1997. Mongolian Oral Epic Poetry: An Overview. *Oral Tradition* 12: 322–36.

Chilton, Bruce. 1986. *Targumic Approaches to the Gospels: Essays in the Mutual Definition of Judaism and Christianity.* Lanham, Md.: University Press of America.

———. 1987. *The Isaiah Targum.* The Aramaic Bible 11. Edinburgh: T&T Clark.

Chuvin, Pierre. 1990. *A Chronicle of the Last Pagans.* Translated by B. A. Archer. Cambridge: Harvard University Press.

Clauss, Manfred. 2000. *The Roman Cult of Mithras: The God and His Mysteries.* New York: Routledge.

Cole, Michael. 1990. Cultural Psychology: A Once and Future Discipline? Pages 279–335 in *Cross-Cultural Perspectives: Nebraska Symposium on Motivation 1989.* Edited by J. J. Berman. Lincoln: University of Nebraska Press.

Collins, Adela Yarbro. 1976. *The Combat Myth in the Book of Revelation.* HDR 9. Chico, Calif.: Scholars Press.

Collins, John J. 1984. *The Apocalyptic Imagination: An Introduction to the Jewish Matrix of Christianity.* New York: Crossroad.

Comaroff, Jean, and John L. Comaroff. 1991. *Of Revelation and Revolution: Christianity, Colonialism and Consciousness in South Africa.* Chicago. University of Chicago Press.

Conzelmann, Hans. 1961. *The Theology of St. Luke.* Translated by Geoffrey Buswell. New York: Harper & Row.

Coplan, David B. 1994. *In the Time of the Cannibals: The Word Music of South Africa's Basotho Migrants.* Chicago: Aldine.

Couloubaritsis, Lambros. 1998. *Histoire de la philosophie ancienne et médiévale: Figures illustres.* Paris: Grasset.

Cramer, J. 2001. Shakespeare's Globe Theatre, Like It Oughta Be. Cited 4 May. Online: http://www.bergen.com/travel/globe199903286.htm.

Cumont, Franz V. 1896–99. *Textes et monuments figurés relatifs aux mystères de Mithra.* 2 vols. Brussells: Lamertin.

———. 1956a. *The Mysteries of Mithra.* New York: Dover. [Orig. *Les mystères de Mithra.* Brussells: Lamertin, 1913.]

———. 1956b. *The Oriental Religions in Roman Paganism.* New York: Dover. [Orig. *Les religions orientales dans le paganisme romain.* Paris: Leroux, 1929.]

Daniels, C. M. 1975. The Role of the Roman Army in the Spread and Practice of Mithraism. Pages 249–74 in vol. 2 of *Mithraic Studies: Proceedings.* Edited by John R. Hinnells. Manchester: Manchester University Press.

Davidson, Olga M. 1994. *Poet and Hero in the Persian Book of Kings.* Ithaca, N.Y.: Cornell University Press.

Davies, Anna Morpurgo. 1986. Forms of Writing in the Ancient Mediterranean World. Pages 50–77 in *The Written Word: Literacy in Transition.* Edited by Gerd Baumann. Oxford: Clarendon.

Davies, Sioned. 1992. Storytelling in Medieval Wales. *Oral Tradition* 7:231–57.

Decharneux, Baudouin, and Luc Nefontaine. 1999. *L'initiation: Splendeurs et misères.* Brussells: Labor.

Degenhardt, Hans-Joachim. 1965. *Lukas, Evangelist der Armen.* Stuttgart: Verlag Katholisches Bibelwerk.

Denny, J. Peter. 1991. Rational Thought in Oral Culture and Literate Decontextualization. Pages 66–89 in *Literacy and Orality*. Edited by D. R. Olson and N. Torrance. Cambridge: Cambridge University Press.

Derrida, Jacques. 1972. La Pharmacie de Platon. Pages 69–197 in idem, *La Dissémination*. Paris: Seuil.

———. 1976. *Of Grammatology*. Translated by Gayatri Chakravorty Spivak. Baltimore: Johns Hopkins University Press.

Detienne, Marcel. 1989. *L'écriture d'Orphée*. Paris: Gallimard.

Detienne, Marcel, and Georgio Camassa, eds. 1988. *Les savoirs de l'écriture: En Grèce ancienne*. Lille: Presses universitaires de Lille.

de Vet, Therese. 1996. The Joint Role of Orality and Literacy in the Composition, Transmission, and Performance of the Homeric Texts: A Comparative View. *Transactions of the American Philological Association* 126:43–76.

Doane, A. N. 1994. The Ethnography of Scribal Writing and Anglo-Saxon Poetry: Scribe as Performer. *Oral Tradition* 9:420–39.

Draper, Jonathan A. 1983. A Targum of Isaiah in 1QS III,2–3. *RevQ* 42:265–69.

———. 1988. The Apostles as Foundation Stones of the Heavenly Jerusalem and the Foundation of the Qumran Community. *Neot* 22:41–63.

———. 1993. The Development of the "Sign of the Son of Man" in the Jesus Tradition. *NTS* 39:1–21.

———. 1997. Temple, Tabernacle and Mystical Experience in John. *Neot* 31:263–88.

———. 2000. Holy Seed and the Return of the Diaspora in John 12:24. *Neot* 34:347–59.

———. 2002. What Did Isaiah See? Angelic Theophany in the Tomb in John 20:11–18. *Neot* 36:63–76.

———. 2003a. *Orality, Literacy, and Colonialism in Southern Africa*. SemeiaSt 46. Atlanta: Society of Biblical Literature; Leiden: Brill.

———. 2003b. What Did Isaiah See? Angelic Theophany in the Tomb in John 20:11–18. *Neot* 36:63–76.

DuBois, Thomas A. 1995. *Finnish Folk Poetry and the* Kalevala. New York: Garland.

———. 1998. Ethnopoetics. Pages 123–35 in Foley 1998b.

Duchesne-Guillemin, Jacques. 1960. *Aiôn et le léontocéphale*. Nouvelle Clio 10. Paris: Presses universitaires de France.

———. 1973. *Religion of Ancient Iran*. Bombay: Tata.

Duggan, Joseph J. 1973. *The Song of Roland: Formulaic Style and Poetic Craft*. Berkeley and Los Angeles: University of California Press.

Dumézil, Georges. 1977. *Les dieux souverains et les Indo-Européens*. Paris: Gallimard.

Dupont-Sommer, André. 1976. *L'énigme du dieu Satrape et le dieu Mithra: Lecture faite dans la séance publique annuelle du 26 novembre 1976, Institut de France, Académie des inscriptions et belles-lettres*. Paris: Institut de France.

Duthoy, Robert. 1969. *The Taurobolium: Its Evolution and Terminology*. Études préliminaires aux religions orientales dans l'empire romain 10. Leiden: Brill.

Eagleton, Terry. 1986. The Revolt of the Reader. Pages 181–84 in idem, *Against the Grain: Essays 1975–1985*. London: Verso.

Echols, L. D., R. F. West, K. E. Stanovich, and K. S. Zehr. 1996. Using Children's Literacy Activities to Predict Growth in Verbal Cognitive Skills: A Longitudinal Investigation. *Journal of Educational Psychology* 88:296–304.

Erzgräber, Willi, and Sabine Volk, eds. 1988. *Mündlichkeit und Schriftlichkeit im englischen Mittelalter.* Script Oralia 5. Tübingen: Narr.

Evans, Craig A. 1993. *Word and Glory: On the Exegetical and Theological Background of John's Prologue.* JSNTSup 89. Sheffield: Sheffield Academic Press.

Farrell, Thomas J. 1977. Literacy, the Basics, and All That Jazz. *College English* 38(5):443–59.

Finnegan, Ruth H. 1974. How Oral Is Oral Literature? *Bulletin of the School of Oriental and African Studies* 37:52–64.

———. 1977. *Oral Poetry: Its Nature, Significance and Social Context.* Cambridge: Cambridge University Press.

———. 1988. *Literacy and Orality: Studies in the Technology of Communication.* Oxford: Blackwell.

———. 1992. *Oral Traditions and the Verbal Arts: A Guide to Research Practices.* London: Routledge.

Flender, Helmut. 1967. *St. Luke: Theologian of Redemptive History.* Translated by Ilse and Reginald Fuller. Philadelphia: Fortress.

Foley, John Miles. 1985. *Oral-Formulaic Theory and Research: An Introduction and Annotated Bibliography.* New York: Garland. Updated electronic version online: http://www.oraltradition.org.

———, ed. 1986. *Oral Tradition in Literature: Interpretation in Context.* Columbia: University of Missouri Press.

———. 1988. *The Theory of Oral Composition: History and Methodology.* Bloomington: Indiana University Press.

———. 1990. *Traditional Oral Epic: The Odyssey, Beowulf, and the Serbo-Croatian Return Song.* Berkeley and Los Angeles: University of California Press.

———. 1991. *Immanent Art: From Structure to Meaning in Traditional Oral Epic.* Bloomington: Indiana University Press.

———. 1995. *The Singer of Tales in Performance.* Bloomington: Indiana University Press.

———. 1998a. The Impossibility of Canon. Pages 13–33 in Foley 1998b.

———, ed. 1998b. *Teaching Oral Traditions.* New York: Modern Language Association.

———. 1999. *Homer's Traditional Art.* University Park: Pennsylvania State University Press.

———. 2001. Editing and Translating Oral Epic: The South Slavic Songs and Homer. Pages 3–28 in *Epea and Grammata: Oral and Written Communication in Ancient Greece.* Edited by John Miles Foley and Ian Worthington. Leiden: Brill.

———. 2002. *How to Read an Oral Poem.* Urbana: University of Illinois Press. E-companion at http://www.oraltradition.org.

Fontaine, Carole R. 1982. *Traditional Sayings in the Old Testament: A Contextual Study.* Sheffield: Almond.

Fossum, Jarl E. 1995a. In the Beginning Was the Name: Onomanology as the Key to Johannine Christology. Pages 109–33 in idem, *The Image of the Invisible God: Essays on the Influence of Jewish Mysticism on Early Christology.* Göttingen: Vandenhoeck & Ruprecht.

———. 1995b. The Son of Man's Alter Ego: John 1:51, Targumic Tradition and Jewish Mysticism. Pages 135–51 in idem, *The Image of the Invisible God: Essays on the Influence of Jewish Mysticism on Early Christology*. Göttingen: Vandenhoeck & Ruprecht.

Franks, Bridget A. 1996. Deductive Reasoning Narrative Contexts: Developmental Trends and Reading Skill Effects. *Genetic, Social and General Psychology Monographs* 122(1):75–105.

Freyburger-Galland, Marie-Laure, Gérard Freyburger, and Jean-Christian Tautil. 1986. *Sectes religieuses en Grèce et à Rome dans l'antiquité païenne*. Paris: Belles Lettres.

Fried, Lisbeth S. 2001. "You Shall Appoint Judges": Ezra's Mission and the Rescript of Artaxerxes. Pages 63–89 in Watts.

Friedmann, Meir, ed. 1963. *Pesiqta Rabbati*. Tel-Aviv: n.p. [Orig. 1880]

Gennep, Arnold van. 1960. *The Rites of Passage*. Translated by M. B. Vizedom and G. L. Caffee. Chicago: University of Chicago Press. [Orig. *Les rites de passage*. Paris: Nourry, 1909.]

Gerhardsson, B. 1998. *Memory and Manuscript: Oral Tradition and Written Transmission in Rabbinical Judaism and Early Christianity, with Tradition and Transmission in Early Christianity*. Translated by Eric J. Sharpe. Grand Rapids: Eerdmans. [Orig. 1961]

Gershevitch, Ilya. 1959. *The Avestan Hymn to Mithra*. Cambridge: Cambridge University Press.

Gieschen, Charles. A. 1998. *Angelomorphic Christology: Antecedents and Early Evidence*. AGSU 42. Leiden: Brill.

Gill, Sam D. 1987. *Native American Religious Action: A Performance Approach to Religion*. Columbia: University of South Carolina Press.

Goetsch, Paul, ed. 1990. *Mündliches Wissen in neuzeitlicher Literatur*. Script Oralia 18. Tübingen: Narr.

Goodman, M. 1998–2002. Palestinian Rabbis and the Conversion of Constantine to Christianity. Pages 1–9 in vol. 2 of *The Talmud Yerushalmi and Graeco-Roman Culture*. Edited by Peter Schaefer and Catherine Hezser. TSAJ 71, 79, 93. Tübingen: Mohr Siebeck.

Goody, Jack. 1973. Evolution and Communication: The Domestication of the Savage Mind. *British Journal of Sociology* 24:1–12.

———. 1977a. *The Domestication of the Savage Mind*. Cambridge: Cambridge University Press.

———. 1977b. Literacy, Criticism, and the Growth of Knowledge. Pages 226–43 in *Culture and Its Creators*. Edited by Joseph Ben-David and Terry Nichols Clark. Chicago: University of Chicago Press.

———. 1986. *The Logic of Writing and the Organization of Society*. Cambridge: Cambridge University Press.

———. 1987. *The Interface between the Written and the Oral*. Cambridge: Cambridge University Press.

———. 1989. Oral Culture. *International Encyclopedia of Communication* 3:226–29.

———. 1996a. Cognitive Contradictions and Universals: Creation and Evolution in Oral Cultures. *Social Anthropology* 4:1–16.

———. 1996b. *The East in the West*. Cambridge: Cambridge University Press.

———. 2000. Canonization in Oral and Literate Traditions. Chapter 8 in idem, *The Power of the Written Tradition*. Washington: Smithsonian Institution

Press. Repr. of Canonization in Oral and Literate Cultures. Pages 3–16 in *Canonization and Decanonization: Papers Presented to the International Conference of the Leiden Institute for the Study of Religions, Held at Leiden, 9–10 January 1997*. Edited by Arie van der Kooij and Karol van der Toorn. Leiden: Brill, 1998.

Goody, Jack, Michael Cole, and Sylvia Scribner. 1977. Writing and Formal Operations: A Case Study among the Vai. *Africa* 47:289–304.

Goody, Jack, and Ian P. Watt. 1963. The Consequences of Literacy. *Comparative Studies in Society and History* 5:304–45.

Gottwald, Norman K. 2000. *The Politics of Ancient Israel*. Louisville: Westminster John Knox.

Grabbe, Lester L. 1998. *Ezra-Nehemiah*. Old Testament Readings. London: Routledge.

———. 2001. The Law of Moses in the Ezra Tradition: More Virtual Than Real? Pages 91–114 in Watts.

Graf, Frtiz. 1994. *La magie dans l'antiquité gréco-romaine: Idéologie et pratique*. Paris: Belles Lettres.

Greenfield, Patricia M. 1972. Oral or Written Language: The Consequences for Cognitive Development in Africa, the United States and England. *Language and Speech* 15:169–78.

Griffith, Alison B. Mithraism, une page en anglais intégrée dans *The Early Church On-Line* Encyclopedia (Ecole) Initiative.

Gunkel, Hermann. 1895. *Schöpfung und Chaos in Urzeit und Endzeit: Eine religionsgeschichtliche Untersuchung über Gen 1 und Ap Joh 12*. Göttingen: Vandenhoeck & Ruprecht.

———. 1964. *The Legends of Genesis, the Biblical Saga and History*. Translated by W. H. Carruth. New York: Schocken.

Habermalz, Sabine. 1998. "Signs on a White Field": A Look at Orality in Literacy and James Joyce's Ulysses. *Oral Tradition* 13: 285–305.

Hadot, Pierre. 1995. *Qu'est-ce que la philosophie antique?* Paris: Gallimard.

Harris, Roy. 1986. *The Origin of Writing*. London: Duckworth.

Harris, William V. 1989. *Ancient Literacy*. Cambridge: Harvard University Press.

Havelock, Eric Alfred. 1976. *Origins of Western Literacy*. Toronto: Ontario Institute for Studies in Education.

———. 1982. The Oral and the Written Word: A Reappraisal. Pages 3–38 in idem, *The Literate Revolution in Greece and Its Cultural Consequences*. Princeton: Princeton University Press.

———. 1986. *The Muse Learns to Write: Reflections on Orality and Literacy from Antiquity to the Present*. New Haven: Yale University Press.

Haynes, W. Lance. 1988. Of That Which We Cannot Write: Some Notes on the Phenomenology of Media. *Quarterly Journal of Speech* 74:71–101.

Heath, Shirley Brice. 1982. What No Bedtime Story Means: Narrative Skills at Home and School. *Language in Society* 11:49–76.

———. 1983. Ways with Words. New York: Cambridge University Press.

Hedrick, Wanda B., and James W. Cunningham. 1995. The Relationship between Wide Reading and Listening Comprehension of Written Language. *Journal of Reading Behavior* 27:425–38.

Heissig, Walther. 1996, The Present State of the Mongolian Epic and Some Topics for Future Research. *Oral Tradition* 11:85-98.

Hemstreet, Keith, et al. 2000. *nycSLAMS*. New York: Zoom Culture. [video]

Henderson, Ian H. 1992. *Didache* and Orality in Synoptic Comparison. *JBL* 111:283–306.

Hengel, Martin. 1974. *Judaism and Hellenism*. Philadelphia: Fortress.

Hezser, Catherine. 1997. *The Social Structure of the Rabbinic Movement in Roman Palestine*. TSAJ 66. Tübingen: Mohr Siebeck.

———. 1998–2002. The Codification of Legal Knowledge in Late Antiquity: The Talmud Yerushalmi and Roman Law Codes. Pages 581–642 in vol. 1 of *The Talmud Yerushalmi and Graeco-Roman Culture*. Edited by Peter Schaefer and Catherine Hezser. TSAJ 71, 79, 93. Tübingen: Mohr Siebeck.

———. 2001. *Jewish Literacy in Roman Palestine*. TSAJ 81. Tübingen: Mohr Siebeck.

Hinnells, John R. 1975. *Mithraic Studies*. 2 vols. Proceedings of the International Congress of Mithraic Studies: Manchester: Manchester University Press.

Holton, Milne, and Vasa D. Mihailovich, eds. and trans. 1997. *Songs of the Serbian People: From the Collections of Vuk Karadžić*. Pittsburgh: University of Pittsburgh Press.

Honko, Lauri. 2000. Text as Process and Practice: The Textualization of Oral Epics. Pages 3–54 in *Textualization of Oral Epics*. Edited by Lauri Honko. Berlin: de Gruyter.

Hoogestraat, Jane. "Discoverers of Something New": Notes on Ong, Derrida, and Post-Colonial Theory. Pages 26–55 in Weeks and Hoogestraat.

Horsley, Richard A. 1984. Popular Messianic Movements around the Time of Jesus. *CBQ* 46:471–93.

———. 1985. "Like One of the Prophets of Old": Two Types of Popular Prophets at the Time of Jesus. *CBQ* 47:435–63.

———. 1987. *Jesus and the Spiral of Violence*. San Francisco: Harper & Row.

———. 1991. Empire, Temple, and Community—But No Bourgeosie. Pages 163–74 in *Second Temple Studies 1: Persian Period*. Edited by Philip R. Davies. JSOTSup 117. Sheffield: Sheffield Academic Press.

———. 1995. *Galilee: History, Politics, People*. Valley Forge, Pa.: Trinity Press International.

———. 2000. Social Relations and Social Conflict in the Epistle of Enoch. Pages 100–115 in *For a Later Generation: The Transformation of Tradition in Israel, Early Judaism, and Early Christianity*. Edited by Randal A. Argall, Beverly A. Bow, and Rodney A. Werline. Harrisburg, Pa.: Trinity Press International.

———. 2001a. *Hearing the Whole Story: The Politics of Plot in Mark's Gospel*. Louisville: Westminster John Knox.

———. 2001b. The Politics of Cultural Production in Second-Temple Judah. Paper delivered to the Wisdom and Apocalypticism Group at the Society of Biblical Literature 2001 Annual Meeting, Denver, Colorado.

Horsley, Richard A., with Jonathan A. Draper. 1999. *Whoever Hears You Hears Me: Prophets, Performance, and Tradition in Q*. Harrisburg, Pa.: Trinity Press International.

Horsley, Richard A., and Patrick Tiller. 2002. Ben Sira and the Sociology of the Second Temple. Pages 74–107 in *Second Temple Studies 3: Studies in Politics,*

Class, and Material Culture. Edited by Philip R. Davies and John Halligan. JSOTSup 340. Sheffield: Sheffield Academic Press.

Hurtado, Larry W. 1988. *One God, One Lord: Early Christian Devotion and Ancient Jewish Monotheism.* London: SCM.

Hutchins, Edwin. 1980. *Culture and Inference: A Trobriand Case Study.* Cambridge: Harvard University Press.

Hymes, Dell H. 1981. *"In Vain I Tried to Tell You": Essays in Native American Ethnopoetics.* Philadelphia: University of Pennsylvania Press.

———. 1989. Ways of Speaking. Pages 433–51, 473–74 in *Explorations in the Ethnography of Speaking.* Edited by Richard Bauman and Joel Sherzer. 2nd ed. Cambridge: Cambridge University Press.

———. 1994. Ethnopoetics, Oral-Formulaic Theory, and Editing Texts. *Oral Tradition* 9:330–70.

Irwin, Bonnie D. 1995. What's in a Frame? The Medieval Textualization of Traditional Storytelling. *Oral Tradition* 10:27-53.

———. 1998. The Frame Tale East and West. Pages 391–99 in Foley 1998b.

Irwin, Marc H., and Donald H. McLaughlin. 1970. Ability and Preference in Category Sorting by Mano School Children and Adults. *Journal of Social Psychology* 82:15–24.

Issacharoff, Michael. 2001. Jakobson, Roman. In *The John Hopkins Guide to Literary and Theory and Critisism.* Cited 7 May. Online: http://www.press.jhu.edu/books/hopkins_guide_to_literary_theory/entries/roman_jakobson.

Jaffee, Martin S. 1994a. Writing and Rabbinic Oral Traditiion: On Mishnaic Narrative, Lists and Mnemonics. *Journal of Jewish Thought and Philosophy* 4:123–46.

———. 1994b. Figuring Early Rabbinic Literary Culture: Thoughts Occasioned by Bomershine and J. Dewey. *Semeia* 65:67–73.

———. 1998. The Hebrew Scriptures. Pages 321–29 in Foley 1998b.

———. 1999. Oral Tradition in the Writings of Rabbinic Oral Torah: On Theorizing Rabbinic Orality. *Oral Tradition* 14:3–32.

———. 2001. *Torah in the Mouth: Writing and Oral Tradition in Palestinian Judaism 200 BCE–400 CE.* Oxford: Oxford University Press.

Jahandarie, Khosrow. 1986. Effect of Schooling on Categorization Preferences: A Picture-Classification Study. *Perceptual and Motor Skills* 63:331–38.

Jakobson, Roman. 1971. Two Aspects of Language and Two Types of Aphasic Disturbances. Pp. 69–96 in Roman Jakobson and Morris Halle, *Fundamentals of Language.* 2nd edition. The Hague: Mouton.

Janko, Richard. 1990. The *Iliad* and Its Editors: Dictation and Redaction. *Classical Antiquity* 9:326–34.

Jastrow, Morris. *A Dictionary of the Targumim, the Talmud Babli and Yerushalmi, and the Madrashic Literature.* Brooklyn: Traditional Press.

Jeanmaire, Henri. 1951. *Dionysos; histoire du culte de Bacchus: L'orgiasme dans l'antiquité et les temps modernes, origine du théâtre en Grèce, orphisme et mystique dionysiaque, èvolution du dionysisme après Alexandre.* Paris: Payot.

Jensen, Minne Skafte. 2000. The Writing of the *Iliad* and the *Odyssey.* Pages 57–70 in *Textualization of Oral Epics.* Edited by Lauri Honko. Berlin: de Gruyter.

Johnson, Luke T. 1977. *The Literary Function of Possessions in Luke-Acts.* SBLDS 39. Missoula, Mont.: Scholars Press.

Jousse, Marcel. 1990. *The Oral Style*. Translated by Edgard Sienaert and Richard Whitaker. New York: Garland.

———. 1997. *The Anthropology of Geste and Rhythm: Studies in the Anthropological Laws of Human Expression and Their Application in the Galilean Oral Style Tradition*. Edited by Edgard Sienaert. Translated by Edgard Sienaert and Joan Conolly. Durban, South Africa: Centre for Oral Studies.

Joyce, Jamres. 1966. *Finnegan's Wake*. New York: Viking. [Orig. 1939]

Kaku, Michio. 1998. *Visions: How Science Will Revolutionize the Twenty-First Century and Beyond*. Oxford: Oxford University Press.

Kaplan, Stuart J. 1989. Communication Technology and Society. Pages 205–34 in *Speech Communication: Essays to Commemorate the Seventy-Fifth Anniversary of The Speech Communication Association*. Edited by Gerald M. Phillips and Julia T. Wood. Carbondale: Southern Illinois University Press.

Karadžić, Vuk S., ed. 1975. *Srpske narodne pjesme*. Belgrade: Nolit. [Orig. 1841–65]

Kaschula, Russell H. 1995. Mandela Comes Home: The Poets' Perspective. *Oral Tradition* 10:91–110.

———. 2000. *The Bones of the Ancestors Are Shaking: Xhosa Oral Poetry in Context*. Cape Town: Juta.

Kelber, Werner H. 1979. *Mark's Story of Jesus*. Philadelphia: Fortress .

———. 1980. Mark and Oral Tradition. *Semeia* 16:7–55.

———. 1983. *The Oral and the Written Gospel: The Hermeneutics of Speaking and Writing in the Synoptic Tradition, Mark, Paul and Q*. Philadelphia: Fortress.

———. 1997. *The Oral and the Written Gospel: The Hermeneutics of Speaking and Writing in the Synoptic Tradition, Mark, Paul, and Q*. Voices in Performance and Text. Bloomington: Indiana University Press. [Orig. 1983]

Koehler, Ludwig, and Baumgartner, Walter. 1958. *Lexicon in Veteris Testament Libros*. 2nd ed. Leiden: Brill.

Kraemer, David. 1989. On the Reliability of the Attributions in the Babylonian Talmud. *HUCA* 60:175–90.

Krauss, Matthew, ed. Forthcoming. *How Should Late Antique Rabbinic Literature Be Read in the Modern World? Hermeneutical Limits and Possibilities*. Piscataway, N.J.: Gorgias.

Kraybill, J. Nelson. 1996. *Imperial Cult and Commerce in John's Apocalypse*. JSNTSup 132. Sheffield: Sheffield Academic Press.

Lakoff, George. 1987. *Women, Fire, and Dangerous Things: What Categories Reveal about the Mind*. Chicago: University of Chicago Press.

Lampe, G. W. H. 1961. *A Patristic Greek Lexicon*. Oxford: Oxford University Press.

Lancy, David F. 1983. Cross-Cultural Studies in Cognition and Mathematics. New York: Academic Press.

Lane Fox, Robin. 1986. *Pagans and Christians*. New York: Random House.

Lerner, M. B. 1987a. The External Tractates. Pages 369–79 in *The Literature of the Sages*. Edited by Shemuel Safrai. CRINT 2/3. Assen: Van Gorcum; Philadelphia: Fortress.

———. 1987b. The Tractate Avot. Pages 263–81 in *The Literature of the Sages*. Edited by Shemuel Safrai. CRINT 2/3. Assen: Van Gorcum; Philadelphia: Fortress.

Lévi-Strauss, Claude. 1962. *The Savage Mind*. Chicago: University of Chicago Press.

————. 1976. *Tristes Tropiques*. Translated by Hohn and Doreen Weightman. Harmondsworth, U.K.: Penguin.

Levine, Lee I. 1992. The Sages and the Synagogue in Late Antiquity: The Evidence of the Galilee. Pages 201–23 in *The Galilee in Late Antiquity*. Edited by Lee I. Levine. New York: Jewish Theological Seminary of America.

Liddell, Henry George, and Robert Scott. 1968. *A Greek-English Lexicon*. Oxford: Oxford University Press.

Liefferinge, Carine van. 1999. *La théurgie des Oracles Chaldaïques à Proclus*. Liège: Centre international d'étude de la religion grecque antique.

Loraux, P. 1992. L'art platonicien d'avoir l'air d'écrire. Pages 420–55 in Detienne and Camassa.

Lord, Albert Bates. 1960. *The Singer of Tales*. Cambridge: Harvard University Press.

————. 1986. The Merging of Two Worlds: Oral and Written Poetry as Carriers of Ancient Values. Pages 19–64 in Foley 1986.

————. 1989. Theories of Oral Literature and the Latvian *Dainas*. Pages 35–48 in *Linguistics and Poetics of Latvian Folk Songs*. Edited by Varia Vikis-Freibergs. Kingston, Ont.: McGill-Queen's University Press.

Loubser, J. A. 1986. Die belang van die konteks in die lees van 'n teks. *NGTT* 27: 154–57.

————. 1993. Orality and Pauline Christology: Some Hermeneutical Implications. *Scriptura* 47:25–51.

————. 1995. Orality and Literacy in the Pauline Corpus: Some New Hermeneutical Implications. *Neot* 29:61–74.

————. 1996. Shembe Preaching: A Study in Oral Hermeneutics. Pages 265–82 in *African Independent Churches Today*. Edited by Michael C. Kitshoff. Lewiston, N.Y.: Mellen.

————. 1999. Review of Jousse 1997. *Voices, a Journal for Oral Studies* 2:205–12.

Luke, Allan. 1996. Genres of Power? Literacy Education and the Production of Capital. Pages 308–38 in *Literacy in Society*. Edited by Rugaiya Hasan and Geoffrey Williams. London: Longman.

Luria, Aleksandr R. 1976. *Cognitive Development: Its Cultural and Social Foundations*. Translated by E. Hanfmann and G. Vakar. Cambridge: Harvard University Press.

————. 1981. *Language and Cognition*. Edited by James V. Wertsch. New York: John Wiley & Sons.

MacCoull, Leslie S. B. 1999. Oral-Formulaic Approaches to Coptic Hymnography. *Oral Tradition* 14:354–400.

MacMullen, Ramsay. 1984. *Christianizing the Roman Empire (A.D. 100–400)*. New Haven: Yale University Press.

Maines, David R. 1984. Suggestions for a Symbolic Interactionist Conception of Culture. *Communication and Cognition* 17:205–17.

Malina, Bruce J. 1982. The Social Sciences and Biblical Interpretation. *Int* 37: 229–42.

————. 1991a. Interpretation: Reading, Abduction, Metaphor. Pages 253–66 in *The Bible and the Politics of Exegesis*. Edited by David Jobling, Peggy L. Day, and Gerald T. Sheppard. Cleveland: Pilgrim.

————. 1991b. Reading Theory Perspective: Reading Luke-Acts. Pages 3–24 in *The Social World of Luke-Acts: Models for Interpretation*. Edited by Jerome H. Neyrey. Peabody, Mass.: Hendrickson.

————. 1996. Rhetorical Criticism and Social-Scientific Criticism: Why Won't Romanticism Leave Us Alone? Pages 72–101 in *Rhetoric, Scripture and Theology: Essays from the 1994 Pretoria Conference*. Edited by Stanley E. Porter and Thomas H. Olbricht. JSNTSup 131. Sheffield: Sheffield Academic Press.

Mason, Steve. 1991. *Flavius Josephus on the Pharisees: A Compositional-Critical Study*. StPB 39. Leiden: Brill.

Mattéi, Jean-François. 1995. *L'Etranger et le Simulacre*. Paris: Presses universitaires de France.

Matthias, John, and Vladeta Vučković, trans. 1987. *The Battle of Kosovo*. Athens: Ohio University Press/Swallow.

McCarthy, William B. 1990. *The Ballad Matrix*. Bloomington: Indiana University Press, 1987.

————, ed. 1994. *Jack in Two Worlds: Contemporary North American Tellers and their Tales*. Chapel Hill: University of North Carolina Press.

McDowell, John H. 1989. *Sayings of the Ancestors: The Spiritual Life of the Sibundoy Indians*. Lexington: University Press of Kentucky.

McLean, Mervyn, and Margaret Orbell. 1975. *Traditional Songs of the Maori*. Wellington: Reed.

McLuhan, Marshall. 1962. *The Gutenberg Galaxy: The Making of Typographic Man*. Toronto: University of Toronto Press.

————. 1994. *Understanding Media: The Extensions of Man*. Cambridge: MIT Press. [Orig. 1964]

McLuhan, Marshall, and Quentin Fiore. 1967. *The Medium Is the Massage*. Coordinated by Jerome Agel. New York: Bantam.

Medjedović, Avdo. 1974. *The Wedding of Smailagić Meho*. Translated by Albert B. Lord and David E. Bynum. Cambridge: Harvard University Press.

Meillet, M. A. 1907. Le dieu indo-iranien mitra. *JA* 10/10:143–59.

Melkman, Rachel, and H. Deutsch. 1977. Memory Functioning as Related to Developmental Changes in Bases of Organization. *Journal of Experimental Child Psychology* 23:84–97.

Melkman, Rachel, Barbara Tversky, and Daphana Baratz. 1981. Developmental Trends in the Use of Perceptual and Conceptual Attributes in Grouping, Clustering and Retrieval. *Journal of Experimental Child Psychology* 31:470–86.

Merkelbach, Reinhold. 1984. *Mithras*. Königstein/Ts.: Hain.

Miletich, John S. 1978a. Oral-Traditional Style and Learned Literature: A New Perspective. *Poetics and the Theory of Literature* 3:345–56.

————. 1978b. Elaborate Style in South Slavic Oral Narrative and in Kačić-Miošić's *Razgovor*. Pages 522–31 in *Linguistics and Poetics*, vol. 1 of *American Contributions to the Eighth International Conference of Slavists (Zagreb and Ljubljana, September 3–9, 1978)*. Edited by H. Birnbaum. Columbus, Ohio: Slavica.

Millard, Alan R. 2000. *Reading and Writing in the Time of Jesus*. Biblical Seminar 69. Sheffield: Sheffield Academic Press.

Morgenthaler, Robert. 1985. *Statistik des Neutestamentlichen Wortschatzes*. Zurich: Gotthelf-Verlag.

Morray-Jones, Christopher R. A. 1992. Transformational Mysticism in the Apocalyptic-Merkabah Tradition. *JJS* 43:1-31.

———. 1993a. Paradise Revisited (2 Cor 12:1-12): The Jewish Mystical Background of Paul's Apostolate. Part 1: The Jewish Sources. *HTR* 86:177–217.

———. 1993b. Paradise Revised (2 Cor 12:1-12): The Jewish Mystical Background of Paul's Apostolate. Part 2: Paul's Heavenly Ascent and Its Significance. *HTR* 86:265–92.

Morvan, Thomas. 2001. Le problème des règles d'écriture pour le dialogue. Pages 189–208 in *La forme dialogue chez Platon*. Edited by Frédéric Cossutta and Michel Narcy. Grenoble: Millon.

Mosala, Itumeleng J. 1989. *Biblical Hermeneutics and Black Theology in South Africa*. Grand Rapids: Eerdmans.

Mueller, Ian. 1987. Mathematics and Philosophy in Proclus' Commentary on Book I of Euclid's *Elements*. Pages 305–18 in *Proclus, lecteur et interprète des anciens*. Edited by Jean Pépin and Henri D. Saffrey. Paris: Editions du Centre national de la recherche scientifique.

Mulder, Jan W. F. 1994. Written and Spoken Languages as Separate Semiotic Systems. *Semiotica* 101:41–72.

Murphy, Karen L., and Mauri P. Collins. 2001. Communication Conventions in Instructional Electronic Chats. Cited 8 May 2001. Online: http://www.firstmonday.dk/issues/issue2_11/murphy/.

Nagy, Gregory. 1996. *Homeric Questions*. Austin: University of Texas Press.

Narcy, Michel. 1992. La leçon d'écriture de Socrate dans le *Phèdre* de Platon. Pages 77–92 in *Chercheursde sagesse: Hommage à Jean Pépin*. Edited by M.-O. Goulet-Cazé, G. Madec, and D. O'Brien. Paris: Institut d'Etudes Augustiniennes.

Nasta, Mihaïl. 2001. *Les êtres de paroles: Herméneutiques du Langage figuré*. Brussells: Ousia; Paris: Vrin.

Neusner, Jacob. 1972. *From Politics to Piety: The Emergence of Pharisaic Judaism*. Englewood Cliffs, N.J.: Prentice Hall.

———. 1987. *The Oral Tradition in Judaism: The Case of the Mishnah*. New York: Garland.

Nida, Eugene A. 1996. *The Sociolinguistics of Interlingual Communication*. Brussels: Les Éditions du Hazard.

Niditch, Susan. 1995. Oral Register in the Biblical Libretto: Towards a Biblical Poetic. *Oral Tradition* 10:387–408.

———. 1996. *Oral World and Written Word: Ancient Israelite Literature*. Library of Ancient Israel. Louisville: Westminster John Knox.

Niles, John D. 1998. British American Balladry. Pages 280–90 in Foley 1998b.

———. 1999. *Homo Narrans: The Poetics and Anthropology of Oral Literature*. Philadelphia: University of Pennsylvania Press.

Obiechina, Emmanuel. 1992. Narrative Proverbs in the African Novel. *Oral Tradition* 7:197–230.

Odeberg, Hugo. 1929. *The Fourth Gospel: Interpreted in Its Relation to Contemporaneous Religious Currents in Palestine and the Hellenistic-Oriental World*. Uppsala: Almqvist & Wiksell.

O'Keeffe, Katherine O'Brien. 1990. *Visible Song: Transitional Literacy in Old English Verse*. Cambridge: Cambridge University Press.

Okpewho, Isidore. 1992. *African Oral Literature: Backgrounds, Character, Continuity.* Bloomington: Indiana University Press.

Olson, David R. 1977. From Utterance to Text: The Bias of Language in Speech and Text. *Harvard Educational Review* 47:257–81.

———. 1980. On the Language and Authority of Textbooks. *Journal of Communication* 30:186–96.

———. 1985. Introduction. Pages 1–15 in *Literacy, Language, and Learning.* Edited by David R. Olson, Nancy Torrance, and Angela Hildyard. Cambridge: Cambridge University Press.

———. 1987. An Introduction to Understanding Literacy. *Interchange* 18:1–8.

———. 1988a. Interpreting Texts and Interpreting Nature: The Effects of Literacy on Hermeneutics and Epistemology. Pages 123–38 in *The Written World: Studies in Literate Thought and Action.* Edited by Roger Säljö. Berlin: Springer-Verlag.

———. 1988b. Mind and Media: The Epistemic Functions of Literacy. *Journal of Communication* 38(3):27–36.

———. 1994. *The World on Paper: The Conceptual and Cognitive Implications of Writing and Reading.* Cambridge: Cambridge University Press.

———. 1995. Conceptualizing the Written Word: An Intellectual Autobiography. *Written Communication* 12:277–97.

———. 1996. Literate Mentalities: Literacy, Consciousness of Language, and Modes of Thought. Pages 141–51 in *Modes of Thought: Explorations in Culture and Cognition.* Edited by David R. Olson and Nancy Torrance. Cambridge: Cambridge University Press.

Olson, David R., and Angela Hildyard. 1983. Literacy and the Comprehension and Expression of Literal Meaning. Pages 291–325 in *Writing in Focus.* Edited by Florian Coulmas and Konrad Ehlich. Berlin: Mouton.

Ong, Walter J. 1967. *The Presence of the Word: Some Prolegomena for Cultural and Religious History.* New Haven: Yale University Press.

———. 1970. *The Presence of the Word: Some Prolegomena for Cultural and Religious History.* New York: Simon & Schuster. [Orig. 1967]

———. 1977a. *Interfaces of the Word: Studies in the Evolution of Consciousness and Culture.* Ithaca, N.Y.: Cornell University Press.

———. 1977b. Maranatha: Death and Life in the Text of the Book. Pages 230–71 in idem, *Interfaces of the Word: Studies in the Evolution of Consciousness and Culture.* Ithaca, N.Y.: Cornell University Press.

———. 1982. *Orality and Literacy: The Technologizing of the Word.* London: Methuen.

———. 1987. Orality-Literacy Studies and the Unity of the Human Race. *Oral Tradition* 2:371–82.

Opland, Jeff. 1980. *Anglo-Saxon Oral Poetry: A Study of the Traditions.* New Haven: Yale University Press.

———. 1983. *Xhosa Oral Poetry: Aspects of a Black South African Tradition.* Cambridge: Cambridge University Press.

———. 1998. *Xhosa Oral Poets and Poetry.* Cape Town: David Philip.

———. 1999. The Image of the Book in Xhosa Oral Poetry. Pages 90–110 in *Oral Literature and Performance in Southern Africa.* Edited by Duncan Brown. Oxford: Currey.

Painter, Clare. 1996. The Development of Language as a Resource for Thinking: A Linguistic View of Learning. Pages 50–85 in *Literacy in Society*. Edited by Rugaiya Hasan and Geoffrey Williams. London: Longman.

Parry, Milman. 1971. *The Making of Homeric Verse: The Collected Papers of Milman Parry*. Edited by Adam Parry. Oxford: Clarendon.

Patterson, Orlando. 1982. *Slavery and Social Death: A Comparative Study*. Cambridge: Harvard University Press.

Payne Smith, Robert. 1903. *A Compendious Syriac Dictionary*. Oxford: Clarendon.

Pennington, Anne, and Peter Levi., trans. 1984. *Marko the Prince*. New York: St. Martin's.

Perrin, Norman. 1976. *Jesus and the Language of the Kingdom: Symbol and Metaphor in New Testament Interpretation*. Philadelphia: Fortress.

Peters, Julie Stone. 1998. Orality, Literacy, and Print Revisited. Pages 27–50 in Weeks and Hoogestraat.

Pihel, Erik. 1996. A Furified Freestyle: Homer and Hip Hop. *Oral Tradition* 11:249–69.

Popper, Karl R. 1972. *Objective Knowledge: An Evolutionary Approach*. Oxford: Clarendon.

Proclos. 1968–97. *Théologie platonicienne*. Edited and translated by Henri D. Saffrey and Leendert G. Westerink. 6 vols. Paris: Belles Lettres.

Ranger, Terence. 1983. The Invention of Tradition in Colonial Africa. Pages 211–62 in Eric Hobsbawm and Terence Ranger, *The Invention of Tradition*. Cambridge: Cambridge University Press.

Rausis, Philippe-Emmanuel. 1993. *L'initiation*. Paris: Cerf.

Reim, Günter. 1974. *Studien zum Alttestamentlichen Hintergrund des Johannesevangeliums*. SNTSMS 22. Cambridge: Cambridge University Press.

Resseguie, James L. 1998. *Revelation Unsealed. A Narrative Critical Approach to John's Apocalypse*. Biblical Interpretation Series 32. Brill: Leiden.

Richard, Marie-Dominique. 1986. *L'Enseignement oral de Platon: Une nouvelle interprétation du platonisme*. Paris: Cerf.

Ries, Julien, ed. 1986. *Les rites d'initiation*. Homo religiosus 13. Louvain-la-Neuve: Centre d'historie des religions.

Rivkin, Ellis. 1978. *A Hidden Revolution*. Nashville: Abingdon.

Robb, Kevin. 1994. *Literacy and Paideia in Ancient Greece*. Oxford: Oxford University Press.

Robbins, Vernon K. 1994. Oral, Rhetorical, and Literary Cultures: A Response. *Semeia* 65:75–94.

———. 1996a. *Exploring the Texture of Texts: A Guide to Socio-rhetorical Interpretation*. Valley Forge, Pa.: Trinity Press International.

———. 1996b. *The Tapestry of Early Christian Discourse: Rhetoric, Society and Ideology*. London: Routledge.

Robin, Léon. 1908. *La théorie platonicienne des Idées et des nombres d'après Aristote*. Paris: Vrin.

Rogoff, Barbara, and Pablo Chavajay. 1995. What's Become of Research on the Cultural Basis of Cognitive Development? *American Psychologist* 50:859–77.

Rosenberg, Bruce A. 1988. *Can These Bones Live? The Art of the American Folk Preacher*. Urbana: University of Illinois Press.

————. 1994. Forrest Spirits: Oral Echoes in Leon Forrest's Prose. *Oral Tradition* 9: 315–27.

Rossing, Barbara R. 1999. *The Choice between Two Cities: Whore, Bride, and Empire in the Apocalypse*. Harrisburg, Pa.: Trinity Press International.

Rowland, Christopher C. 1981. *The Open Heaven: A Study of Apocalyptic in Judaism and Early Christianity*. London: SPCK.

————. 1984. John 1.51, Jewish Apocalyptic and Targumic Tradition. *NTS* 30:498–507.

————. 1985. A Man Clothed in Linen: Daniel 10:6ff and Jewish Angelology. *JSNT* 24:99–110.

Safrai, Shemuel. 1976. Education and the Study of Torah. Pages 945–70 in vol. 2 of *The Jewish People in the First Century*. Edited by Shemuel Safrai and Menahem Stern. Philadelphia: Fortress.

Saussure, Ferdinand de. 1993. *Troisième cours de linguistique générale (1910–1911)* = *Saussure's Third Course of Lectures on General Linguistics (1910–1911)*. Translated by Roy Harris. New York: Oxford University Press.

Schaefer, Ursula. 1992. *Vokalität: Altenglische Dichtung zwischen Mündlichkeit und Schriftlichkeit*. ScriptOralia 39. Tübingen: Narr.

————. 1993. Alterities: On Methodology in Medieval Literary Studies. *Oral Tradition* 8:187–214.

Schaper, J. 1995. The Jerusalem Temple as an Instrument of the Achaemenid Fiscal Administration. *VT* 45:534–39.

Schechter, Solomon, ed. 1967. *Aboth de Rabbi Nathan*. New York: Feldheim.

Schiffman, Lawrence H. 1990. The New Halakhic Letter (4QMMT) and the Origins of the Dead Sea Sect. *BA* 53:64–73.

Schmandt-Besserat, Denise. 1977. An Archaic Recording System and the Origin of Writing. *Syro-Mesopotamian Studies* 1:1–32.

Schnackenburg, Rudolf. 1968–82. *The Gospel according to John*. Translated by Kevin Smyth. 3 vols. New York: Seabury.

Schwartz, Seth. 2001. *Imperialism and Jewish Society: 200 BCE to 640 CE*. Princeton: Princeton University Press.

Scinto, Leonard F. M. 1986. *Written Language and Psychological Development*. Orlando: Academic.

Scott, James C. 1977. Protest and Profanation: Agrarian Revolt and the Little Tradition. *Theory and Society* 4:3–32, 159–210.

————. 1990. *Domination and the Arts of Resistance: Hidden Transcripts*. New Haven: Yale University Press.

Scribner, Sylvia. 1997. The Practice of Literacy: Where Mind and Society Meet. Pages 190–205 in *Mind and Social Practice: Selected Writings of Sylvia Scribner*. Edited by Ethel Tobach, Rachel Joffe Falmagne, Mary Brown Parlee, Laura M. W. Martin, and Aggie Scribner Kapelman. Cambridge: Cambridge University Press. [Orig. 1984]

Scribner, Sylvia, and Michael Cole. 1978. Literacy without Schooling: Testing for Intellectual Effects. *Harvard Educational Review* 48:448–61.

————. 1981a. *The Psychology of Literacy*. Cambridge: Harvard University Press.

————. 1981b. *Unpackaging Literacy*. Pages 71–87 in *Variation in Writing: Functional and Linguistic-Cultural Differences*. Vol 1. of *Writing: The Nature, Development, and Teaching of Written Communication.* Edited by Marcia Farr Whiteman. Hillsdale, N.J.: Erlbaum.

Schüssler Fiorenza, Elisabeth. 1998. *The Book of Revelation: Justice and Judgment.* Minneapolis: Fortress.

Segal, Alan F. 1977. *Two Powers in Heaven: Early Rabbinic Reports about Christianity and Gnosticism.* SJLA 25. Leiden: Brill.

——. 1992. The Risen Christ and the Angelic Mediator Figures in the Light of Qumran. Pages 302–28 in James H. Charlesworth, *Jesus and the Dead Sea Scrolls.* ABRL. New York: Doubleday.

Smith, Colin, ed. 1964. *Spanish Ballads.* Oxford: Pergamon.

Smith, John D., ed. and trans. 1991. *The Epic of Pabuji: A Study, Transcription, and Translation.* Cambridge: Cambridge University Press.

Smith, Jonathan Z. 1998. Canons, Catalogues and Classics. Pages 295–312 in *Canonization and Decanonization: Papers Presented to the International Conference of the Leiden Institute for the Study of Religions, Held at Leiden, 9–10 January 1997.* Edited by Arie van der Kooij and Karol van der Toorn. Leiden: Brill, 1998.

Smith, Mahlon H. 2001. Friedrich Schleiermacher. Cited 3 May 2001. Online: http://religion.rutgers.edu/nt/primer/schleier.html .

Solère-Queval, Sylvie. 1988. A l'image de l'âme. Essai sur l'organisation des dialogues de Platon. Doctoral thesis. Université de Lille III.

——. 1995. Lecture du *Lysis* de Platon. Lille: n.p.

Speyer, Wolfgang. 1971. *Die literarische Fälschung im heidnischen und christlichen Altertum: Ein Versuch ihrer Deutung.* Munich: Beck.

Stanovich, Kevin E. and Anne E. Cunningham. 1992. Studying the Consequences of Literacy within a Literate Society: The Cognitive Correlates of Print Exposure. *Memory & Cognition* 20:51–68.

Stemberger, Günter. 1995a. *Introduction to the Talmud and Midrash.* Translated by Markus Bockmuehl. 2nd ed. Edinburgh: T&T Clark.

——. 1995b. *Jewish Contemporaries of Jesus: Pharisees, Sadducees, Essenes.* Translated by Allan W. Mahnke. Minneapolis: Fortress.

Stock, Brian. 1983. *The Implications of Literacy: Written Language and Models of Interpretation in the Eleventh and Twelfth Centuries.* Princeton: Princeton University Press.

——. 1990. *Listening for the Text: On the Uses of the Past.* Baltimore: Johns Hopkins University Press.

Street, Brian V. 1984. *Literacy in Theory and Practice.* Cambridge: Cambridge University Press.

Svenbrö, Jesper. 1988. *Phrasikleia: Anthropologie de la lecture en Grèce antique.* Paris: La Découverte.

——. 1991. La lecture à haute voix. Le témoignage des verbes grecs signifiant "lire." Pages 539–48 in Baurain.

Tannen, Deborah. 1982. The Oral/Literate Continuum in Discourse. Pages 1–16 in *Spoken and Written Language: Exploring Orality and Literacy.* Edited by Deborah Tannen. Norwood: Ablex.

Taylor, Andrew. 2001. Was There a Song of Roland? *Spec* 76:28–65.

Tedlock, Dennis. 1983. *The Spoken Word and the Work of Interpretation.* Philadelphia: University of Pennsylvania Press.

——, trans. 1996. *Popol Vuh: The Mayan Book of the Dawn of Life.* Rev. ed. New York: Simon & Schuster.

——. 1999. *Finding the Center: The Art of the Zuni Storyteller.* 2nd ed. Lincoln: University of Nebraska Press.

Thomas, Rosalind. 1989. *Oral Tradition and Written Records in Classical Athens.* Cambridge: Cambridge University Press.

——. 1992. *Literacy and Orality in Ancient Greece.* Cambridge: Cambridge University Press.

Titon, Jeff Todd. 1988. *Powerhouse for God: Speech, Chant, and Song in an Appalachian Baptist Church.* Austin: University of Texas Press.

——. 1994. *Early Downhome Blues: A Musical and Cultural Analysis.* 2nd ed. Chapel Hill: University of North Carolina Press.

Tov, Emanuel. 2001. *Textual Criticism of the Hebrew Bible.* 2nd ed. Minneapolis: Fortress.

Tuman, Myron C. 1983. Words, Tools and Technology. *College English* 45:769–79.

Turcan, Robert. 1981. Le sacrifice mithriaque. Pages 341–80 in *Le sacrifice dans l'antiquité.* Edited by Jean-Pierre Vernant et al. Entretiens sur l'antiquité classique 27. Genève: Fondation Hardt.

——. 1989. *Les cultes orientaux dans le monde romain.* Paris: Belles Lettres.

——. 2000. *The Gods of Ancient Rome: Religion in Everyday Life from Archaic to Imperial Times.* New York: Routledge. [Orig. *Rome et ses dieux.* Paris: Hachette Littératures, 1998.]

Ulansey, David. 1989. *The Origins of the Mithraic Mysteries: Cosmology and Salvation in the Ancient World.* Oxford: Oxford University Press.

Ulrich, Eugene C. 1999. *The Dead Sea Scrolls and the Origins of the Bible.* Grand Rapids: Eerdmans.

Urbach, Ephraim E. 1988. *MeOlamam shel Khakhamim.* Jerusalem: Magnes.

Vansina, Jan. 1985. *Oral Tradition as History.* Madison: University of Wisconsin Press.

Vegetti, Mario. 1988. Dans l'ombre de Thoth; dynamiques de l'écriture chez Platon. Pages 387–419 in Detienne and Camassa.

Vermaseren, Maarten J. 1963. *Mithras, the Secret God.* New York: Barnes & Noble.

——. 1971–78. *Mithraica.* 4 vols. Leiden: Brill.

Vikis-Freibergs, Vaira. 1989. Text Variants in the Latvian Folk-Song Corpus: Theoretical and Practical Problems. Pages 49–72 in *Linguistics and Poetics of Latvian Folk Songs.* Edited by Vaira Vikis-Freibergs. Kingston, Ont.: McGill-Queen's University Press.

Vocate, Donna R. 1987. *The Theory of A. R. Luria: Functions of Spoken Language in the Development of Higher Mental Processes.* Hillsdale, N.J.: Erlbaum.

Vygotskiĭ, Lev S. 1986. *Language and Thought.* Translated by Alex Kozulin. Cambridge: MIT Press. [Orig. 1934]

Walters, Vivienne J. 1974. *The Cult of Mithras in the Roman Provinces of Gaul.* Leiden: Brill.

Warner, Elizabeth A. 1974. Pushkin in the Russian Folk-Plays. Pages 101–7 in *Oral Literature: Seven Essays.* Edited by Joseph J. Duggan. Edinburgh: Scottish Academic Press; New York: Barnes & Noble.

Watts, James W., ed. 2001. *Persia and Torah.* SBLSymS 17. Atlanta: Society of Biblical Literature.

Webber, Ruth H. 1986. The *Cantar de Mio Cid:* Problems of Interpretation. Pages 65–88 in Foley 1986.

Weeks, Dennis L., and Jane Hoogestraat, eds. 1998. *Time, Memory and the Verbal Arts: Essays on the Thought of Walter Ong.* Selinsgrove: Susquehanna University Press.

Wehmeyer-Shaw, Debra. 1993. Rap Music: An Interview with DJ Romeo. *Oral Tradition* 8:225-46.

Wellhausen, Julius. 2001. *The Pharisees and the Sadducees: An Examination of Internal Jewish History.* Translated by Mark E. Biddle. Macon, Ga.: Mercer University Press.

West, Gerald O. 1995. *Biblical Hermeneutics of Liberation: Modes of Reading the Bible in the South African Context.* Pietermaritzburg: Cluster; Maryknoll, N.Y.: Orbis.

Westerink, Leendert Gerrit, Jean Trouillard, and A. Ph. Segonds, eds. and trans. 1990. *Prolégomènes à la philosophie de Platon.* Collection des universités de France. Paris: Les Belles Lettres.

Wheelwright, Philip E. 1962. *Metaphor and Reality.* Bloomington: Indiana University Press.

Widengren, Geo. 1945. *The Great Vohu Manah and the Apostle of God: Studies in Iranian and Manichaean Religion.* Uppsala: A.-b. Lundequistska bokhandeln; Leipzig: Harrassowitz.

Wilson, Bryan R. 1973. *Magic and the Millennium: A Sociological Study of Religious Movements of Popular Protest among Tribal and Third-World Peoples.* London: Heinemann.

Yang Enhong. 1998. A Comparative Study of the Singing Styles of Mongolian and Tibetan Geser/Gesar Artists. *Oral Tradition* 13:422-34.

Zemke, John M. 1998. General Hispanic Traditions. Pages 202–15 in Foley 1998b.

Zipes, Jack D. 1988. *The Brothers Grimm: From Enchanted Forest to the Modern World.* New York: Routledge.

Zlotnick, Dov. 1988. *Iron Pillar Mishnah: Redaction, Form, and Intent.* Jerusalem: Bialik Institute.

Zotović, Ljubica. 1973. *Le Mitraizam na tlu Jugoslavije.* Translated by Ćurde Bošković. Edited by Milutin Garašanin. Belgrade: Arheološki institut.

Zumthor, Paul. 1987. *La Lettre et la voix: De la littérature médiévale.* Paris: Editions du Seuil.

———. 1990. *Oral Poetry: An Introduction.* Translated by Kathryn Murphy-Judy. Minneapolis: University of Minnesota Press. Originally published as *Introduction à la poésie orale.* Paris: Editions du Seuil, 1983.

Zumwalt, Rosemary Lévi. 1998. A Historical Glossary of Critical Approaches. Pages 75–94 in Foley 1998b.

Zussman, Yaakov. 1982. The Inscription in the Synagogue at Rehob. Pages 146–51 in *Ancient Synagogues Revealed.* Edited by Lee I. Levine. Detroit: Wayne State University Press.

———, ed. 2001. *Talmud Yerushalmi.* Jerusalem: Hebrew Language Academy.

CONTRIBUTORS

Pieter J. J. Botha is Professor of New Testament at the School of Theology and Religion, University of South Africa, Pretoria, where he has taught for eighteen years. He completed his graduate studies in New Testament at the University of Pretoria. He has written on the development of the Gospel traditions and various historical aspects of early Christianity, including *Everyday Life in the World of Jesus* (1999). He may be reached at bothapjj@unisa.ac.za.

Claudia Camp is Professor of Religion at Texas Christian University. Her research interest is in feminist literary and social-historical analysis of biblical wisdom and narrative literature, with recent work in canon formation in oral culture. She is the author of two books, *Wisdom and the Feminine in the Book of Proverbs* (1985) and *Wise, Strange and Holy: The Strange Woman and the Making of the Bible* (2000), and numerous articles, and was editor (with Carole R. Fontaine) of *Women, War, and Metaphor: Language and Society in the Study of the Hebrew Bible* (1993). She can be reached at c.camp@tcu.edu.

Baudouin S. Decharneux is Professor and Head of the Department of Philosophy and Religious Sciences at the Free University of Brussels, Belgium. He is also visiting Professor in the University of Natal (South Africa) and the University of the Val d'Aoste (Italy). He has written on Hellenistic Jewish philosophy and early Christianity. His major works are *L'ange, le devin et le prophète: Chemins de la Parole dans l'œuvre de Philon d'Alexandrie dit "le Juif"* (1995) and, with Luc Nefontaine, *Le symbole* (2003) and *L'initiation* (2000). He may be contacted at bdecharn@ulb.ac.be.

Jonathan A. Draper is Professor of New Testament at the School of Theology, University of Natal, Pietermaritzburg, where he has taught for eighteen years. He completed his graduate studies in New Testament at Cambridge University. He is the author (with Richard A. Horsley) of *Whoever Hears You Hears Me: Prophets, Performance, and Tradition in Q* (1999) and editor of *The Didache in Modern Research* (1996) and *The Eye of the Storm: Bishop John William Colenso and the Crisis of Biblical Interpretation* (2003). He may be reached at draper@nu.ac.za.

John Miles Foley is Curators' Professor of Classical Studies and English, W. H. Byler Distinguished Chair in the Humanities, and founding Director of the Center for Studies in Oral Tradition at the University of Missouri-Columbia, where he edits the journal *Oral Tradition*, the *Blackwell Companion to Ancient Epic*, and two series of books. His major publications include *The Theory of Oral*

Composition (1988), *Traditional Oral Epic* (1990), *Immanent Art* (1991), *The Singer of Tales in Performance* (1995), *Teaching Oral Traditions* (1998), *Homer's Traditional Art* (1999), and *How to Read an Oral Poem* (2002), which is complemented by the web site www.oraltradition.org. He can be reached at FoleyJ@missouri.edu.

Richard A. Horsley is Distinguished Professor of Liberal Arts and the Study of Religion at the University of Massachusetts, Boston. He is author of *Hearing the Whole Story: The Politics of Plot in Mark's Gospel* (2001) and (with Jonathan A. Draper) *Whoever Hears You Hears Me: Prophets, Performance, and Tradition in Q* (1999) and of many other books and articles on Jesus, the Gospels, and their historical context. He may be reached at Richard.Horsley@umb.edu.

Martin S. Jaffee is Professor of Comparative Religion and Jewish Studies in the Henry M. Jackson School of International Studies of the University of Washington. He is the author of *Torah in the Mouth: Writing and Oral Tradition in Palestinian Judaism 200 BCE–400 CE* (2001), *Early Judaism: Religious Worlds of the First Judaic Millennium* (1997; 2nd ed. forthcoming), and several other books on early rabbinic Judaism. He may be reached at jaffee@u.washington.edu.

Werner H. Kelber is the Isla and Percy E. Turner Professor of Biblical Studies and the Director of the Center for the Study of Cultures at Rice University. He is the author of *The Oral and the Written Gospel: The Hermeneutics of Speaking and Writing in the Synoptic Tradition, Mark, Paul and Q* (1983; repr., 1997; French trans., 1990), which examines points of transition and conflict in the transmission of early Christian traditions. He can be reached at kelber@rice.edu.

J. A. (Bobby) Loubser is Professor of New Testament at the Faculty of Theology and Religion Studies, University of Zululand, KZN, South Africa, where he has taught since 1990. He completed his graduate studies at the University of Stellenbosch and is the author of ninety academic publications, addressing issues such as the hermeneutics of oral and literate cultures. He is the author of *The Apartheid Bible* (1986). He may be reached as jloubser@pan.uzulu.ac.za.

Jean-Luc Solère is a searcher of the Centre National de la Recherche Scientifique (Paris) and teaches at the Université Libre de Bruxelles (Belgium). He is a specialist of Western philosophy (ancient, medieval, and early modern). He has recently co-edited *La Servante et la Consolatrice: La philosophie dans ses rapports avec la théologie au Moyen Âge* (2002), *Le Contemplateur et les Idées: Modèles de la science divine, du néoplatonisme au XVIIIe siècle* (2002), and the *Dictionnaire du Moyen Age* (2002). He may be reached at jsolere@ulb.ac.be.